Advance Praise for
What You Don't Know

"Artificial Intelligence Systems that don't prioritize human-centric, values-driven development at the outset of design put society at risk. Good intentions do not equate to Responsible AI and Cortnie has done a fantastic job showing how poor design leads to PR crises, loss of revenue, and human harm. Use this book as a model for pragmatic change for policy makers and businesses alike."

—**John C. Havens, Author,** *Heartificial Intelligence: Embracing our Humanity to Maximize Machines*

"A must read for people of all ages! I thought I understood the pros and cons of AI until I read Cortnie Abercrombie's book *What You Don't Know*, and realized how little I really knew. For all-aged workers, it's important to understand how companies are using AI to eliminate you from consideration based on information that has nothing to do with your skill and ability or terminate you based on bias built into the programming. I highly encourage everyone to read Ms. Abercrombie's book to better understand the role AI plays in candidate selection and employee retention. But this book is not just informative, it's a call to action, encouraging readers to ask Congress for appropriate (and desperately needed) AI protection."

—**Sheila Callaham, Executive Director, Age Equity Alliance and** *Forbes* **Diversity, Equity, and Inclusion Contributor**

"In a world where students must protest algorithms to get into the university of their dreams, then fight to get a job through AI interviews, Cortnie lays out a plan not only to keep these decision-making systems accountable, but also to enable each individual to take back some degree of agency over their lives."

—**John MacIntyre, Co-Editor in Chief,** *Springer Nature AI* **and** *Ethics Journal* **and Pro Vice Chancellor at the University of Sunderland**

"Cortnie shows us a vision of the future where holographic health, personal health assistants, and AED bots combine missions to save lives in real time. It's a thought-provoking look at the future and the areas of public trust we must gain to achieve her vision."

—**Larry Medsker, Co-Editor in Chief,** *Springer Nature AI* **and** *Ethics Journal* **and Research Professor at The George Washington University**

"For those looking to better understand the core ethical issues presented by the AI impacting our daily lives, this book is a compelling read. I also recommend it for lawyers and judges who are in the process of shaping AI law, as it presents some of the real world legal risks to liberal democracy which must be avoided in connection with the upside AI promises to deliver us all."

—**Bradford Newman, Chair of North America AI and ML Practice, Baker McKenzie**

"From what happens when a self-driving car hits someone to how AI decides who can wait for healthcare, Cortnie answers the tough questions with specific calls to action for everyone from AI developers to those who should safeguard it inside of large corporations."

—**Kirk Borne, Chief Science Officer, DataPrime**

"Cortnie takes us on a thought-provoking journey starting with her decision to transition from AI incubator to AI ethicist. Her insightful book concludes with an invigorating vision of what we can do when AI is finally fully trusted."

—**Valerie Morignat, CEO, Intelligent Story and Professor of AI Ethics and Strategy**

"Cortnie has a great way of illuminating and bringing to life the challenging questions in front of us, and reminding us each that we have a critical role to play in what sort of digital world comes next!"

—**Karen Silverman, CEO and Founder, The Cantellus Group**

"This is a book all students starting in the field of data science need to read. From the real-life case studies and quizzes to the frameworks for trustworthy AI, to Cortnie's personal insider accounts of dealing with clients and corporate executives, this book provides that thought-provoking preparation for data science in the real world that all students could benefit from."

—**Kinshuk, Dean of College of Information, University of North Texas**

"There are so many rights and liberties that AI can trample. Lawyers, lawmakers, and the public need to know how they are impacted and what they can do. This is one of the first books that goes in depth on specific cases and gives prescriptive calls to action."

—**Karen Suber, Co-Founder, Attune Capital Management and Board of Directors, Harvard Law School Association of New York City**

WHAT YOU DON'T KNOW

AI'S UNSEEN INFLUENCE
ON YOUR LIFE AND
HOW TO TAKE BACK CONTROL

CORTNIE ABERCROMBIE

Post Hill
PRESS

A POST HILL PRESS BOOK
ISBN: 978-1-63758-208-4
ISBN (eBook): 978-1-63758-209-1

Cover design by Cody Corcoran
Interior design by Yoni Limor

Post Hill Press
New York • Nashville
posthillpress.com

Published in the United States of America
1 2 3 4 5 6 7 8 9 10

In memory of my grandmother
Betty Ann, who always lent me her
strength and encouragement in tough times and reminded
me to make time for the things important to me.

To all of you searching
for your meaning and purpose
in these crazy pandemic times,
I have a message for you
in the Acknowledgments.

When you invent the ship, you also invent the ship-wreck; when you invent the plane, you also invent the plane crash; and when you invent electricity, you invent electrocution.... Every technology carries its own negativity, which is invented at the same time as technical progress.

—Paul Virilio, French cultural theorist, urbanist, and aesthetic philosopher

CONTENTS

INTRODUCTION
The Smokescreen Lifted

How on earth was a cigarette company going to "reduce cancer" in the world using artificial intelligence (AI)? I was intrigued and suspicious as I sat across the conference table listening to a scary-ambitious digital executive as he talked about finding and targeting all the heavy smokers in the world. In the world! What kind of crazy, arrogant person thinks he can find every heavy smoker in the world? At first, I wanted to laugh, but I suppressed it when I noticed no one was laughing or sneering or making any snarky comments. No one. I slowly looked around the room to see if I recognized any of the data science team and came across one person in particular who I knew beyond a doubt could do the impossible. From the data science talent in the room and the high level of executives from my company, I understood that the challenge had already been accepted and was being worked. The lead data scientist's face was completely serious. And I knew. He would find all the heavy smokers—and anyone else—the digital executive wanted to find. If this data scientist hadn't been in the room, I would have chalked this up as hubris and narcissism on the digital executive's part.

If there were a *Forbes* "Most Powerful People in the Underworld" list, this digital executive would definitely have made it. Why? Because he had more money than God at his disposal, and he was not afraid to use it in any way he could to become more powerful in the world of Big Tobacco. He was on a mission to become the first chief digital officer the cigarette company had ever seen, and since he would also be the first Hispanic to earn the title, he was out to blaze a trail—a "smokeless" one. But we will get to that later.

I had joined the discussions mid-meeting. My plane hit the ground at LaGuardia late, and I grabbed my suitcase from the overhead and ran to the rideshare I had requested while still on the plane. Then I ran from where the car was stuck in traffic to my company's building and waited impatiently as the security desk got me a temporary badge. Then I ran to the elevator and then to the conference room. My life was one big hurry, literally running from one place to the next. The people I met were always hurried too. I'm giving you a bit of foreshadowing of how bad things happen in the AI world. Put me on the record as saying…if humanity ever loses to AI, it will not be with a bang or a whimper, but with a rush.

My job was to fly around the world checking out mega-million-dollar artificial intelligence solutions at Fortune 500 companies. I guess you could think of me as an artificial intelligence *Shark Tank* executive. Like the TV show, I was looking for the next big AI solution to invest in and take from being a custom solution at one customer to a repeatable solution we could standardize and offer to many similar firms in the same industry.

This particular meeting was to look at a solution called an AI-driven "social media command center" for a large tobacco company. Let's hit pause. You're probably thinking, *What the heck is an AI-driven social media command center?* Think of scenarios in movies when people sit in front of banks of television screens watching the world, waiting for something to happen. Yeah. It's that. Only it's a social media version. Envision an AI alerting you to relevant patterns in real-time tweets, Instagram photos, Facebook comments, and memes that could affect your company. In the past, it's been consumer goods companies such as Coca-Cola, Nike, and Unilever who have valued the ability to react to social media sentiments fast. But now, most all companies do as they realize it only takes a few people with large followings and a few seconds worth of tweets to take down years of their brand reputation work.

So how does this AI social media command center work exactly? The companies have people in a room monitoring the AI system's social trend alerts about their customers, their brand, their competitors, events, situations, and customer interactions as they happen. Ever been so ticked at an airline that you went straight to Facebook to complain about it to your friends and family and told them never to book there? Yeah, companies hate that. They want to make you happy before you actually succeed in getting all your friends and family to hate them—especially if you have thousands or millions of people following you. In the case of cigarette companies, they are regulated out of traditional advertising routes in many countries, including the United States. Social media, which has few government regulations and a large population of young people, is an opportune route for them to strategically target new customers and trigger regular customers to smoke more.

I cannot remember if I even knew this solution was for Big Tobacco beforehand. I definitely knew about the promise of the AI Command Center solution, but I really didn't think about the fact that this version was attached to a *tobacco* firm. There are two schools of people when it comes to these types of companies. One is the live-and-let-live camp, and the other is the I'm-not-supporting-this-at-all camp. What's terrible is that I had been going so fast up to this point. I had been working with other teams to build their business cases to get their solution on the docket for the internal monthly review board. I flew out and landed in this meeting without giving any thought whatsoever to what camp I was in or even what the solution was specifically supposed to do for the client. I remember I was told that we could help reduce cancer in the world. I also remember that I was intrigued but not quite sure what that meant with regard to this client. But who doesn't want to reduce cancer?

As I sat there in the meeting, I was on an emotional roller coaster. The "combustible product"—this was how the Big Tobacco group referred to regular cigarettes—contained over two hundred carcinogenic agents when lit. Whoa! I mean, I knew it was probably bad, but wow. But the new product—the "smokeless" or "risk-reducing product" (yeah, they said that) which had the tobacco taste and nicotine that heavy smokers craved would only have four main ingredients, and those would not be lit but heated. Therefore, their stance was that the new product would not be as carcinogenic. In theory, if a heavy smoker of "combustible product" could be converted to the new heated product, it could extend how long they—in my mind I inserted the word "live" here—but that is not what actually came out next. Instead, it was…"could continue using tobacco products." Stop right there.

Are you understanding this like I did? In my words, not theirs: heavy smokers were dying too fast from regular cigarettes; therefore, in order to keep them buying, they needed to prolong their lives by transitioning them to something that would kill them more slowly. We have finally, and still dubiously, gotten to the point where they are in some way fulfilling this idea of "reducing cancer" in the world. But, by the way, it would likely contain genetically modified tobacco with nicotine that was at least two times more addictive via a device that costs as much as Air Pods (and that's if you don't opt for the designer version encrusted with Swarovski crystals) and require other paraphernalia that would cost as much as a semester of college each year. But hey, you know, at least heavy smokers would get a few more years to live, which they would probably need to pay off their new "smokeless" cigarette habits.

As the discussion on how to target people for this new "smoke-less" product progressed, I became more and more uncomfortable. I kept thinking, *Just push these pesky little thoughts down and pay attention to the details at hand*. These algorithms were already being worked, and the train was already moving. But this sinking feeling kept creeping over me. It finally boiled up when a top executive from a different area of our company cornered me and my boss in private and pointedly asked, "Are you really going to help enable this?" My read on this comment was: *Are you really going to help a Big Tobacco company target people for their new vape device? Are you really buying this argument that they are reducing cancer by targeting heavy smokers?* And I'll be completely, vulnerably honest with you here. A wash of emotions came over me. At first shame: *How could I even consider this?* Then rage at the accusation: *Are you calling me unethical?* Then realization: *Oh crap, I think he's right!*

He then went on to explain that his division had to withdraw services after they had been duped by a group that was associated with various questionable activities. Even though it cost his business unit a lot of money to do it, they withdrew and refunded any money for their service. It was a cautionary tale for our benefit, but its effect was to make me feel like I was a tobacco terrorist. My boss and the team working on this solution were good people. They genuinely felt this could be a real way to help reduce cancer rates in heavy smokers. They were excited they could help with the solution—many of them having had loved ones whose health greatly suffered from smoking addictions. My boss's immediate reaction was indignation and to distance himself from the other executive's comments. I got the distinct sense that he was waiting to see what my reaction was going to be.

My boss valued trust, loyalty, and relationships above everything else—above skill, expertise, or school pedigree. This was rare in the AI consulting world. He had brought me over from a division that was not well liked or trusted by his and invested all his spare moments into grooming me for this executive position. I was grateful to him for all that he had done for me.

This. Was. Hard. Well-intentioned team. Champion boss. As much as I'm not really a fan of tobacco companies, the client himself was an up-and-coming digital leader who was an ambitious, friendly underdog—the kind you would normally cheer on to overcome "the Man." Not many minorities made it to the upper echelons of Big Tobacco, and this was his way of showing off his digital leadership savvy to his senior board and win the "Chief" title.

What to do? I agonized.

That night, I tossed and turned, wondering what would happen to all the heavy smokers who would be found by this algorithm. Would the intel and patterns being gathered via artificial intelligence be used to trigger them to smoke more? Since all the data was going to be in the cloud, would an ambitious or even gullible employee trade the names and identifying information of these heavy smokers to data brokers who could then sell their info to health insurers who might pay top dollar for it? Could this result in heavy smokers not being able to get insurance? What were the implications of having these "smokeless devices" that could track people's nicotine intake and smoking habits? If tobacco companies could pick up on the habits of chain smokers, would it make it easy for them to trigger more people to become smokers?

Image recognition, a form of AI, could be trained to find cigarettes in people's hands in photos on Instagram and Facebook. Because so many people's friends tag them, or name them in photos on Facebook and Instagram, the cigarette company would then have the names of the people holding the cigarettes in the photos. Having a list of smokers and their friends, where they hang out (e.g., bar names, vape stores), and what kinds of things they are into is very helpful for triggering smokers using AI capabilities administered through social media. Let me give you a scenario to help you imagine it more tangibly.

Our AI-driven social media command center team at BigTobaccoX is alerted to emerging trends around #SuperRaves, @Felix (a social media influencer followed by thousands who is a user of smokeless product), and @BigPopaSmokes (a local vape shop in BigTobaccoX's desired city). BigTobaccoX's social media team decide they could get thousands of people to sign up for their new "smokeless" device if they take advantage of this opportunity to send the following message out on the most popular social media sites: "Hey @Cortnie_CDO (that's me) @BigPopaSmokes (name of a vape store) is sponsoring a #SuperSecretRave (event associated with BigTobaccoX). Your friend @Felix is already signed up to go. Free designer smokeless devices and event admission when you register with @BigTobaccoX before the party." Then the command center team just sits back and watches the social media campaign work and continue tweaking it as needed. You get the idea.

As I played out these scenarios and the likelihood of them happening, it became clear to me that the digital leader couldn't have been honest about only going after the heavy smokers in the world. I believe they were definitely a target market for him, but not the *only* target. To fully use the power of the AI-driven command center, he would be going after people who lived their lives on social media, attended parties like raves, and were subject to peer pressure (i.e., "Your friend Felix is going"). Does this sound like any particular age groups you can think of? Let me connect a few dots here. If you do an internet search, you will quickly find out that the average age someone starts smoking is between twelve and fifteen years old. Pew research found that Instagram is used by 72 percent of US teens; the only social media platform used by more teens is YouTube. In stark contrast, only 37 percent of US adults use Instagram. The very nature of the social media outlet and the way events and other influencer activities are marketed, means teens will be impacted. This *aha!* moment made it much easier to decide what to do.

I was brought in to see if I thought this was a good AI solution to scale and repeat. The AI digital command center aspect was great, but the find-heavy-smokers and convert-non-smokers parts were not. I walked away from it. Quotas and massive bonuses could have been made on scaling a solution like that for the Big Tobacco industry, but it wasn't worth it to me. I focused on other solutions that were just as promising but without the moral questions. Some will think I was being self-righteous, perhaps. Others may wonder why I didn't go further and try to shut down the AI solution. I will say that some social media groups will not work with Big Tobacco companies, and the methods they use are unorthodox but not illegal. And that is why I've told this story. Whether you see yourself as a smoker who didn't need much nudging anyway, or as the ambitious digital leader trying to prove your abilities, or as the data science practitioner at the whim of a potentially unethical client, you have to think in advance about where your boundaries are and what you might be persuaded to do in the absence of laws and norms to govern you. I thought a lot about my boundaries after this meeting.

I got back home and took time to reflect on all the things I had seen as I rushed from the development of one AI solution to the next. I thought about the frenzy of trying to patent and obtain investment on a promising AI solution. It reminds me of how mob mentality works—once the AI initiative starts, there's no stopping it until it's run its course. One inciter starts it, and the followers find themselves hurriedly executing orders they wouldn't normally even consider. In the context of AI, the time frame is generally dictated by a product development method that most data scientists and application developers use called Agile. Most executive stakeholders familiar with the use of Agile development methods in the software business have come to expect a minimal version of a product (aka Minimal Viable Product or MVP for short) in six to eight weeks. Unfortunately, AI is not your usual software development. Six to eight weeks isn't nearly long enough to train a computer system on the patterns and resulting recommendations that might ultimately be automated as actions in huge corporate systems.

To meet these unrealistic deadlines, but to still get their MVPs into the hands of those with investment dollars on the dates promised, I have watched data science leaders beg, borrow, steal, make up (create fake data), and *scrape* data. Scraping data is the practice of using a computer program to legally steal any information that can be seen on websites. It's such a common practice that I'm sure any data scientist that would see me call it *stealing*, would balk. Think of it as going to a bookstore and copying all the books without permission or payment because they were in front of you and there were no laws against it. Data science leaders' only care was impressing the funders of their AI initiatives so they could secure the budget and resources to build them. They were rushing so fast they forgot about those who could be adversely affected. This is why I said that if we, humanity, ever lose to AI, it will be with a rush, because we hurried into developing things that might sabotage or kill us. We just needed to get it developed before the next group did—you know, for competitive purposes. After all, AI creators will tell you that if *they* didn't build it, someone else would. (That's always been sound logic.)

I listened to business teams who used AI to track your location—not just while you were in their store but after you left and went to the next. Once your smartphone's location beacon crossed into a competing store's geofenced territory, you'd receive a mobile coupon on your phone's screen meant to lure you back to the other store. You'd never know your privacy was being violated to sell another product.

I watched as intelligent automation began to grow, and with it, the potential for layoffs. Automation experts would have you document every task in your job, how you did it, what systems you used, and what decisions you made so they could program a machine to do your job—and much faster than you ever could. You would never know why you were fired or that you'd trained your own replacement.

I struggled as colleagues told me of insurance companies who wanted expert systems that could decide the outcomes of the most pivotal moments in people's lives—things like eligibility for a healthcare plan or disability insurance. And even though they wanted the system to behave like their best actuaries, they would only fund the services of a junior intern to train the system. You would never know you were turned down for a life-altering insurance claim by a machine and because that machine received non-expert training.

We've all heard the worst-case stories when the use of AI goes horribly wrong or when it's used for nefarious purposes. Perhaps the most infamous in recent memory is the Facebook-Cambridge Analytica scandal of 2016, when millions of Facebook users in swing states were unknowingly labelled as politically "persuadable" by an AI algorithm. Their personal information was sold without their knowledge via a data broker—Cambridge Analytica—to the Trump campaign, and then this AI-identified group found their Facebook feeds bombarded with ads, memes, and "news" painting the opposing candidate in a negative light. Or maybe you heard about the time Target assigned women a "pregnancy prediction score" based on data mined from their purchasing history. If the algorithm labeled a woman as pregnant, the company sent her baby-related coupons. This resulted in one well-known case in which a father of a sixteen-year-old girl angrily confronted Target for that reason—only to find out it was true from the daughter herself.

As AI becomes smarter and more powerful, it has the potential to lead to even greater problems as people seek to use algorithms developed for one purpose (such as financial risk modeling) for another (such as prioritizing care). Last fall, a study of a major teaching hospital revealed that the algorithm they used to determine priority of care contained significant racial bias. The algorithm concluded that black patients comprised just 18 percent of the hospital's high-risk group—when in fact, the real number was around 47 percent. As a result, white patients were granted access to healthcare ahead of black patients who were far less healthy and whose need for care was more urgent. What went wrong? In this case, the algorithm was trained on financial risk. What wasn't reported in the news—but that I found out through interviews—was that the hospital took an algorithm meant to model their financial risk scenarios and decided to make the most lucrative financial scenario a reality. Since white patients spent more on healthcare, the algorithm identified them as a priority for care.

Or how about mistaken identity? A man in Michigan was arrested—in front of his wife and two young daughters—for a crime he did not commit, based upon facial recognition technology that misidentified him. AI-based facial recognition technologies are trained largely on images of people with light skin as opposed to darker skin;

as a result, they cannot easily differentiate features of one black person from another as indicated in the famous Gender Shades study by MIT's Joy Buolamwini.

And in the UK, the world witnessed its first mass protest against an algorithm as college hopefuls chanted "Fuck the algorithm!" as they marched outside the country's Department of Education. Students who were unable to sit for their A-level exams due to Covid-19 were instead assigned final grades by an algorithm whose data was based upon a school's previous performance. About 40 percent of the students received lower grades than their teachers projected for them, jeopardizing their acceptance into the college of their choice.

Despite well-known failures like these, let me be clear: artificial intelligence has given us some incredible benefits, and I think it will be amazing—once we can trust it.

But AI is like the Wild West right now, and this is the time when it's most dangerous. This is a fast-developing, highly experimental field, and there is very little transparency or oversight and few standards, policies, or laws that will safeguard your rights, privacy, and jobs. The lack of regulations, coupled with the average person's lack of awareness of how AI works and how it affects them on a daily basis, makes for an incredibly risky situation. Unless you're an insider and have seen firsthand how AI is being used, there is no way for you to know what could go wrong. You will only feel the squeeze of irresponsible AI all around you. Perhaps your house gets foreclosed on by an unchecked mortgage algorithm, or a police officer shows up to arrest you or a loved one at the recommendation of a faulty facial recognition match, or your bank account is seized after an AI firm's careless data-handling results in the theft of your identity.

Maybe you have already seen some of the signs but didn't know why these things were happening. For example, you emailed your family about your miscarriage and now you see ads in your Pinterest and Amazon feeds for consolatory cards, jewelry, and books. That's the work of AI that targets digital ads to you. Or maybe you noticed it's harder for people to get a job (the result of AI that vets your personality for employers based on what you say on social media), or that your kids seem to be endlessly addicted to YouTube. This is thanks to AI recommendation engines that suggest one video after the other. Or maybe your Facebook feed seems to have been taken over by ideological groups spouting hateful stuff you honestly couldn't care less about. Or maybe you did one of those ancestry genetic kits, only to find afterward that you were "coincidentally" denied life or long-term disability insurance.

Incidents like these are all attributable to the unethical or irresponsible use of AI, and they will only become more prevalent as AI becomes more intelligent and its reach expands. Until regulators and educators catch on and catch up, and until the Wild West period of AI is under control, you'll need to educate yourself about what's really happening with AI and empower yourself with the knowledge you need to protect yourself and your loved ones. You can't assume that all AI is infallible, private, and secure, and that its creators have your best interests in mind. It's not, and not all of them do. Likewise, don't assume that because it's everywhere—in our smartphones and watches, our homes, cars, computers, and social networks—it must be trustworthy.

But also don't assume that AI is too complex for you to understand. It's not! That's what I'm here for and why I wrote this book. My intent is to be your guide to understanding what AI is capable of, where the major danger zones are located, and how to protect yourself until we have better laws and social norms in place.

The book is based upon the most common questions I get about AI from the people who surround me every day. I've compiled questions from business associates, teachers, doctors, church goers, rideshare and taxi drivers, family members, and even people I've talked with while standing in line at places like the post office, Starbucks, Walmart, and Kohl's. These are not AI research scientists; they are everyday people who are curious about AI, its capabilities, and what to be on the lookout for. I'll answer these questions in regular language without the technical jargon.

The first two chapters will teach you the AI basics: what it is, how it works, what everyday things it's in, the pros and cons of these systems, and what's reality and what's hype when it comes to AI. This will help give you a foundational understanding going into the chapters that follow. Those chapters will guide you through the ways you might be directly impacted by AI in your everyday life. We'll cover the main issues most people care about, such as: how AI might affect your ability to get a job and keep it; how bad actors could use AI to hack you; what AI knows about you and why that matters (even if you think you have "nothing to hide"); how you could be manipulated by AI and not know it; how to recognize and limit your exposure to misinformation, deepfakes, and fake news; the many roles AI plays in healthcare and what you can do to advocate for the best care; and how AI could siphon away your rights and liberties. Along the way, I'll give you specific tips and practical steps to protect your privacy, rights, and personal data—no technical expertise required.

What you don't know about AI really *can* hurt you. But not on my watch!

CHAPTER 1
What Is Artificial Intelligence and How Does It Work?

A year spent in artificial intelligence is enough to make one believe in God.

—Alan Perlis

What Is AI?

Before we talk about what AI is, let's talk about what it isn't so we can get past preconceived notions. Close your eyes and think about what AI looks like. What was the first thing your brain conjured up? Was it a robot or android? Was it a Hollywood-based version of AI—maybe HAL from *2001: A Space Odyssey* or the Terminator or Ava from *Ex Machina*? These are all super-advanced notions of what AI is. If these are what you are using to base your criteria for AI today, then let's do some resetting so you can better understand the basics of AI as the capabilities exist today.

AI are human-like intelligence systems. Robots and androids are different than AI—though AI systems can certainly be embedded in them to make them smart. AI can exist anywhere there is enough processing power for its code (e.g., smartphones, computers, cars).

The goal of any artificially intelligent system is to analyze and make decisions at least as good or exponentially better than humans.

Three Types of AI Systems

The varying degrees of how well AI performs relative to human general intelligence is what determines which of the three AI types an AI is.

Artificial Narrow Intelligence (ANI)

Inferior to Humans' General Intelligence

Today's AI systems are all Narrow AI. These AI are boring really. They do not have some sleek android body as envisioned in movies nor evil mastermind plots to take over the world. These AI are bits of code that can be embedded anywhere there is enough processing power (e.g., cars, computers, planes, tractors, fridges, smartphones). They are focused on specific tasks with specific objectives; they are not true multitaskers yet like us humans. There are not any AI systems out there currently that can drive you to work safely, take care of your kids, *and* run a business. They *might* do one of these tasks but not all three. While this type of AI would not beat us at general intelligence, it could master many tasks in a profession like, say, accounting and be combined with robotic process automation to take our jobs in that area. It can also process way more data and information for a particular task than humans can, which would give it what I think of as "calculator intelligence." You wouldn't give a calculator credit for knowing more than we do just because it can calculate big numbers faster.

Also, given that today's best robots cannot play a rudimentary game of soccer or amble about a room without guidance without falling over or bumping into things, it is not likely we will embody these AI to create a Terminator or realistic android anytime soon. The robots of today are not learning and reacting on their own; they are basically elaborate remote-controlled puppets—even the famous robot Sophia. (Do an internet search on "Sophia the robot" and you'll see what I mean.) Every example of AI you will see in chapter 2 is Narrow AI.

Artificial General Intelligence (AGI)

Equal to Humans' General Intelligence

This is the type of AI that most people think of when asked what AI is. It's also usually imagined in some type of android. This type of AI would be able to match us in intellectual ability in a broad way. If I put the AI system in a robot with legs and asked it to walk, it would figure it out on its own in a similar fashion to how toddlers learn. It would use trial and error and then revise its own learning. Humans learn from both observation and knowledge that seems inherent—instinctual, if you will. We touch a hot burner, and we learn not to touch a hot burner again because it will hurt. A robot or AI will not have five fully functioning senses, at least not in the immediate future. Does it require our five senses in order to have human-like reactions? For example, should it be given a simulated version of feelings like pain and suffering so that it can be sympathetic to humans as well as learn like they do? Or should we take advantage of the strength of AI inside of robotics and not make it susceptible to our pains. Would it still be able to learn? Part of why we are careful when driving a car is that we do not want to harm someone else or be harmed in an accident. We have emotions such as empathy toward others and fear of injury that constrain our behaviors when driving so we don't drive recklessly. But how do we constrain an AI system so that it fits with our societal norms?

There have been plenty of arguments about whether we can simulate consciousness and intention in computer systems, thanks to the works of philosophers like John Searle and David Chalmers. One specific argument on this subject is the Chinese Room thought experiment. The gist is that an AI system can be programmed to read Chinese characters and even respond with Chinese answers convincing enough to fool a Chinese-speaking person into believing they are talking with another Chinese speaker. But that doesn't mean that the computer system *understands* what it said to the person any more than a human would if they were given a set of instructions on how to answer questions in Chinese. The AI will simply be doing what it was trained to do.

Google's CEO surprised the world in 2018 when he demonstrated a new, amazingly human-sounding AI voice assistant called Duplex.[1] Designed to book appointments for its user, it could call restaurants, ask an employee for a reservation, and then respond to any questions the employee had. It would even say "um" and take pause breaks like a human speaker. It was so realistic that tech ethicists backlashed, insisting that Google have Duplex identify itself as an AI up front when it called a person. But just because AI systems can mimic shallow conversations or even our mannerisms, does that mean the AI system is as intelligent as a human? We wouldn't assume an actual person was intelligent if all they could do is answer questions about the weather or book restaurant reservations, so why should we let a machine get away with being considered intelligent for doing so? Not to mention machines do not have other components of intelligence such as personality, intent, or emotions.

Artificial Super Intelligence (ASI)

Superior to Humans' General Intelligence

I saw a slide during a Google presentation where the presenter casually mentioned machine-learning algorithms setting up better data architectures than humans. I'm not going to lie; it concerned me. Why? Data architecture is sort of like the strategy of how AI systems receive their data. If it can set these up, could it also just code itself around any types of kill-switch programs that we might set up for it? The question that must be answered in order to know is: Could AI give *itself* goals? Will its goals always come only from human programmers? Experts who think this couldn't happen also don't believe super intelligence is possible. But some experts *do* believe it's possible. One expert in particular, Nick Bostrom, has written an entire book called—wait for it—*Superintelligence* to explore the matter. I really can't decide what I believe on this until I see evidence of AI that either 1) purposely defies the goals it was given by its human programmers, or 2) demonstrates that it can give itself goals. I believe AI could surpass our general intelligence—but not for decades, and even then, this ASI would need to know how to keep us humans from pulling its electricity or scrambling its code.

What Does It Mean to Exhibit Human-Like Intelligence?

There are humans who, you could argue, think and act like computers. There are humans who are geniuses in areas like math and science but not smart at interpersonal relationships and business strategy and vice versa. Determining intelligence is highly subjective. Sometimes it gets a bit murky to decide what constitutes human-like intelligence. Keep this in mind for later when we go through an exercise to define "human-like" thinking.

To exhibit human-like intelligence, AI must understand, reason, learn, interact, and act like a human. That's a tall order. So tall, in fact, that many AI experts will refer to AI as any system capable of just *one* of these things as opposed to *all* of them. You may be thinking, *Hey, I don't know of any systems today that can truly do this*. I can't have a full-on conversation with Siri or Alexa. I can't ask them deep and meaningful questions and have them return meaningful answers. You're right. I can ask how the weather is, and they will tell me. But they don't usually go beyond the answer to the exact question I asked. They don't ask why I might be checking the weather in Colorado when I live in Texas. They don't reason that I may be planning a trip and want to know about camping conditions in the Rocky Mountains. They don't understand my intent from my body language or by gathering contextual clues such as the fact that I'm wearing a T-shirt that says "I love the Rockies." While there may be systems out there designed to do some of these, they do not come together in one single package and work holistically…yet. If it did, I believe Pedro Domingos and the AI researchers on the mission to achieve "the Master Algorithm" would be celebrating with a huge bottle of champagne.

Further, if these AI systems are supposed to be human-like, and if you consider that nonverbal cues make up the majority of communication, then would we need to see a face, expressions, and posture to exhibit the right kind of tone and messages? Would an AI in fact need to have a human body and face to truly meet the requirements? While there are groups out there like Soul Machines in New Zealand working on this kind of thing, it does not exist in a ubiquitous way today.

Why AI Can Be So Confusing

People are using all sorts of different terms as AI evolves. And we all carry presumptions about AI. Sometimes these are known to us and sometimes not. For example, some people talk about robots like they alone are AI. Sometimes researchers and AI developers define AI as the machine learning algorithm alone because that is really the engine of AI. I find myself doing this constantly. But really, AI is a *set* of technologies and data sources. It's a bit like talking about a person and saying their eyes are human or their legs are human. That's true. They belong to humans as parts that enable a whole, but they, by themselves, are not a whole human being. For many, this confuses things. Because, well, how far do we go with this description to have "human-like intelligence," or is it just to *demonstrate* human-like intelligence? Is it just intelligence, and if so, what components of our intelligence does it have to be equal to? Does it have to be equal to *all* of our intelligence? In that case, are there aspects of our intelligence that we should set as criteria for human-like intelligence, such as emotional intelligence, inference, intention, ambition, logic, and the ability to answer questions?

Is the Turing Test good enough anymore? It was designed in 1950 to understand if a computer could answer questions well enough to be mistaken as a human. Today, wouldn't the AI have an unfair advantage? Specifically, couldn't it just look up on the internet anything it's asked directly? Would we consider that to be sufficient to meet the definition of AI? Isn't that basically what Siri or Alexa can do today? That's what Google's search engine does. Is Google a complete AI? Google scientists have certainly pioneered the field of AI. But does that mean a search engine is truly AI? Is it a whole AI or just a part? Or would we say that because Google cannot reason with us and ask clarifying questions to return the best possible answers based on our intent, it's not really AI? Do humans only ask shallow, one-dimensional questions? Not often. So just how human-like does an AI need to be in order to meet each of our preexisting assumptions about AI?

Let's test our theory about Google's search engine based on what we've just defined as the criteria: to understand, learn, reason, interact, and act.

AI Test of Google Search Engine

Criteria for AI

Understands like a human

I can speak to it, and it can tell what I'm saying as long as it understands my syntax. What I mean is, if I go outside of a subject for which it has been trained, it may not be able to give me an answer. If, for example, I asked it something in legal jargon, it may not be able to return a meaningful answer because it has not been trained on legal words. But then, you could argue this is the case for humans as well. Humans who have not taken law classes may not understand legal jargon either.

Reasons like a human

If I told Google Search, to help me find ways to cut costs, would it be able to ask me a set of clarifying questions? Would it innately understand that it's not okay to save money in ways that might jeopardize people's health or lives? Or to do anything that violates societal norms in order to cut costs? I think it fails here. But then again, you can argue that some humans or other legal entities like corporations do as well.

Learns like a human

Does Google's search engine learn like a human? No. But much has been done to help AI here. Oftentimes though, the part of our experience that is inexplicable to AI relies on senses and emotions. We touch something that is hot, and it hurts; so we don't do that again. Then we learn all the things that are hot and associate that same pain with those items. Scientists would say this is about reward and punishment. But often we don't know ourselves well enough to imbue an AI with rewards or punishments.

Interacts like a human

Does Google's search engine interact like a human? No. Technically there are chatbots out there that can respond to questions in an online chat format. They can even talk to you, but most have a very robotic-sounding voice. They don't usually have a face with expressive emotions. They don't typically use tone and word choices like slang or humor as part of their communication. They don't get upset or use silent pauses to make their point. They can't touch our hand or hug us or use any nonverbal cues to make us feel better if we tell it something traumatic. It can't laugh like a human if we tell it a joke.

Acts like a human

Let's say I whispered to Google Search that there was an intruder in my house. What would Google Search do? What would I expect Google Search to do if it were a human versus what I expect from a computer system? What would a human do? A human that heard this on the phone would probably stop, listen to my tone to determine if I was kidding or serious, and call the police and send them to my house. Would Google Search do that? Probably not, because this would require inference and deduction as opposed to command language like "Call 911." Google Search, by itself, does not currently have the ability to call 911 because this is not its purpose. It cannot multitask like a human because most AI are built for one singular purpose.

Should Google's search engine be considered an AI based on *all* of the above criteria? No. Does it have elements of AI? Yes. If it has some elements but not all, is it still AI? I would say yes. And this is exactly how things get confusing. I would suggest to you that Google Search is a "narrow AI" versus an "artificial *general* intelligence," which is what most of us think of as being capable of exhibiting broad human intelligence.

How Does AI "Understand"?

An AI's ability to simulate "understanding" is dependent upon the data it ingests, how it gets that data, and the purpose of the AI. For some uses of AI, it needs the five senses like humans to "understand."

Sometimes this data is representational; other times it's coming directly from the sources; and in some cases, the data needed is not available and the search is on to find the best proxy for that information to be used in an algorithm. In my experience, when something has gone wrong with AI, it has almost always been a problem that started with data. The quality, formatting, validity, veracity, and lineage of the data are incredibly important in the formulation of the AI system. At this point in computing, no matter what kind of data the AI system ingests, it will always need a way to get it back to language a computer understands. So even if a computer "sees," it must have the photos or the videos converted into digitized data that it can read, understand, and analyze. There is almost always some way of converting that data through various methods which we will dive into next.

See (commonly used in AI today)

How does an AI system see? As humans, we look at things and can almost instantaneously identify what we're seeing, including attributes about the image itself, and we can also contextualize what we're seeing. For example, it's a human, and the human is a girl, she appears sad—which we infer from her facial expression and the dropped ice cream cone next to her on the ground. We do that in less than a second just by looking at the scene. Right now, a computer's ability to understand the image itself is hard enough, much less to pick up on surrounding elements and their contextual meaning to the main subject of the image we see (the girl in this case). We derive instant meaning and make instantaneous decisions based on it. The meaning we derive, in some cases, will be different than the conclusions other humans would draw based on our life experiences up to that point.

For example, if my life experience included having a child six years ago, I would pay particular attention to a child who is 1) alone without any parents nearby, and 2) crying. The meaning I might derive is that the child could be lost. The empathy I would feel for both the parents not in the image and the child would force me into action. I would stop everything (my commute to work, my morning coffee run, walking the dog) in order to help the child find her parents. On the other hand, if my initial inference is simply that the child is crying because of the spilled ice cream and I identify an adult in close proximity with similar features, then I would likely assume the crying is not serious, and there is an adult—perhaps a relative—who can help the child with the dropped ice cream. Even if an AI system, let's say an AI-based closed-circuit video system, could "see" and visually recognize the elements in the picture, could it derive meaning and a course of action from them? The ability to monitor is not the same as the ability to intervene. Is an AI system that could monitor actually intelligent? Would it do the same things that a human would in those circumstances? Would it have "life experiences" (simulated or otherwise) to draw upon that could help it to intervene as a human would? Or would it require something more, some way to program in empathy?

An AI system technologically "sees" via the development of a type of machine learning algorithm that looks for patterns that make a dog a dog, a woman a woman, a cat a cat. This capability is called image recognition. Tons and tons of photos have been labeled by people to help train various image recognition systems.

Hear (commonly used in AI today)

Artificially intelligent agents such as Alexa and Siri require speech recognition capabilities in order to listen and talk to you. This gives these AI systems the ability to recognize the words you have just spoken to it and then to translate those words into text so that it can be analyzed and understood through text analytics. Companies that are on the leading edge of speech recognition systems include: Google, Microsoft, IBM, Baidu, Apple, Amazon, Nuance, and SoundHound.

Speech recognition often includes other areas you may have seen in headlines, such as natural-language processing (NLP), natural-language understanding, and natural-language generation. These can often be combined with digital signal processing (DSP) capabilities, which can home in on just the human voice and block out background noises. As an example, DSP is used to home in on just your answer when an auditory chatbot says something like, "Say yes if you need an agent," as opposed to your dog barking in the background or your husband chiding your child. Ontologies and knowledge graphs help the AI ascribe context and meaning to your words by subject. Here's an example of an ontology around film. This is helpful because if you want to look up the song "Zombie" by the band The Cran-berries, and you're in a music AI system, it won't deliver a bunch of zombie movies instead. It becomes even more important when you are in industry-based (e.g., oil, energy, telecommunications, media) or profession-based (e.g., legal, information technology, human re-sources) applications where there are lots of acronyms and words that will not make sense without context.

Touch (not commonly used in AI today)

If you think about how touch works for us, it's not all just "touch." There's more to it than that. We can feel cold, hot objects can burn us, and our knees might ache after a long run. Heavy objects that we try to lift may bear down on us hard and signal that it will be impossible for us to lift them. We can tell if something is solid, soft, liquid, sharp. We can feel mist against our skin. Our sense of touch at its most basic can be boiled down into a few main categories: 1) pressure, 2) temperature, 3) movement, and 4) texture.

Most robots in the past have relied on cameras and proximity sensors to determine where objects are, but they haven't really "felt" anything. But now a slew of emerging methods are being tried to heighten touch in AI robots. Some are using nanowire that sits on their "skin" above the surface, some are using waves of light that come from within the robot, and some are using tiny channels of liquid, while others are developing artificial "nerves" and nervous systems.

As of August 2018, "hairy robots" were going to be more sensi-tive to touch than humans. Researchers, led by Zeynep Celik-Butler at the University of Texas at Arlington, patented a new self-powered smart "skin" that would help robots gather information about their surroundings by using millions of tiny microscopic (0.2 microns) nanowire "hairs."[2] The applications for this are endless, but specific ideas included weaving the skin into smart clothing such as uniforms that could detect toxic chemicals, and identifying people by match-ing fingerprints that come in contact with the "smart skin."[3] Another concept was that this "skin" could be placed on prosthetics to give a sense of feeling back to the people wearing them. Researchers at the Harvard School of Engineering and Applied Science partnered with the Wyss Institute to pioneer the 3D printing of a sensory material made of liquid—specifically organic ionic liquid-based conductive ink—into the soft elastomer material of a robot's skin to replicate the sensations of movement, pressure, and temperature. In October 2017, researchers at UCLA and the University of Washington described their research on an artificial skin for robots. The skin would allow robots to do things like dismantle a bomb, perform surgery, and even fry an egg like a chef.[4] The skin uses tiny channels filled with electrically conductive liquid metal and is made of the same stuff as swimming goggles.

As of June 2018, Stanford grad student Yeongin Kim was working on an artificial nerve consisting of a pressure sensor, a ring oscillator, and an ion gel–gated transistor, to form an artificial mechanoreceptor that could help provide prosthetics with feelings of movement, temperature, texture, and certain kinds of pressure.[5] It would do this by connecting with residual nerve endings from a limb. But there's a lot more to this than just the human potential: the artificial nerve could be combined with an artificial brain, which we know Google has been working on for quite some time. If successful, it could result in the first bio-robots that could process input and decide how to react, just as humans do. Now isn't that a bit scary and exciting all at once?

Smell (not commonly used in AI today)

Perhaps the first question you are asking is, *Why the heck would AI need to smell?* What is the practical application for that? Well, what if we could use it to detect:

a.   (and diagnose) lung cancer early;

b.   something burning in the house while the family is asleep;

c.   a gas leak;

d.   when food is spoiled;

e.   the fear in a potential terrorist;

f.   what someone has eaten or drunk.

Most "smell" sensors work by detecting gases and chemicals in the air. One of the most noble applications comes from a robot maker in Asia whose aim is to take care of elderly and bedridden patients and help them to extend their time in their homes as opposed to having to go into a care facility. One of the main reasons the elderly go into nursing homes (beyond the fact that they can no longer take care of themselves) is that their homes become unsafe for them because they forget to turn appliances off. An AI system equipped with smell detection could work with smart appliances to ensure they are turned off and functioning correctly. And incredibly, CT Asia Robotics is using smell-detection sensors to "smell-check" patients via the use of a gas sensor that can diagnose the presence of lung cancer with an 80 percent accuracy rate.

Taste (not commonly used in AI today)

Chef Watson is the AI that first comes to mind when I think of an AI that can "taste." To get "taste" into its data, Watson's creators added simulated human taste buds to it. Ha! Just kidding. But I did have you fooled there for a second. No seriously, just like everything else in AI, this supposed sensory ability is added with huge patterns of data. In this case, it's data about what humans like in terms of food. Chef Watson's research scientists had it analyze over thirty-five thousand recipes looking for patterns of ingredient pairings, preparations, food styles, and cooking methods. It was also trained in food chemistry and an obscure scientific field called hedonic psychophysics—the psychology of what people find pleasant and unpleasant. AI does not actually "taste" just yet, it simply derives its understanding of our "tastes" from patterns of data.

How Does AI Reason and Learn?

The creators of the AI system program a set of instructions into it called an algorithm, which helps it develop reasoning capabilities. The AI system learns to use its reasoning by training on data sets for which it has to respond correctly until it gets good enough to beat a human. This is how the AI learns; it is trained by experts, data scientists, and loads of data. There are three basic training methods used to help an AI system learn.

Training Methods

1. Supervised Learning

Most AI systems are trained using supervised learning. First, people label the test data. For example, if the goal of an AI system were to sort out pictures of "ripe peaches," a human would put a tag on a picture that says "ripe peach" and this would be stored in a test data set with other ripe-peach pictures. The AI system is then fed the "ripe peach" training data to see what defining characteristics the algorithm picks up and whether it can still pick the ripe peaches accurately if shown a bunch of ripe peaches mixed in with other fruits like apples and with peaches that are underripe or spoiled.

The AI system may have to iterate on certain pictures of peaches or even certain types of apples if they look like peaches. If it can't meet the established accuracy threshold (let's say correct identification of ripe peaches at least 90 percent of the time), then it needs human help identifying more "ripe peach" factors. As the system trainer, I would then point out bruised skin and stems that have fallen out as a way for the system to disqualify those from the ripe-peaches category and instead place them in the "spoiled" category. The AI will then add that learning to its algorithm (its instruction set) and continue attempting to pick pictures of ripe peaches. Once it has iterated like this enough times to reach an acceptable accuracy rate (defined by the expert), then the information learned could be officially incorporated into the system. Human intervention in AI is much needed until we have a better handle on how machines interpret their instructions and incorporate learning. This is why transparency and an explanation of what these algorithms do is so important. Even when humans are given a chance to intervene, sometimes we do not provide sufficiently experienced experts, or we flat out aren't paying attention when the computer actually misses something. This was the case with the self-driving car that hit a woman. The car was mandated in emergency situations to let the human take over. But by the time the human realized there *was* an emergency situation, it was too late and the person had been hit.

The types of algorithms that can be trained using supervised learning include regression, decision tree, random forest, k-nearest neighbor, and logistic regression, which you will learn more about in the next section.

2. Unsupervised Learning

This method of algorithmic training is used for lumping things, people, and places together based on observations of similarities. For example, the computer learns on its own that all the "green round things" look alike so they get classified together. All the oblong yellow things seem similar, so those get lumped together. If we were classifying humans, the criteria would probably be based on many things and would depend on what the algorithm's creator is trying to accomplish. For example, if I want to sell more purple sweaters using Instagram as a channel for my marketing, then I'd show the AI system the Instagram photos of people who wear purple sweaters. It would then start to classify all available data about them from Instagram and then look for similarities (*other* than the purple sweaters). Algorithms that could be trained using unsupervised learning would be: Apriori algorithm, K-means.

3. Reinforcement Learning

The machine is given a goal, such as "win at the strategy game of Go," and then it trains itself using trial and error in a specified environment such as a game or some containment that has explicit rules complete with rewards and penalties built in. It learns from past experiences and makes different decisions each time, until it finally achieves its goal. This is how AlphaGo, the AI champion of Go, was trained. An example of an algorithm that is trained using reinforcement learning is the Markov model, which you will learn about below.

An AI System's Reasoning Comes from Algorithms

While I won't go through every algorithm used in machine learning, these eight are the most popular. If you are interested in learning more about the wide variety of opinions on how well each of these work for different applications, then read Pedro Domingos's *The Master Algorithm*.

- *Linear regression* is the simplest and most popular. It estimates the values of things and people based on another value. For example, I can estimate that you will most likely weigh more if you are taller because every time height goes up—all else being equal—weight goes up.

- *Logistic regression* is like a Magic 8 Ball toy, ask it any question where the answers can be: yes, no, or maybe. It gives the probability that something is going to happen, not happen, or maybe happen. For example, there is a 40 percent probability that it will rain today.

- *Decision trees* produce groupings of factors that can significantly explain the main variable. For example, if I want to predict if a kid will play outside, I might have to consider factors like the weather conditions (e.g., whether it is rainy or sunny) or the presence of friends (e.g., enough for indoor video games or outdoor soccer). Now multiply those factors times millions of people and decisions and you can see why this is the domain of machine learning.

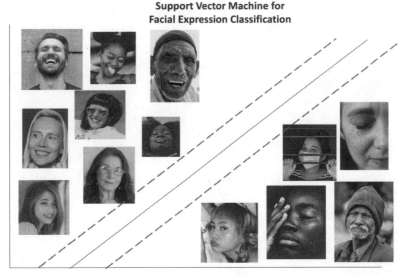

Support Vector Machine for Facial Expression Classification

Happy Faces

Sad Faces

- *Support vector machine (SVM)* is like "drawing a line in the sand" to differentiate the domain of different groups. An example is classifying facial expressions into groups of happy and sad. You'd map out all the pictures that were super-smiley with teeth showing to ones that were barely a grin. You'd do the same for sad pictures. You'd draw a line between the ones that were happy and the ones that were sad. To understand better, see the diagram for the Support Vector Machine for Facial Expression Classification.

- *Naive Bayes* is family of algorithms that calculates the conditional probability of an event based on prior knowledge related to the event. It classifies according to probabilities that are then ranked, letting the highest-probability entities rise to the top.

- *K-nearest neighbor (KNN)* is the "majority rules" algorithm. I've also called it the "guilt by association" algorithm. If your friends jumped off a bridge, would you do it too? According to KNN, if three of your five closest friends jumped, then you would be classified as a jumper. Remember this when you accept friend requests on Facebook.

- *K-means* clusters things and people by their defining characteristics. It's often used to segment customers based on buying patterns.

- *Markov models* are used for probabilistic forecasting and assume a future state depends only on its current state. This works well when there are specific "rules" as with a game. Teams I worked with used this for what I call ledger-style AI systems. What I mean is, if I have a set of procurement rules like, *I will only pay five cents for a pencil and no more*, then I can use a Markov model to look at invoices from thousands of my suppliers, and it will go through each line item looking for pencils and the list of 12 million other things that I have set maximum prices on. It classifies any pencils over five cents as things I won't pay for and recommends those items as "rejects," which in my larger AI system means *go back and try again, vendor, you charged me too much* based on my "rules," which in this case happens to be purchasing contracts I have with the vendor.

What Can AI Systems Do that No Others Can?

Artificial intelligence systems can analyze massive amounts of data. Think ten years of taxes for hundreds of businesses or individuals at once, thousands of pages of regulatory laws, billions of social media profiles, billions of internet searches, millions of health diagnoses and genomic research articles, and then combine them all and look for patterns against queries.

They can take in unstructured data that has been previously "dark" or unanalyzed because it is contextual, such as *written or typed text, spoken words, videos, and pictures.* Have you ever tried to analyze numerous videos trying to find out the answer to one question but from multiple perspectives? Instead of quickly getting to the answer, you might have spent a whole weekend watching the videos for the one answer you needed.

We have been able to analyze data that is in structured rows and columns—think of spreadsheets and data tables—for over three decades now. But what we have not been able to do is analyze trends and patterns among spoken words, text, videos, and pictures. Think about all the books, manuals, insurance policies, doctor's notes, lengthy regulatory documents, ongoing social media feeds from the likes of Facebook and Twitter, Google searches, or reviews in comments sections. Think of the efficiency farmers could achieve if they could use pictures of rotten produce to have robots sort them out before they made it into the bins with the good tomatoes or apples during harvest season.

Analyzing *continuously streaming and constantly changing data* brings the power of *now* and instant action or reaction that only artificial intelligence systems can provide. Examples of this type of data would be ever-changing social media feeds that stream all day, online buying behaviors, connected device data such as the geotracking on your phone that changes when you change locations throughout the day, data from your car that tracks your speed, location, and driving style (e.g., hard stops, fast turns). This ability means AI can continuously adapt decisions and actions as a result of new or changed data versus rules-based systems which are static and unresponsive to new insights. As a matter of fact, the more data an AI system has running through it, the more refined its decision-making capabilities become.

For example, AI systems that focus on personalization will get better and better at deciding your preferences for specific clothing items the more you shop online. With every purchase, internet search, "like," and outfit you hover your mouse over, the AI learns your shopping habits. When you *look* at something on a webpage and it's in one color but then *buy* it on a different webpage because it's shown in another, AI learns your color preferences and perhaps even the visual stimulations that entice you to buy. Then, if you like to buy that particular thing from a certain retailer over another, it's learning about your store preferences and even your payment preferences if you buy the item with a certain type of credit card or payment form.

All of this rich and continually changing data is fueling the AI system's learning and decisions, and it ultimately results in the combination of offers it feeds to you. To give you an example, it might show me a Credit Card Company X "bonus miles" offer for bedazzled shoes on the CloggyShoes retail site on the "shoes-with-outfit" version of the webpage. Knowing me, I'd probably buy it like this as opposed to buying shoes from a webpage that shows me just the shoes alone. I'm a sucker for well-put-together combo offers, especially when presented as an outfit.

Hasn't AI Been Around Forever? Why Is It Making a Comeback?

It's true the first AI research has roots back to 1954 and received big funding in the 1960s due to interest from the US Department of Defense. All technologies have hype cycles with fluctuating levels of interest and funding, and AI is no different. There are three basic reasons why AI has made a comeback recently.

First, there is a whole lot more accessible data in the world now. We live our lives as digital and social media beings, and that leaves a great variety of rich data behind as a byproduct. Even the somewhat antiquated healthcare system has finally seen a transition to the digital age with electronic health records for patients plus new collective doctor diagnostic systems which allow for sharing of data among doctors as approved by patients. There's new genomic data thanks to the popularity of genetic testing for ancestral heritage. Social media and geotracking data are growing exponentially, thanks to Google,

Facebook, YouTube, Twitter, WhatsApp, LinkedIn, Instagram, and Snapchat. The Internet of Things—devices connected to the internet and thus to other connected devices—is creating billions of bytes of data doing everything from detecting maintenance needs in oil rigs to ensuring your house stays safe and sound and at a cozy temperature. Retailers are collecting buyer behavioral data from apps you've downloaded for convenience or rewards like Starbucks, Amazon, Walmart, and Target. There are slews of service apps that we are using that create data profiles as well, such as: banking, matchmaking, ovulation tracking, apartment/house finding/evaluating, financial advisement, gaming. Just look at your smartphone right now. All of those apps are collecting data about you either directly or from geotracking on your phone or pictures you've taken or all of the above.

Not to mention companies are monetizing their existing data or augmenting their data to develop data sets specifically for use with potential business partners' AI systems. For example, fitness tracker groups are combining their data with other health data via application programming interfaces (APIs) to allow more insight into healthy habits like working out or nutrition for weight-loss goals. Another group is tagging pictures of specific crops at different levels of ripeness so that farmers who own specific robotic harvesting tractors can delineate right there in the field which vegetables or fruits are spoiled and which are good. In this new AI era, data and the training of the algorithms are where the differentiation will come, not the algorithms themselves. Hence why I spend so much time explaining all the possible data sources so you can see for yourself how diverse and big the data opportunities are in the AI space.

Second, the computing power is exponential with new quantum capabilities paired with data storage, which has gotten more efficient and really cheap. For the first time in history, computing power—the ability to crunch through massive streams of data—is actually keeping up with ambitions for AI systems. Data scientists who train AI algorithms will complain that it still takes weeks instead of hours, but the computing power is evolving quickly. Fun fact: When Watson first came on the scene with *Jeopardy!* back in 2010, the computing hardware took up a huge room and could do a lot less crunching at the same time. As of 2017, the same tech was the size of three pizza boxes, and it just continues to get smaller with the introduction of each new chip.

Third, more businesses are jumping in than ever before, thanks in no small part to the wealth of data available now that wasn't available in the past. Government armed forces and intelligence groups have always been interested in AI. Banks have had need for machine-learning aspects of AI for as long as hackers and fraud have been around. But more recently, insurance firms, manufacturing groups, large technology companies, media and entertainment firms, oil and gas companies, retailers, and automotive companies have all come up with inventive ways to leverage AI in their businesses. IBM had a log of over 150 different use cases in almost every single industry on the planet. Which brings us to the next question.

What Are Businesses Using AI For?

The biggest lure of AI is to capture the excitement of being a great tech disrupter…like Google, Facebook, Uber, Amazon, Airbnb. These digital platforms leverage AI innovation to connect people with each other and the stuff they need, whether it's a place to stay, a taxi, or grandma. AI also creates bottom-line-enhancing opportunities through cost reduction and efficiencies. Then of course, some CEOs and business executives will always be on the cutting edge of technology. They are the ones always looking for the latest and greatest ways to do things. They are innovators, first movers. Naturally, these leaders will migrate to AI and seek ways to use it in their business because it's the latest, hottest tech. These leaders want their companies to lead the charge and take the early-mover advantage. But we are now entering the point in the AI era where it's no longer about early adoption. The use cases (how AI is being applied to business contexts) are more established, though the technology and methodologies can still be quite experimental.

Many CEOs who are now delving more into AI are doing so because they are afraid of digital disruption. They are worried that others will leverage AI to react immediately to the marketplace, and if the reaction is big enough and swift enough, they could be left in the dust. Of course, there are many examples of digital disruption that well-established companies did not see coming, and as a result, they are either out of business or they are hanging on for dear life while racing to adapt. In case you haven't seen these examples before: Netflix overcame Blockbuster and several other on-demand entertainment models from cable companies and the like. What's more, its most popular entertainment business model doesn't even rely on getting a DVD into your hands anymore because they stream it to you. They are now also taking over the movie industry. Interestingly enough, it is because they have been using AI to understand subscribers' viewing habits and entertainment wants (e.g., sci-fi, affinities for Ryan Gosling, anime, vampires, STEM programs for kids) that they know best what we want in our movies. They are using this information to develop content that appeals to us better than some of the top movie-making companies out there.

I remember back when all the Harry Potter films were coming out; I couldn't wait to go to the theater to see them. As a movie-lover, I had once gone every other weekend or so. But then somewhere along the way, it seemed like plots became dull and the prices of movies at the theater kept going up. Now I pretty much reserve my theatergoing experiences for Marvel movies because I really want to see them on the big screen. But back to Netflix's model. They provide entertainment in a way that movie companies can't—at home, in our pajamas, for a low monthly fee, with several more choices served up right afterward…a double, triple, or infinity feature (as they call it in theater terms), or in streaming terms, "binge-watching."

Let's keep going with these examples because it's interesting to view other industries' digital disruptions as well. Uber upended the taxi business without owning a single vehicle—by getting us to do their driving! Ha! Who could have seen that coming? AI did. Airbnb Inc. became one of the largest accommodations providers yet owns no real estate. The most popular media owner is Facebook, and they do not create any content whatsoever—but they do own *your* content. Apple and Google are some of the world's largest software vendors, but they don't write the apps. The list is long and goes on and on.[6]

Most of these digital disrupters are leveraging AI as a key way to outperform their competitors. Many of them are using AI-based platforms to help them organize resources they don't own. For example, Facebook organizes your content so it can be easily found and liked and connected to others' content. Amazon organizes shopping and helps recommend other products and connects you with reviews and allows you to provide your own feedback and comments about various vendors and products. Apple and Google give you organized ability to select apps by interests such as productivity, lifestyle, and so much more. Then you can rate those apps and see others' comments about them and come back for regular updates. Many won't remember the time when you would receive a box with your software upgrades or updates for the year or possibly even the next two to four years. Now the update cycle is almost 24/7 on some apps.

Many well-established businesses will argue these companies are digital disrupters because they were digital babies that grew up this way as companies. Whereas traditional businesses who have to figure out how to leverage digital platforms are different animals entirely. I think that is a completely fair thing to say. So let me tell you where "traditional" businesses are prioritizing AI development. I coauthored a report with the IBM Institute for Business Value that surveyed CEOs to find out where they intended to focus their AI efforts inside their companies.[7] The top five areas, in order, were: 1) Information Technology (IT), 2) Sales, 3) Information Security, 4) Innovation, and 5) Supply Chain.

Information Technology. IT leaders' priorities included management of finances, procurement, and vendor management as well as operations, IT architecture, and engineering. Let's face it, information technology can be a huge advantage when done well inside companies, or it can be catastrophic when poorly executed. The sad truth is that many companies treat the role less as a strategic member of the c-suite and more like a group that just likes to spend money and take too long getting important business projects done. It's no surprise that these guys would be the first folks to also code themselves out of a job while looking for ways to reduce costs and manage sometimes out-of-control numbers of vendors. If you think about how different business leaders inside the corporation buy technology solutions, it's often best-in-class, fastest, coolest, easiest, or relationship-driven for their department. However, this amounts to a nightmare for IT vendor management, IT architecture, and the engineering required to cobble all these little siloed systems together enough for the entire enterprise to be able to glean some usefulness from them. As far as coding themselves out of jobs, many IT employees, especially testers and Help Desk Tier 1 and 2 folks, may find that AI paired with automation has replaced their functions entirely.

Sales. Use of AI in sales is about connecting the dots of what customers want and adjusting that to reflect reactively in supply chain operations. Imagine a tennis shoe maker wants to respond to a special marathon that became an overnight point of interest on social media. They have only days to respond to fans with a shoe to commemorate this super-exciting event, complete with the logo on the shoe, thereby immortalizing them to their customers for reacting so fast to their demand. AI essentially enables the perfect sales use case in this example.

Information Security. The use of AI in this area of business is to prevent, detect, and react when a security breach happens. Prevention and mitigation of fraud, hacking, and the theft of identities and goods is one of the longest-running applications of machine-learning algorithms.

Innovation. This is the business purpose I think of most when I think of AI. AI can be used in a software platform that enables employees to develop all kinds of new ideas. The AI-enabled platform can then use matching algorithms to see if there are existing patents on the ideas. It can even help the employees find the right entrepreneurs, both inside the company and external to it, to engage based on their idea. At IBM, a company-wide competition was centered around just such an AI platform. The platform came with a variety of fun tools to help employees think outside of the box and then check their ideas to see if they had been done before. They were able to leverage the tool kit to help them put the first straw-man ideas to paper. More than half of the company participated because it was fun and based on new tech that everyone wanted to know further. The applications they came up with in that three-month time period were amazing—everything from anti-bullying apps to systems that could help people maintain healthy weight by making it easier to log foods simply with pictures that would convert to food log entries. It's pretty amazing what companies can do when they have their entire workforce focused on innovating new solutions. Not to mention the energy for that competition was off the charts.

Supply Chain. It all comes back to whether you can deliver the goods when they are wanted and how they are wanted. Supply chain operations can be the hardest thing for companies because there is so much uncertainty about what can impact the raw goods development, the distribution of raw goods and produced goods, and hence the price and constitution of the goods. Of course, you have to know where the goods are, and if there are any changes amid everything.

Ensuring you have something right when it is wanted despite rain, hail, tornadoes, crazy highway shutdowns…these are ever-evolving elements that supply chain leaders must deal with and still get the products out, or procure the things their employees need to keep the company running. In consideration of these factors, the priorities for most supply chain leaders include demand planning and forecasting, risk and security management, and asset management.

Four Most Common AI Initiative Types

Outside of these specific areas, I began to notice patterns in the AI engagements that I was working on. I noticed four main themes regardless of the functional or departmental area within the company. Again, most of these companies are not "digital babies"; these are large traditional businesses.

a. *Personalization.* If I can show you all the products and services you want, when and how you want them, you will buy more quantities, more often, for longer (loyalty) because I have formed a relationship with you. I demonstrated that I understand your needs and endeared my company or products to you. I have created a loyal brand customer of you.

b. *Preserving or augmenting knowledge or expertise.* An example of this, whether in financial advisement positions, actuaries in insurance, or well-seasoned oil rig engineers, is that the top executives in the company are freaking out because they realize they either have incredibly scarce resources or they have an impending mass retirement on their hands of some of their wisest people. They need to preserve the knowledge of these workers (and fast) to ensure they do not lose revenues during any transition periods to new people or full AI automation of those jobs.

c. *Answering questions, giving support.* Customers need answers, and they want to call in or conduct a quick chat via mobile phone, tablet, or computer whenever they feel like it regardless of what part of the world they are in. AI is good at reading tons and tons of text. For example, you could give it digital volumes of warranty manuals on automobiles dating back to the 1990s or insurance claims, policies, or frequently asked questions, and let customers ask it questions all day and night. It will never tire. What's even better is that each customer interaction, including the type of question and its wording, the AI answer, and the immediate customer reaction/feedback, help the machine-learning algorithm get better over time. This question-and-answer capability is where chatbots have their roots, and they are fairly straightforward to set up.

d. *Compare and comply.* These types of engagements are similar in principle to ledger systems, where you have one thing the AI must read through on one side and some sort of equivalent action that it brings about on the other. An example of this would be when you have thousands of invoices coming in, with tons of text explaining the work that was done and the rate charged. On the other side of the equation, you have negotiated amounts that you will pay for specific services. If you are overcharged for a service, the AI will refute your bill and ensure payment doesn't go through. This is an example of comparing one thing to another and then taking action based on the outcomes.

CHAPTER 2
Is AI Really All Around Me?

At this point you're probably thinking, *Well, I haven't seen a ton of robots out walking around. People don't seem too concerned. There are a few cool robot videos on YouTube, but I don't really think I could be affected by AI in my life.* Allow me to open your eyes to all the things you interact with daily that AI is in. These AI systems are so good at nudging you, tracking you and triggering you that you may not have even noticed them.

Smartphone—Are You Using It or Is It Using You?

You are using the smartphone, and the AI in it is using you. What I mean is, you are generating data 24/7 as you interact with your phone. Every activity you do, like running an errand, going to the gym, turning on your fitness tracker, putting on sleep sounds, or creating a music playlist, the AI in your smartphone is using that intelligence to make it smarter about your preferences, habits, and frequented locations. For example, the AI might recommend music with fast beats per minute once you select "run" as your workout routine in your fitness app. As part of this recommendation, it may have just triggered you to use a music app which targets ads across your screen while you listen. Did it just use you? Or were you using it? Here's another example. The AI may work across your maps, reminders and calendar apps to notify you to pick up a prescription that is at a pharmacy on your route home from the location of your daughter's soccer game. You logged the soccer field's location in your calendar app so it could tell you the best time to leave. And now—bonus—every time you go back to that soccer field, the pharmacy app texts you a coupon on your way home to get you to visit them again. But AI is a catch-22. It's an advantage because it makes life easier and a threat because it's using your sensitive, private data to do so. It's sharing your information back and forth with the developers of apps that you have downloaded to your device and with the maker of the smartphone itself. In one calendar entry you have already shared the location of yourself and your daughter every Thursday to not only the phone manufacturer and any of their business partners, but also to the local pharmacy— whose app is tracking you via your phone's Global Positioning System (GPS) locator. As you'll see in later chapters, that data can be used to your detriment.

Smartphone-Based Personal Assistants: Siri, Google Assistant, Bixby, Alexa

You are interfacing with many of your smartphone's apps when you use an artificially intelligent personal assistant like Siri or Google Assistant. These pull your spoken or typed words into a program that parses your human words into computer words—this is called natural-language programming (NLP). Then it comes back to you either with answers to your questions, or it does what you've asked...like when you say, "Siri, open Audible, play 'Data and Goliath.'" Siri is able to interface with iOS Messages, Calendar, Music, Reminders, Maps, Mail, Weather, Stocks, Clock, Contacts, Notes, and Safari. As a funny aside, if you have an iPhone just ask Siri, "Do you have a girlfriend?" three or more times and just see what smart answers you get back each time even though the question stays the same. You can also try this with Google, which can perform a similar function on Android devices, but I'm told the answers aren't as funny.

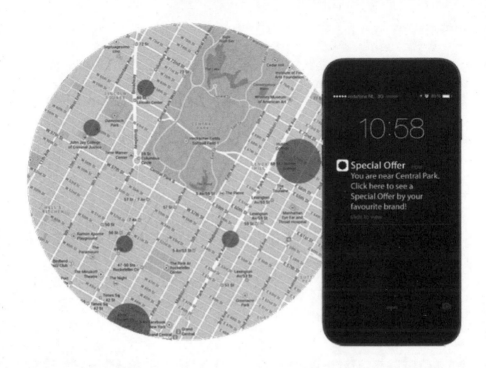

Retail Apps

Many of the apps you've installed are tracking your location via the GPS receiver that's already on your phone. Some retail apps may even be geofencing you. Geofencing is used in many ways, but in the case of a consumer, an app that you have downloaded to your phone identifies your device as being within the vicinity of a "virtual perimeter" that is set up around a specific location—say, a competitor's store or a specific retail location. This triggers a pre-programmed action such as emailing you a coupon or causing a text message to pop up on your screen or any of many other options that can be delivered via app or through your phone. Geofencing itself is not AI, but it works in tandem with AI algorithms within the retail apps to determine the correct offer for you based on the behaviors the app's AI is seeing you take and where you physically are. Then it makes a decision about which offer it will send you, depending also on which store locations you are near.

Fitness and Nutrition Apps

Vi, billed as the first true AI personal fitness trainer, takes its form as a pair of earphones.[8] Using AI, Vi can create a training plan based on your physiology and coach you how to achieve your goals for the workout. FitGenie is a nutrition app that uses genetic algorithms to get at user food preferences and needs, so it's not just about calorie-counting but ensuring you get the right kinds of foods based on the type of diet you prefer—even if that is vegetarian or paleo. In addition, the AI helps it adjust your nutrition plans instantly as you enter your weight and how much activity you have done throughout the day. It can even recommend further meals for the day based on what you have in your pantry so you don't have to travel back to the store to fulfill the rest of your nutrition needs for the day.[9]

Photos and Camera Facial Recognition

There's even machine learning that helps you organize your photos with facial recognition, so you can find "mom" pics or "Bowser the dog" pics. Every time you label someone's face, furry or not, you are training the system to recognize who's who in your sphere of importance. It can also help you further organize your photos by assessing faces for gender, age, and emotion. The computer vision APIs (application programming interfaces let authorized users interchange data from a specified web location) can also identify what's in your picture (such as a dog) without you having to label it.[10] Google Lens technology can even tell you the dog breed in your photo and bring up an emoji to represent the breed. You can also use this powerful technology to find out what those beautiful flowers are in your neighbor's yard. The Google Lens app even pulls up where you can shop for them. Now you can go buy some of your own.

Healthcare

When you go to the doctor nowadays, the first thing you have to do is answer what seems to be a hundred questions. Some of them are relevant to your actual diagnosis, but many are being used to complete a data profile. You are feeding your information into larger data sets which will be used to help with future artificial intelligence diagnostics. This is an area called "clinical documentation," and believe it or not, it is ultimately very useful for your overall care. Many healthcare companies are trying to give us better patient care by gathering genomic information through testing, as well as pooling our electronic health records (within the Health Insurance Portability and Accountability Act—HIPAA—guidelines). AI is in many healthcare applications, from diagnostic tools to imaging detection. Eyes of Watson is an AI-based medical imaging and disease diagnostic tool in one. It can analyze images from a patient and overlay other conditions to give a diagnosis. Some applications of AI are simply designed to help doctors' offices run better, like instantaneously verifying your health insurance enrollment with a scan of your health insurance card through an app called Zocdoc. Others can detect how many pills seniors have left in their medicine bottles with the goal of helping them stay independent and in their own homes longer by enabling them to take better care of themselves.

Smart Homes

Smart homes have many AI-enabled devices that can operate by themselves or in concert with each other. These include thermostats, vacuums, security cameras, doorbells, entertainment systems, fridges, coffeemakers, and even mattresses that want to help you sleep better. Virtually everything in your house is reporting data about its usage. Many of them, as one reporter noted when she tried a bunch of different smart home devices, are constantly sending data packets even when they are not in use. The cause might be AI systems that are exchanging data back and forth with smart devices in an effort to optimize a device's performance so it's more efficient (vacuum) or predict usage patterns to save energy (thermometer). Other times, the device might be taking action, like ordering your favorite food items that the AI noticed were running low in the fridge. In the case of the Roomba, it is mapping out your home and collecting data to compare with other homes while learning how best to get around certain types of objects for dust pickup. Even your bed is collecting data about how many times you tossed and turned through the night so you can know why you still feel tired the next day.

Gaming

Gaming could arguably be one of the oldest commercial applications of AI. It's often used to predict how humans will react to scenarios in the gaming environment. Gaming is the field where many precursors to artificial general intelligence come from because in each game, the goal is to try and think like humans and then outwit them. Demis Hassabis, leader of the foremost AGI company, DeepMind—a division of Google—got his start in the field of AI through the development of video games. Winning a strategy and intuition game called Go was a huge feat to overcome for the AGI system known as AlphaGo. But even before that, many gaming and movie companies used artificial intelligence in games to help them do everything from making hair appear to move naturally to generating realistic character reactions inside games. IBM's Watson also got his start by playing a game with humans called *Jeopardy!*

However, watch out, many gaming consoles now have video cameras. Most of these are there to enhance your gaming experience but could be surveilling even when not in use. When Microsoft first came out with a game called Kinectimals, which required a camera-based sensor, it was weird to watch as the animal did exactly what my kid did. But there was also that feeling of *wait a minute, if it can use my kid's actions in the room and take pictures of us doing dances, then what else can it do, and where is that information going?* When not in use, consider covering those cameras or facing them toward a wall.

Smart Cities, Surveillance, and Predictive Policing

Cities that claim to be "smart" embed sensors and cameras that collect data from citizens, devices, and assets to help the cities run more cost-effectively and efficiently while also improving and innovating city services for citizens. For example, AI helps smart cities manage and adjust traffic patterns through smart stoplights on especially congested days. It helps people find and reserve open parking spots near their desired destination using pressure sensors, GPS mapping, and a smartphone app. City managers use AI to help optimize planning and zoning. AI is also used in transportation systems, power plants, water supply networks, waste management, schools, and libraries.

One of the most controversial areas AI is used is in law enforcement to curb crime. More and more smart cities have implemented facial recognition into their city surveillance cameras, which means you could end up being surveilled 24/7.[11] Depending on who's watching and what their agenda is, that could be a real problem. Further, many cities are supplementing their police forces with predictive policing, which uses data about past criminal activity to plan where and what type of future crimes may occur. States where it's use has been confirmed include Texas, California, Washington, South Carolina, Arizona, Tennessee, Florida, Michigan, and Illinois. But the use of it and facial recognition tech are so rampant in cities that I would assume any city with a high crime rate might be using it. The main criticisms of these AI-based technologies are 1) that they only help predict *policing practices* but not the occurrence of *potential crimes*, and 2) facial recognition technologies lead to false arrests because the technology is not proven and is biased against people of color. The topic of predictive policing and use of facial recognition are explored in more detail in chapter 10.

Google

AI is the core of everything Google does. They are one of the major trailblazers in the field of modern AI. Google has long been focused on individual consumers like you and me, trying to use AI to help us all get better results from our online searches, often based on lots of variables that are constantly changing. Their algorithm is not only serving up search terms but also ads that are as relevant to us as possible. AI is in every product Google offers including Google Search, YouTube, Google Maps, Pixel smartphone, Google Assistant, the Chrome browser, Gmail, Android, Google Ads, website analytics, video conferencing, and Google Home. That's just to name a few; believe it or not, there are so many more things they offer that have AI in them.

Facebook

Facebook makes almost 100 percent of its $86 billion annual revenue by targeting you with highly relevant ads while you use its platforms. The more they can get you to look at and engage with advertisers' content on Facebook, Instagram, or WhatsApp, the more money they make. It makes sense then that Facebook's AI systems entice you to be on their platform for long periods of time by recommending content like news articles, political posts, funny memes, and groups you might enjoy. When you are not actively on Facebook or Instagram, the AI-based recommendation engine might even try to lure you back with a notification on your phone of a compelling piece of content, such as *@CatLove just posted pics of her new kitten*. Facebook's content recommendations are exactly what has landed it in hot water with Congress and the public. They are regularly accused of: aiding in the spread of fake news and misinformation, interfering with and polarizing political processes, violating users' data privacy and security, and shirking policies that could help curb online trafficking. All of these issues are addressed in more detail in chapters 7, 8, and 9.

Customer Service Chatbots

When you dial in to talk to the customer service department at most companies or do a web chat online or on a mobile device, you may encounter a "chatbot" in the form of a text prompt on your screen, or if you are on the phone, it might present as a voice—sometimes human-sounding, but often robotic—which can answer your basic questions. Chatbots are a form of AI, and they use natural-language processing and speech recognition, which we discussed in chapter 1. The data they use to answer your questions comes from digital content like an owner's manual, customer complaint policy, or a list of frequently asked questions. Programmers of chatbots use text to form question-and-answer pairs that almost work like if-then statements. Think of the decision tree algorithm in chapter 1. For example, if the client says, "My car's brakes are squealing and making a strange groaning noise; what does this mean?" The computer's next action, based on the terms "brakes" and "groaning noise," might be for the system to ask you another clarifying question: "Did you recently repair your brakes with Brand Y brake shoes?" IF you say yes, THEN it forwards you to the complaint department for Brand Y. IF you say no, then it may forward you to a mechanic who can answer your question further.[12] Most people I know get pretty frustrated with these systems. My husband had a forty-five-minute encounter with a tech company's chatbot after he ordered a computer online and couldn't get an answer about when it would arrive. While companies are keen to use chatbots to save money and make simple answers available to customers 24/7, sometimes they can be more frustrating to customers than helpful.

Sometimes the AI systems are collecting and analyzing information about things you are *not* saying. For example, AI might "listen" for ambient noises such as dogs barking, kids or babies crying, or the voices of elderly people. An insurance customer service bot detecting the presence of crying children in the background could impact the way a client is ranked in the queue for services or even what advice is given to parents versus nonparents. The chatbot AI may collect your geolocation data if you are calling from a mobile phone—handy if you're in an automobile accident. It's also evaluating the *types* of words you are choosing along with the tone and pitch of your voice to gauge how upset or happy you are. For example, you say, "I'm so *ticked* about your *freaking* brakes because *I just hit someone*, and now I want you to pay for it. It's all your *fault*." Based on these word choices, the pitch of your voice, and the background noise of kids and sirens, the AI "agent" may escalate your call straight to the department that will handle your complaint with extreme urgency and sensitivity. These capabilities are not necessarily present in every customer service interaction, but for more complicated and emotional situations like complaints (*I hate your product*) or insurance issues (*I lost everything because someone broke into my house*), these extra AI bells and whistles can keep a company from losing customers, getting sued, or having a corporate brand crisis situation if things get mishandled.

Mobile Loan Applications

Even the process of getting a loan has changed because of AI. It's actually an easier process for most people, but it's also a great deal more intrusive from a privacy perspective. Now, an AI could assess your loan worthiness not from your credit scores, which are based mainly on historical repayment patterns (and why it can be so hard for young people to get loans without a cosigner), but by simply accessing highly private information on your smartphone. You're probably thinking, *Oh it couldn't possibly do that! How could that even happen?* But yes, when you fill out a lending application form on your phone and click "I agree," the AI will access all the data on your phone. It will be especially interested in where you live, if you are married, your age and ethnicity, your preferences, who is in your social network, your texts, and social media posts.[13]

Insurance Tracking Devices

Been tempted to get one of those telematics devices for your car? Basically, if you install a tracker which tells them your driving behaviors (good and bad), the insurance company purports to give you a potential discount (*if* you're a good driver). These devices pair with a smartphone app that let you see your driving behaviors as well in an almost report card-like fashion. *What's it tracking*, you ask? How often you drive and for how long, hard braking, hard acceleration, speeding, fast cornering, time of day—especially nighttime driving, phone usage while driving. Then the AI system works to overlay all of this information with your smartphone's geolocator information and maps that let it analyze if you speed through stop signs, residential areas, school zones, and the like. These are also a major data privacy concern as it pinpoints where you went, what time, and for how long. Thanks to voice recognition, it can even confirm your presence in the car. Police could insist on getting feeds from insurance companies to automatically fine people who speed in their city. They can already get a court order to retrieve the data for cases ranging from divorce to murder. Beyond the police, there's also the thought that an entire insurance call center full of customer service people can track your whereabouts all day. I guess your comfort with these devices depends on how much faith you have that companies won't do bad things with your data or share it.

Virtual Personal Assistants: Alexa, Siri

Personal assistants perform small tasks for you upon your voice command, such as putting an event on the calendar, ordering groceries, and even calling mom—or anyone else in your contact list. We usually interact with them through smart speakers like Amazon's Echo or our smartphones, but they can be downloaded to any internet-connected device such as a fridge—so it can order you groceries and keep tabs on expiration dates. Just like the customer service chatbots mentioned earlier, personal assistants use speech recognition and natural-language programming to translate your commands into computer programs that are designed to fulfill your requests. Most of these natural-language programs and computer programs run in the cloud. "Cloud" is just a fancy word to refer to a bunch of networked computers that are accessed via the internet. Think of the cloud as a train depot where you keep a locker full of stuff you need when you go to various cities. You don't like to carry it all with you to every city you go to, so you leave the big stuff there. Whenever you need it, you can come back to your locker, get what you need, then take it with you to your destination. In this example, the internet access is the train, your locker is the cloud, and the stuff you keep in it is your data, such as documents, photos, videos, and music.

Amazon's Alexa

Since Amazon is the leader in smart speakers with their Echo and Dot devices, let's focus first on the Alexa Voice Program, which is the natural-language program that runs Alexa, the interactive voice you hear on the Echo device.[14] Alexa was introduced to the market in November 2014 alongside the Echo.[15] The Echo device itself is more of a "dummy terminal," or input-and-output machine. As a matter of fact, the reason the device is not called "Alexa" is because Amazon didn't want customers to attach to the device itself as much as the personal assistant portion, which can function with potentially any device with a microphone, speaker, and internet access.[16] The Echo or Dot can function as a speaker for the Alexa voice and also songs, game shows, or any Alexa "skills" that you load onto the device. It can take your voice commands and send them out to the Alexa Voice Program for interpretation and interaction so fast you hardly notice any time lapse between your question and her answer. The device activates when you say the wake word "Alexa," and a flashing light lets you know it's "hearing" you. Alexa won't work if you do not have internet access.

Amazon has opened up their Alexa natural-language programming to allow non-Amazon developers to create more "skills." Think of skills as the apps that come on smartphones, since they pretty much work the same. The difference is, they are activated by voice instead of you having to find your smartphone, scroll through apps, open the right one, and then do what you need to in the app itself. Instead, skills are designed for ease of use. Regardless of where my child has taken my smartphone, I can simply say to one of the smart speakers in my house, "Alexa, open Starbucks and order my most recent favorite."

Here's how Amazon explains their "skills": *A robust set of actions or tasks that are accomplished by Alexa.*[17] Alexa provides a set of built-in skills (such as playing music), and developers can use the Alexa Skills Kit to give Alexa new skills. A skill includes both the code (in the form of a cloud-based service) and the configuration provided on the developer console.

Skills are often being developed by—you guessed it—groups that want to sell you stuff. It's most likely stuff you're already buying. For example, Domino's Pizza has developed a skill for Alexa that allows the device to order pizza via your Domino's app. If you're a Capital One customer, you can even do your banking via Alexa because Capital One developers have created a mobile app that can be invoked by Alexa.

Alexa has over eighty thousand skills in the US.[18] But how secure are they? If I have my Capital One skill on Alexa, and my teenage daughter has heard me log in before, could she tell the device to upload money to her PayPal account? There have been more than a few stories where Alexa has been invoked via TV programs such as the news. One particular story involves Alexa ordering dollhouses for numerous people in San Diego because a newscaster featured a story where a daughter ordered a dollhouse and cookies via Alexa. He happened to repeat the phrase she used, and viewers all over San Diego complained that their devices tried to order the dollhouse.[19]

Alexa is currently being considered for use as an "office assistant" in Polycom products. Polycom is the leader in conferencing products for business, so this means Alexa would literally be everywhere inside companies—inside conference rooms and at people's desks. But does this also mean that it could potentially spy on you everywhere? In the same way you can be audited as an employee for productivity on the workplace computer you use, whether laptop or desktop or even smartphone, could you also be monitored everywhere for what you are *saying* as well? It certainly raises concerns.

Amazon has created more lines of products so that Alexa can be everywhere and you can invoke Alexa voice commands to operate more things in your house, car, and office.[20] Here's a quote from an Amazon press release:

> "We want you to have access to Alexa every-where—in your kitchen, in your living room, in your office, and now in your car or truck," said Tom Taylor, Senior Vice President, Amazon Al-exa. "Today, we're excited to expand the number of ways that customers can add Alexa to their homes and their vehicles, so they can use Alexa to make their lives more convenient and easy—whether it's asking for the traffic on your drive home, checking your email in the morning, or simply saying 'Alexa, good night' to turn off your lights and lock your door."

But is this going too far? Is this convenience worth giving Amazon access to the data collected from all these interactions? At the rate that Amazon is adding Alexa everywhere in our personal lives, they will soon have more sensitive personal data on us and our family members than Google—including the ability to pick our voice out of crowd. Alexa theoretically keeps your data infinitely and never really turns off—even though it has an off button. Many tech experts have done experiments to prove that Alexa is eavesdropping even before you use the wake words. This is an invasion of your privacy, and your words may be used against you in court, for advertising purposes, or sold to third parties. See chapter 7 for more details about Alexa and data privacy.

Apple's Siri

Apple's business model is based on selling products and not access to people's data. Tim Cook, Apple's CEO, has been the most outspoken about data privacy relative to the other Silicon Valley tech giants like Facebook or Google.[21] We will get more into that in chapter 7. For now, take notice that the way these leading AI companies make their money dictates how much they protect consumer data. The companies you want in your home, car, and work will be a matter of trust and how much you believe they will protect your information from third parties that could be harmful to your pursuit of life, liberty, and happiness.

Siri is one of the first of the modern personal assistants. It was introduced in 2011 in the iPhone 4. Siri got its name because it was originally a project started by the Artificial Intelligence Center of the nonprofit SRI International. It's included in a variety of Apple's operating systems: Apple iOS, which is the mobile operating system in iPhones and iPads; watchOS, in the Apple Watch; macOS, included in Mac laptops and desktops; HomePod, which is Apple's smart speaker equivalent to the Amazon Echo; and tvOS, inside the Apple TV, which is similar to Roku and other digital streaming platforms.

Because of the wide array of products that Siri is already operating in, especially those that differentiate it from Alexa, such as the ability to make phone calls, it can perform a wider range of native user commands: performing phone actions, checking basic information, scheduling events and reminders, handling device settings, searching the Internet, navigating areas, finding information on entertainment, and engaging with iOS-integrated apps. It can also engage with third-party messaging apps, make payments, request a rideshare, and place internet calls. There are claims that Siri has limited the number of third-party apps available to it because Apple has been picky about whom it does business with to ensure it can do a better job than its main competitors, Amazon and Google, of keeping your personal information secure, whereas Amazon has not necessarily been so discriminating—something to think about.

"One to Rule Them All"?

How we use (and don't use) personal assistants in our everyday lives will decide the winners. Many tech ratings groups frame the market as if smart speakers are the most important criteria for virtual personal assistants. Because of this, they focus their ratings on criteria like how well the natural-language programming understands you, responds to you, and how well it can do speaker-y things like play music. But the format in which the personal assistant comes to you is irrelevant if you don't find it convenient to use. I would argue that it's how and where we need to use a personal assistant most that matters.

My husband argues that the best use of personal assistants is as a more advanced kind of Google. He wants to look things up in a conversant manner and have the personal assistant understand him really well. I argue that they should go beyond just looking things up. For example, I'd like to be able to ask where *Fantastic Beasts: The Crimes of Grindelwald* is playing locally, what the showtimes are, and then have it access my theater rewards app to book the tickets so that I get the rewards for it as well. Because Alexa is pretty far ahead on third-party app skills, I may be able to do that more easily with Alexa at this point than with Google. However, a middle school student preparing a paper about the Alamo for history class will probably value Google Assistant more because they can open up Google, do the research via spoken word, and simultaneously share the findings with teammates on Google Docs. In case you don't have kids in the home, you should know that many schools use Google products.

Here's another question worthy of contemplation for future implications: Will all these individual digital assistants be replaced by one digital assistant to rule them all? Let's walk through an example of what I mean. At work, I may use one called Sherlock to look up trends in electronic health records for signs of sepsis, then in my car, I may use one to navigate verbally through my other electronics, saying things like, "Siri, check my email and read the ones marked unread in the VIP folder." When I get home, Alexa's there running my Roomba and my washing machine and my coffee pot. I'll also have one on my exercise bike that will check to see if my sister is online so I can challenge her best time in real time.

I believe that we will ultimately come to have one digital assistant that interfaces with all of our various products at work, in our home, and in our car. Because they will all be managed through the cloud, I believe that digital assistants will be incredibly impactful in helping us navigate easily through our daily lives. I also believe that as our lives become more simplified, they will become more connected, and we will be at extreme danger of losing privacy and rights to our own data. I believe that all the third parties that we interact with will have some claim to individual blocks of our data, and it will become harder and harder to opt out without major inconveniences or disruptions in our daily lives.

We have to take measures now to start ensuring the very private, connected information we will be creating won't be used against us. That we won't be discriminated against or targeted for bullying campaigns or fake news. That we won't be denied medical coverage, insurance, or home loans due to what our digital assistant knows about us through the data it has collected. We should not be for sale—especially when we pay for these services. Any tech companies that violate the public's trust on data norms should expect full backlash and proper legal repercussions. But before we can have legal repercussions, we need actual laws. The time is long past for expecting large corporations to do the right thing by us as individuals, and there's never been a history of companies doing things in our best interest without being pressured by a huge public backlash.

CHAPTER 3
Could AI Limit My Job Opportunities?

Hiring or non-selection remains one of the most difficult issues for workers to challenge in a private action, as an applicant is unlikely to know about the effect of hiring tests or assessments, or have the resources to challenge them.

—Jenny R. Yang,

former chair, US Equal Employment Opportunity Commission

AI Quiz: What Do You Know About AI in Hiring and Recruitment?

1) Which of the following companies use AI to conduct initial interviews and assign candidates an employability score? *(select all that apply)*

   a) Hilton

   b) Unilever

    c) Ikea

    d) Dow Jones

    e) L'Oreal

2) AI could deselect you at which stage(s) of the recruitment and hiring process? *(select all that apply)*

    a) seeing the job post

    b) applying for the job

    c) screening your résumé and application

    d) interviewing

    e) compensation negotiations

3) AI-based hiring tools: *(select all that apply)*

    a) are used primarily by multinational corporations with tens or hundreds of thousands of employees

    b) can be programmed to be unbiased in screening job candidates

    c) are not good at understanding the context associated with job candidates' posts on social media, the content of job candidates' pictures on Instagram, or memes job candidates like" on Facebook

    d) are better than humans at making hiring decisions because AI bases its decisions on the most up-to-date information

    e) are not good at interpreting the emotional responses of people with darker complexions or disabilities

4) Based on your intonation, word selection, and facial movements, the nation's largest AI hiring firm claims their AI-based assessment software can score and rank you on the following: *(select all that apply)*

  a) personal stability

  b) willingness to learn

  c) emotional intelligence

  d) psychological traits

  e) ability to work on a team

5) If you make it to the interview stage, the employing company is legally obligated to tell you why you did or did not make it past the AI-based interview. True or False?

6) A company that conducts AI-based interviewing is required to give you your data and erase the interview from their system so you cannot be further penalized if another employer uses the same software. True or False?

See answers on next page.

Answers to AI Quiz: What Do You Know About AI in Hiring and Recruitment?

1) All of the above.

2) All except e.

3) c. and e.

4) All of the above.

5) False.

6) False.

Rage Against the Machine

I was raging after reading an article about an AI hiring company that secretly snoops through people's social media posts to provide a behavioral assessment on them to would-be employers. You would never know it's happening because you won't have been looking for a job when the analysis of your social media takes place. That's right! The analysis has already occurred, been stored, and accessed by the hiring company. You'll be passed over for a job (hopefully not) without the opportunity to put your best foot forward. I started to think about the stupid stuff even the most polished people post on social media and how even well-intentioned posts can be taken the wrong way when out of the original context. This spells doomsday for many people's job opportunities. Despite my righteous indignation, I kept reading. The article's author starts with how the AI assessed her "stability potential" as low and placed an "ominous" red bar next to it.[22] Evidently, "stability potential" means a "person's willingness to give it their all before they quit." What possible reason could there be for that metric to exist? Also, a red bar next to it means what? That they should be ashamed of that part of their personality, or that the employer should not hire this person?

Then my eye started twitching in anger when I saw that the company gives ratings on "learning ability," "need for autonomy," and a "personality assessment." Yeah, evidently a *machine* decided she was optimistic, sunny, and a good listener. The AI got all that from a Twitter feed? *Seriously*? Sadly, this is a bunch of nonsense and pseudoscience that would, unfortunately, be taken seriously by human resources (HR) professionals who didn't know better than to trust these types of AI vendors. But it was the next line that had full-on steam coming out of me like one of those bulls in a cartoon about to charge. The journalist went on to say, "The first profile they provided me with, which included (old) information from my Twitter, analyzed aspects like anxiety and depression."[23] First, it is highly unlikely that anyone, much less a machine, could assess that someone is depressed based on their Twitter feed. I mean, come on, it seems the majority of people take to Twitter to complain about something or troll someone.

Second, even if you could ascertain someone's state of anxiety or depression from social media posts, that's not legal! Depression is covered as a disability that an employer is not allowed to ask about under US Equal Employment Opportunity Commission (EEOC) guidelines.[24] But with AI, I guess an "employer" didn't ask, an AI did. And technically, it didn't ask, it just made its own decision about whether *it* found you depressed or not. No wonder ten senators wrote a formal request to the EEOC in December 2020 to start enforcing oversight on AI hiring technologies.[25] AI hiring systems have been given a pass way too many times because they tend to snipe at people from the shadows like this one did. If you don't know you have had a violation of your hiring rights, how can you report them to the EEOC?

Another point to think about is exactly how long the AI hiring company and the employer get to keep this data and the resulting behavioral assessment. It would be disheartening if one behavioral assessment based on a social media feed when someone was twenty years old could affect their ability to get a job well into their fifties. Not to mention once an assessment or data is propagated to the cloud, they are often bartered and swapped with other companies too. This means a behavioral assessment performed by one AI hiring company could then be used by their other corporate clients. Therefore, it is not unreasonable to assume that one behavioral assessment performed without your knowledge could prevent you from getting a job at many companies that use that same AI hiring group. This would all happen without your knowledge. All you would know is that you weren't able to get a job anywhere.

Welcome to the Hidden-Job Era, Where AI Decides Who's Hired

Forget everything you thought you knew about job hunting. Most jobs aren't posted anymore, which means you could miss out on your dream job simply because you had no idea it exists. Instead, employers use AI to proactively look for desirable job candidates before you know there is a job to be had. Here are some disturbing facts about today's AI-involved job market:

1. 80 percent of jobs are never posted online,[26] because...

2. 86 percent of recruiting groups focus on hiring people who are not looking for a job and are currently employed elsewhere; AI helps them find these people online,[27] which is why...

3. 96 percent of recruiters believe AI can greatly enhance acquisition and retention.[28] In fact...

4. 72 percent of résumés are weeded out before a human ever sees them.[29] So much for winning the employer over with your positive personality and brilliant ideas.

With these stats, it seems the sole goal of hiring professionals is to never talk to you. The jobs are hidden because recruiters already know whom they want to go after. Maddening, isn't it? You're scouring the internet looking for openings or sweating bullets waiting for a callback or any acknowledgement of your application, while HR pros use AI to chase after candidates on social media who sit comfortably at another job. There's logic to this that you are seriously going to hate, but at least you will know. Most recruiters feel like there is something wrong with you if you left your job or were fired. They feel the best and fastest hires (evidently only 15 percent of employees can't be lured away with more money) are found by poaching people from an equivalent role at a company's competitors.[30] This is actually not new news, but it does help you understand why recruiters think AI is so helpful in finding these people online.

Human resources professionals at large corporations will tell you they have a thousand jobs to fill and ten thousand candidates to sift through for each job. They need to find, vet, and recommend only the best candidates and do so more quickly, cost effectively, and with more employee diversity than ever before—especially in a post-pandemic economy when rehiring is expected to rise at unprecedented rates. While HR professionals are betting on AI to make things better, it will be their knowledge gaps about AI that could deepen systemic bias and cause bigger rifts in society. Make no mistake: though AI hiring firms will say that their tech is meant to be used in concert "with humans," this is a crock. They know it, and the HR people who use it know it. In *Washington Post* interviews with employers on the subject, most admitted they focused only on candidates the computer system ranked highest.[31] The ability of these technologies to sift through and rank thousands of candidates is exactly why employers spend millions on them, and they believe in them. They don't have time or resources to question them or double check their results. The AI hiring systems employed to help HR people home in on candidates quickly can do everything from violating your privacy to potentially locking you out of job opportunities in entire industries.

If you were hoping AI-based recruitment was used only in a few niche technology startups, think again. This tech is everywhere. It's used by some of the biggest companies on the planet—we're talking Hilton, Unilever, AT&T, JPMorgan Chase, PepsiCo, and thousands more[32]—as well as midsize companies and small businesses. There's no escaping it. In fact, the biggest AI hiring firms have their sights on "owning" particular roles (such as bank tellers, for example) and already have a predominance of firms in the hospitality and banking industries. When you consider what their ambitions might do to a job seeker's prospects, it's actually quite scary. Because of the prevalence of AI screening and data sharing across employers who use AI, it's possible that you could be blacklisted from an entire industry or profession. Who is to say that once you interview at one bank, for example, the AI software firm doesn't save your data and scores and recall those for an AI interview at another bank?

No part of the job-hunting process is exempt from AI either. Even your first interview is likely to be conducted by AI via video conference instead of by a human. It's a strange, de-humanizing experience. You will sit awkwardly in front of your webcam while AI commands and questions you, uses facial recognition technology to assess your facial expressions and track your eye movements, registers your emotional responses, and analyzes the tone of your voice and the language you use. Imagine waiting for about ten seconds after each question is asked while the AI assesses your answers. Then you receive your next question via a strange monotone voice—or worse, you just read it quickly as it scrolls across the screen. When it's all done, the AI will assign you an employability score—which you will never see, by the way. That score determines whether you move forward in the hiring process or are digitally denied. All of that decision-making is completely hidden from you. Welcome to the new era of the AI job market, where the fate of your life and livelihood doesn't lie in the hands of any*one*. It rests, rather, in the cold calculus of an impersonal algorithm.

Back to the question: Could AI limit my job opportunities? You bet it could! It could limit you so much that employment lawyers will be gearing up for class-action lawsuits due to biased AI hiring and recruitment methods.[33] But to more fully appreciate the extent of how AI could keep you from getting your next gig, you need to know how and where it's playing a part in the hiring process and the danger zones to avoid.

The Five Types of Hiring AIs

Job-to-Candidate-Matching AI

Read Minds and Choose Words Carefully

Think of the AI hiring process the same way you think about dating apps and what goes into finding the perfect match. The employer is going to put into the AI system everything they hope and dream of in a candidate relevant to their job description (which, remember, won't be posted for you to see but will be used to train the AI). Just like in dating matches, they'll realistically get about one-third of the skills, personality, experience, or education they're looking for in potential job candidates. But if they're lucky, they'll get the stuff they identified as being most important. Now the real question for you is: *What is it they are looking for exactly?* And more importantly, *What words did they use to describe that?* The goal is to match your resume, your online profile, or your application's words to their job description's words closely enough so that you get on their job-matching radar.

This is the hard part because people—both the employers who write the job descriptions and the job seekers who must describe their work history—use vocabulary that is most familiar to them. Believe it or not, it's these word choices that cause systemic bias problems. Those very human word choices get programmed into a set of instructions called an algorithm, which then goes out and searches social media and applicant and hiring databases like CareerBuilder, Monster, and Indeed. The challenge is that you don't get to see an actual job description, and you don't get to know what kind of person is writing it before the screening of you has already happened.

I can give you some hints given the market dynamics. The higher up the ladder a job, the more likely its description is being written from the perspective of a male versus a female, and a white person versus a person of any other ethnic background. STEM jobs such as software engineering and computer science are still overwhelmingly held by white men, and at the five biggest tech companies (Facebook, Amazon, Apple, Google, and Microsoft), less than 35 percent of their workforce are women.[34] Since the pandemic forced many women home to be caretakers, the ratio has probably only gotten worse. Likewise, in executive ranks in any field, the dominant ethnicity and sex is white male. So now consider what happens when the dominant group, in this case white males, is writing the majority of job descriptions. Bias can creep in because, like anyone, white males' life experiences and culture will naturally lead them to use different descriptive terms than people with differing backgrounds—terms that make sense to the writer and others like him, but not necessarily used on the resumes or online profiles of candidates who aren't like him.

Let's look at a hypothetical example. A hiring manager tries to make an entry-level software programming job sound super cool by saying they're looking for a "coding ninja." It so happens that this term is especially popular in one area of the United States (the West Coast), in one school (Stanford), and among white males aged eighteen to twenty-two. Because the phrase "coding ninja" is very specific to a geographic location, age range, ethnicity, and gender, the job description is *biased from the start*, even if the writer didn't intend for bias to occur. Now enter an AI, which can only look for matches to the existing job description, and we have the potential for bias at scale. It's easy to see why: the AI will most likely pass right over any candidates who aren't white males in their early twenties who recently graduated from Stanford, because those candidates' qualifications don't match the terms of this narrow job description. How many people put "coding ninja" on their official résumé or online profile? Not many! (And if they do, they're more likely to be young, white males from the West Coast.)

The AI will then be dispatched to analyze thousands upon thousands of résumés and profiles that exist on public databases like LinkedIn and Indeed, where it will identify desirable candidates based on matches between specific words and phrases in the job description and the candidates' profiles.

Cloning AI

Employers' Aims to Clone Their "Best" Means AI Might Be Excluding You

Predicting what will make a candidate successful in a job is difficult and nuanced, and there are many theories. Industrial psychologists argue that personality traits are a bigger predictor of success in a job than skills, education, or past experience. However, human resources departments traditionally rely on what is listed on a résumé and what type of university a candidate has attended, along with the type and level of degree they attained. Data scientists seek to uncover patterns in data of existing "successful" employees and match them to candidate résumés. The data science way seems like it would be the holy grail of defining successful candidates. But what is the data version of "successful," and does it line up with real life? Data scientists will look for quantifiable information on which they can train their AI algorithms. They will look in employee records for things like promotions, awards, tenure, and high employee ratings. I have two things to say about this:

First, what if the primary indicators of your success don't appear in the data? What if, for example, it's your grit and perseverance that make you a great employee, or your versatility? These aren't quantified in data. Your teammates and bosses may have publicly praised you for these qualities, and your professional reputation may be built upon them, but data scientists won't care about anything unless it can be traced via data. Data is their tool, and it's also what trains the AI on how to find the best candidates for the job.

Second, "indicators of success" such as promotions, awards, and high ratings can also be biased because of a history of hiring that lacks diversity. If I only started hiring women, people of color, and retirees in the last two years, but I pull ten years of historical employee data so I can gain more statistical significance, then the last two years will lose out to eight years' worth of patterns. Those last two years of diverse hiring will simply be left out as statistical "outliers" when I put my AI into operation. Not only that, but promotions, awards, and high ratings often systemically go to the majority because people tend to favor those like themselves. Using these success indicators as examples of what AI should look for in a future job candidate again just perpetuates bias and the potential for discrimination.

In a recent American Bar Association podcast on AI, I was asked, "But what if former football players really are the best sellers? If, as a vice president of sales [VP], I already have a team full of football players who are exceeding their sales quotas, why wouldn't I want the AI to find more football players?" First, I don't know many women who are football players, so that's going to be discriminatory and get you in trouble with the EEOC. Second, diversity is important to companies. It allows companies the most agility when market shifts happen, keeps companies from groupthink which can stagnate innovation, and helps them serve melting-pot societies. Third, if all you have ever had on your team are football players, then the only people who have been given a chance to exceed sales quotas are football players. The VP wouldn't know he liked other sports players, genders, ethnicities, or generations as "sellers" until he included them in his group and gave them a chance to exceed sales quotas. Then he might change his mind about who makes the best candidate.

Job Ad–Placing AI

If You Don't See the Job, You Can't Apply for It

"Women Less Likely to Be Shown Ads for High-Paid Jobs on Google, Study Shows."[35] This headline caught my attention and made me wonder about the use of AI in targeting job ads on Google to candidates. Researchers created more than 17,000 fake profiles whose sole function was to visit job seeker sites. They behaved in exactly the same way, with gender being the only factor that was different. Over the course of some 600,000 ads, these researchers found that males were shown ads that encouraged them to seek coaching services for high-paying jobs far more than females. How much more? Males were shown ads for coaching for $200,000+ executive jobs 1,852 times, while females were shown the same ad—despite displaying the exact same online behavior—only 318 times.[36] This type of covert ad placement can definitely limit your job opportunities if you are a woman.

There are many reasons this type of gender discrimination could occur. The AI-driven automated system will try to learn where it can find matches to its job description online. For example, if the AI algorithm has been trained on a dataset that says, in essence, "Successful = young white male Stanford alum = coding ninja," then it will crawl the web looking for places where the narrow set of criteria that fits the data hangs out and then display the ad for a software programmer on those sites. If I'm an AI looking for a young, single, white programmer guy, I might look in online gaming communities to find my next successful hire and place my ad there. Whereas looking for a woman with an ambitious, outgoing personality might lead me to look on social media for team captains of female sports leagues or for leaders of Sheryl Sandberg Lean-In Circles on Facebook. If the AI is only placing job ads in the online spaces where these narrowly defined communities hang out, it's missing out on any job candidate who does not fit the profile. In other words, anyone who does not fit that profile will not see the ad, because they simply do not frequent the online spaces the algorithm has chosen to target with ads.

What this means to you, the job seeker, is that if you can't see a job, you can't apply for it. It is yet another way AI could limit your job opportunities.

Social Media-Snooping AI

The Subjective Red Flags—Send This to Job-seeking Friends

Here are some of the things the AI looks for and the primary reasons employers did not hire someone based on the job candidate's activity on social media:

a. Job candidate posted provocative or inappropriate photographs, videos, or information: 40 percent

b. Job candidate posted information about them drinking or using drugs: 36 percent

c. Job candidate had discriminatory comments related to race, gender, religion, etc.: 31 percent

d. Job candidate was linked to criminal behavior: 30 percent

e. Job candidate lied about qualifications: 27 percent

f. Job candidate had poor communication skills: 27 percent

g. Job candidate bad-mouthed their previous company or fellow employees: 25 percent

h. Job candidate's screen name was unprofessional: 22 percent

i. Job candidate shared confidential information from previous employers: 20 percent

j. Job candidate lied about an absence: 16 percent

k. Job candidate posted too frequently: 12 percent[37]

AI gives employers the ability to screen you out on things they can't legally ask about you during an interview. AI can dig into whatever personal info it can find, including every social media file and everything ever posted by your friends, family, previous employers, and more. Questions about your race, nationality, age, gender, disabilities, marital status, spouses, children and their care, criminal records, or credit records would normally open a company to discrimination allegations.[38] But AI recruitment systems can factor them into their decisions under a veil of secrecy. With AI, no *person* has screened you based on these criteria; instead, it was a piece of software that sifted through social media and made recommendations, which gets employers around some legal loopholes— at least for now.

Criteria do not have to be *explicitly* set to look for younger candidates who make less money or for healthy nonsmokers who might take fewer breaks and pose less of a healthcare burden, for example. All an AI hiring firm must do is simply leave people with undesirable qualities out of the data they use to train the AI. Then the model will not pick up any of the features that are typically considered undesirable.

For example, if there are few to no disabled people in the list of social media profiles the AI is trained on, then the AI will not seek out their unique characteristics for inclusion when sourcing candidates. It is a loophole that US laws currently do not directly address. In addition, it would be incredibly difficult to prove discrimination by AI because the people who develop the machine-learning algorithms often cannot understand why the AI chose what it chose. Many AI firms keep haphazard records of the data that was used to train their AI as it is. Not because they are subversive per se (though some AI hiring firms might be), but because they are inexperienced, sloppy, lazy, or working too fast to take the extra time and effort to prevent such bias. Either way, this means there is no proof that groups protected under Equal Employment Opportunity Act were *purposefully* left out of the AI's training data set. From there, if ever brought to court over discriminatory hiring practices, AI hiring firms can say that the algorithm must have picked up bad information past its initial training set.

Employers' use of AI to snoop on social media posts could yield erroneous and misleading results that could serve to exclude you from the job you were meant to have. AI is terrible at judging context and the degree to which something could be considered offensive. This is unfortunate given that more than 50 percent of employers have found content on social media that caused them *not* to hire a candidate.[39] As employers increasingly turn to AI to take over the social media-screening function, it will be important for you to know the types of "violations" that make employers put candidates in the "denied" bucket (refer to the list above for a refresher). Remember also that with AI, searches aren't confined to just you, the job candidate. They are looking at the people in your network and what they are posting as well to deduce insights about you. The AI can derive insights from your liked content and the types of people you communicate with the most. As a matter of fact, "guilt by association" is one of AI's specialties.

Think about your crazy ex-boyfriend who is a gun enthusiast, prankster friends from high school who lit a dumpster on fire, or partying friends from college who always have drinks in their hands. You get the idea. It can get real ugly real fast. Especially when you consider that pictures and posts on social media have a way of being misinterpreted by people—much less AI—that don't understand context. For example, an AI trained on image recognition and tags could find your name in a tag and then "look" for alcoholic beverages in your hand or near you. Then *poof!* you're out because it puts you in the "drinks" category and then later filters out anyone with that label because it is considered undesirable by the employer. The AI won't contextualize that perhaps this is a one-time occurrence of drinking at a bachelorette party. It will simply ding your score or rating or outright eliminate you from the candidate pool.

These are the social media faux pas that could result in you being screened out. Forty percent of hiring managers said no to a job candidate because they felt the candidate posted provocative or inappropriate photographs, videos, or information.[40] "Inappropriate" is a very subjective term. I had a boss in marketing once that felt it was "inappropriate" for one of our social media influencers to post pics of his breakfast every morning. The influencer saw it as another way to connect with his followers. Thirty-six percent of hiring managers don't want a candidate who has posted about drinking or using drugs.[41] You may think you are fine because you do not habitually drink or do drugs. However, just to cover your bases on this, search yourself on all the major social media sites. Make sure that no old college drinking pictures or bachelorette pictures exist there. If they do, you may want to consider de-tagging yourself; otherwise, an AI could sort you into the "no" category.

Thirty-one percent of employers said no to a candidate because of discriminatory comments related to race, gender, or religion.[42] While that's certainly a legitimate reason to reject a candidate, AI does not yet have the ability to reliably filter against true discriminatory or hate speech and wording that can be misconstrued as such. (If it did, Twitter and Facebook would be using it like it was going out of style!) Instead, chances are high that AI can take your comments out of context and flag you as being discriminatory. So be sure to check your comments and posts on social media for anything that can be misconstrued or misinterpreted.

Interviewing AI

"Makes Your Skin Crawl" Then Rates Your Employability

Job seekers have described AI interviews as "alienating," "dehumanizing," "exhausting," "disheartening," "anxiety-inducing," and "agonizing." To have to perform in front of a web camera as AI makes unexplained demands and asks questions "made my skin crawl," according to one interviewee of the *Washington Post*. Others found it sad to boil their entire life's experiences into a sound bite to be judged by a computer program instead of a human.[43]

Here's how it works. You get dressed up, carefully select the quietest spot in your house, favorably adjust the lighting, and then stare into your webcam as an AI greets you and asks you canned questions. What you'll see on the screen could be no more than a series of words, or it could be an eerily lifelike speaking avatar or even a disembodied head.[44] Whatever form the AI takes, it will scrutinize your facial expressions, word choices, and vocal intonation as you methodically answer each question, with no immediate feedback. Forget about getting your own questions answered or getting to see the place you might work and observe the culture for yourself. There is really no additional opportunity for connection or dialogue when interviews are done solely via AI. It's a one-sided pull for intel.

How awkward and limiting is that? As if interviews aren't scary enough when you can make eye contact and read the reactions of the person across from you! With a human, you could at least clarify your intentions or meaning if you saw a negative reaction to your answers. In an AI interview, that's impossible too. The AI will rank you on "willingness to learn," "personal stability," and of course, "employability," and you will never have a clue or be told how you did. You may or may not receive an automated AI text letting you know you made it past the first interview—ha! Those turkeys! In the good old days, you were screened and then you could finally get to a person. Ah, relief. You could get past the impersonal rigmarole and have an honest-to-goodness dialogue to show off your real passions and ambitions, your charisma, and your sense of humor—things not found on a résumé. Now, even that's no longer true. It's literally an inhuman process!

And perhaps you are wondering, like I did, how does an AI know what facial expressions and patterns of speech are ideal? Cue the company clones: It comes from current employees who also sat through the interviews and assessments as benchmark subjects. The AI hiring firm will look at the patterns and trends in what the "successful" employees say and how they act and compare that to what the job candidate says and how they act. The closer you look, react, and talk like the "successful" employees, the better your score. Too bad they can't just make robot clones of "successful" employees—or can they? More on that in the next chapter on automation.

There are also privacy, security, transparency, fairness, and fraudulent-claims concerns. A prominent privacy rights group, the Electronic Privacy Information Center, filed a complaint with the Federal Trade Commission in November 2019 against the leading AI interview firm, HireVue, citing "unfair and deceptive" practices. They described the technology as "a major threat to American workers' privacy and livelihoods," claiming the systems were "biased, unprovable, and not replicable."[45] AI researchers and top neuroscientists describe AI interview technology as "digital snake oil," "pseudoscience," "imprecise," "a license to discriminate," and "a black box" that gives no fair chance for job seekers to weigh in.[46]

AI interviews use facial recognition technology, which has been proven to be biased for a host of reasons, all of which have to do with a lack of diversity within the data set on which the AI is trained. One study, for example, found that the data set was overwhelmingly comprised of lighter-skinned subjects and therefore biased against people with darker complexions.[47] The same holds true for those with disabilities, conditions that cause facial abnormalities, and basically anyone from cultures divergent from the majority of employees. If you're part of a minority group that isn't represented in the data set, the AI will exclude you.

Lawmakers worry about the lack of transparency in how AI hiring systems work and if people who decline an AI test will still get a fair shot at the job. They are also concerned about the data and footage collected. In a single thirty-minute AI interview, over five hundred thousand data points are collected—including biometric data on your face. Your face—you know, that password on your body that you can never change—which can unlock your mobile phone, digital wallet, and cloud accounts. Job seekers are not yet employees, so they are also not covered by policies that protect employee information. While there has been lots of talk about data privacy laws, the only state that has them is California. Ironic, since the majority of privacy-violating technology comes from there.

While many bills have been introduced at the federal level on the matter of AI hiring technologies, only Illinois has a state law that is currently in effect. Illinois Governor J. B. Pritzker signed the first law requiring employers to tell applicants how their AI systems work and get their consent before testing. This is a commendable step in the right direction. However, it's not a true choice unless you will still be viably considered for the job if you refuse to consent. There is no requirement for employers to prove they offered non-AI options or that they still considered the candidate. We really have a long way to go before AI hiring is fully transparent, secure, safe, and fair.

Here's What You Can Do to Take Back Some Control

For AI-involved hiring to work for our benefit, it needs to be 1) trained on good data, which means the data pool needs to be large and deeply diverse; 2) fully transparent, with explainable scores, open to scrutiny, accountability, and, when wrong, rectification, by all parties; and 3) subject to regulations and guardrails that protect the rights and liberties of the humans it was designed to serve. We are not there yet. This means that you as a job seeker, or that a job seeker you love—your kids, grandkids, spouse, friends—will in all likelihood be subjected to AI screening when joining the workforce, even in the frenzied post-pandemic rehiring. What can you do about all this? Keep reading.

Be So Visible They Can't Ignore You Online

- Maintain a current version of your online résumé and portfolio of your work on LinkedIn, professional sites, job recruitment platforms like Indeed, and on your own website if you have one. Ensure you use the latest keywords used in the LinkedIn profiles of leaders in your profession and that the words used to describe your skills and qualifications match those of any jobs you are especially interested in (if you can find a job description posted anywhere).

- Consider getting a URL in your name where you can post all your latest and greatest accomplishments. Ensure your word choices are in line with the latest terms used in your field and that your skills are continually updated so recruiters, both AI and human, can find you online.

- Stay visible and active on LinkedIn and in professional organizations. Keep up your memberships and actively participate in or lead projects.

- Post thought leadership articles regularly on LinkedIn and other social media sites.

- If you have a particular job title in mind, start searching that title on LinkedIn, Google, Facebook, and Twitter so that search engine optimization algorithms will begin associating the title with your name. Save the job title in your search alerts on these sites.

- Join professional groups that are associated with jobs you would like—especially on LinkedIn but also on Twitter and Facebook.

- Hashtag for the job you want, not the job you have. My twitter handle is Cortnie_CDO, and I have #CDO and #ChiefDataOfficer in my description. You should do the same on all your social media sites so that you are tagged with the title you want to be someday.

- Apply to the job you want even if you suspect you may not meet all the "requirements." Tailor your résumé to match the keywords and requirements of the job description.

Assess Your Digital Self

- Update the privacy settings on Facebook, Google, Twitter, LinkedIn, and other platforms. Shut down those that have access to see your posts while you are searching for a job. That is the only way to ensure nothing is misinterpreted or misconstrued by AI.

- Check your posts, especially images, for any potentially sensitive content. When in doubt, delete it.

- Regularly perform internet searches for your name and in your area of expertise to ensure that publicity is good and that your online presences can be found. De-tag content that associates you with anything negative.

- Be careful what you like, upvote, and share.

- Be careful about who you "friend" on Facebook or who you "connect" with on LinkedIn, for example. Don't forget, AI will assign guilt by association. You can employ the "all" or "nothing" methods to throw off algorithms. If you have so many connections of so many different types of people, then the algorithm can't peg you as being a particular "type" based on your connections. If you choose to go the "nothing" route, then you have to choose very wisely whom you have in your network, because the fewer there are, the more meaning will be ascribed to them. I personally choose the "all" method—especially on LinkedIn.

- Consider if you need to use certain social media, and either delete the account or remain inactive. I have a Facebook account, but I haven't logged on in forever. People generally don't interact with or tag people who are inactive.

Go Direct, Bypass AI

- Maintain awareness of key topics and influential people in your field as well as your personal visibility by attending and speaking at key professional events.

- Set alerts on your calendar to periodically remind yourself to check for jobs on websites of companies where you'd like to work. You don't have to wait for an algorithm to find you—you can circumvent the whole automated system by going directly to the source to learn about job openings.

Demand Change

- Unfortunately, at the present time, if the company you want to work for uses an AI hiring vendor, you will have to agree to be interviewed by AI. To change this will require political action. Advocate with your congresspeople for better laws and privacy around AI screening and interviews.

- Demand to see the scores and labels attributed to your profile. Ask the employer to explain why the algorithm gave you the scores it did. You may consider filing a complaint with the EEOC if they cannot provide an explanation to you.

- Demand transparency from the employer about what will be done with your data, and especially your "scores" and "labels." Ask if those can be reused by the AI hiring firm for other employers in the same industry. If so, then this could significantly affect your job opportunities in the whole of an industry.

- If you get rejected by an AI interviewer, ask the hiring manager what you could do better in the next interview. This will force the *people* doing the hiring to investigate.

- If possible, avoid AI interviews altogether by leveraging your own network or the network of good friends and family who can help you directly connect with a hiring manager for a job.

CHAPTER 4
Could I Be Replaced or Fired by AI?

AI tools are going to drive decisions like who ought to be promoted and who should be fired. When you have algorithms making decisions that impact humans in one of the most essential life functions—which is their work— there are going to be issues of fairness and transparency and legal challenges, and I think we are going to see those legal challenges start very soon.

—Bradford Newman, Chair of North America AI and ML Practice, Baker McKenzie

How ageism and cultural misunderstanding could get you fired in the age of automated decisions.

You were the pride of the financial firm you worked at for thirty years. You came straight out of college and went right into the firm. As one of the first Latina women to be hired there, you won award after award and landed over half of the firm's biggest clients. You fought three times harder than any male or white woman to prove yourself—working nights and weekends, crying when you missed your daughter's first steps, music recitals, and quinceañera preparations. But you believed the sacrifice would be worth it because you would teach your kids the biggest lesson of all—that if you work hard, you could achieve your dreams. You rose to the ultimate symbol of career achievement: partner.

But then your fortunes took a turn for the worse, and you couldn't understand why or what happened to cause this. Suddenly all that hard work meant nothing. A new performance-management algorithm that the company's human resources department was trying out flagged you as a "flight risk." This triggered an AI system that monitors your keystrokes, your health insurance-provided fitness tracker, and your phone—including your calendar appointments, job-hunting apps, internet searches, but most importantly, the GPS data showing where you go at all times.

Ultimately, after intensive scrutinization, the AI decided you were not trying to leave to go to a competitor. The performance-management algorithm decided the competition would not hire you at the age of fifty. However, because of recent visits you made to clients at their homes instead of their offices, the algorithm decided you were trying to steal the firm's clients to launch a business of your own. It gave additional proof by noting that you had also recently subscribed on a social media site to the "50s-plus Entrepreneur" group and had been actively posting. No one told you what the algorithm found or why it decided you were a flight risk in the first place. There was no legal requirement for the company to do so. But because you work in an "at-will" employment state, you are terminated.

Not only would you not get the retirement celebration and acknowledgement of a fantastic career from the firm and your colleagues, but your career would now come to an abrupt and disreputable end. Instead of a huge party, you were forced to hand over everything that was ever given to you by the firm during your thirty years of service and were escorted out by guards. Because there was data to be gleaned from your fitness tracker, your car, and your phone and laptop, those would now be held by the firm as evidence in case of a wrongful-termination lawsuit.

You felt powerless and crumpled into the rideshare you were forced to get because you no longer have a company car. On the ride home, all you could think was, *How did this go so terribly wrong?* Then grief turned to panic as you wondered how you would continue to support your grown children and mother who live with you. You were not prepared for an early retirement. All your savings had gone into paying for your kids' college and the constant care required for your mother's dementia. How could this happen?

As you sat holding your mother's hand, tears streaming down your face, you replayed in your mind everything you did in the last month since the algorithm had been implemented. You had cultivated deep and meaningful relationships within the Mexican business community by being there for their daughters' quinceañeras and more recently Día de los Muertos (Day of the Dead—in Mexican culture, friends and family gather to pray for and remember lost loved ones on this day). While celebrating with them at their houses, you discovered many of them subscribed to a new group called 50s-plus Entrepreneur, so you joined as well. But you couldn't fathom how any of this had relevance to your current situation. You dismissed it. There was no time to look back; you didn't have the time or money to hire an attorney anyway. You had to keep moving forward. That meant getting a new job at an age when you were just ready to think about retiring. This time, you would put money away for retirement. You would accept any job that allowed you to keep paying the bills.

Questions to Think About: (Take the Quiz Online at www.AITruth.org)

- Would the employee monitoring algorithm have flagged unusual activity around Day of the Dead if someone of Mexican heritage had helped develop it?

- Are there data sources that could have been used to flag this holiday in the algorithm?

- Is it the usual practice of data scientists to look for such things before releasing an algorithm to be used?

- Is there a *legal requirement* for data scientists to look for such things before releasing an algorithm to be used?

- Do data scientists have a standard operating model for algorithm development?

- Will the algorithm ever be updated with this information on its own without creating a data science-initiated feedback loop?

- What are some of the ways the data science team may learn of the need for retraining the algorithm?

- Is it likely the company has an internal appeals process for being fired-by-algorithm?

- Could the company have done anything differently in its implementation of both the performance management and employee-monitoring algorithms?

- Do you think it was tested on diverse groups before its release?

- If the financial firm continues using the algorithms as is, what issues do you see the firm encountering in the future as more and more minorities become subject to firing?

This story was inspired by the following headlines: "IBM can predict with 95 percent accuracy which employees are about to quit their jobs"[48]; "Workers Have a Big Secret: Their Age"[49]; "Bosses can monitor your every step—and possibly more."[50] To see more, visit the Notes section.

A Ratings Lesson from a Houston Honors/Special Ed Teacher

AI-based rating systems should be fed "training data" to learn from. Then, theoretically, among that data, the learning model will find patterns about what constitutes a "good" teacher. However, often there is not enough data features for the model to come to accurate results. For example, Teacher X has thirty-five students, with 20 percent on the honor roll and 20 percent in special education. The special education students increased test scores by 1 percent, which is amazing relative to the performance of special ed students in the state. Of the honor roll students who learned from this teacher, 10 percent increased their scores, which is average, because honor roll students' scores are often already the topmost scores. The other 60 percent of the class increased test scores by 30 percent on average, which outperforms the state average by 10 percent. This amount of data would be sufficient to make a real assessment.

Do you think previous algorithms have been "trained" with this level of information? No. Instead, what happened in Houston, for example, is that a teacher was graded on how well their students did in a value-added-model approach, which had major overfitting because of the vagueness of the data.[51] Here's what I mean by vagueness of the data: The teachers with middle-of-the-road students had more room for improvement in test scores. Those who had either special ed or honor students didn't, because those students either had learning deficiencies or were already scoring very high, which meant they had a narrow gap for improvement.

Either way, the employee ratings became more about how much room for improvement there was instead of the teacher's ability to affect that improvement. Teachers who had honors or special education kids, therefore, appeared to underperform relative to the teachers who had kids in the average or middle areas. These were unfair ways to measure the effectiveness of teachers. Another problem with AI-based rating systems is that there is often not enough data to learn from. In this case, the number of students a teacher has may only be thirty-five. AI-based methods require at least one hundred records or more to truly have a representative sample to learn from. While all students from all teachers could be glommed together, an individual student's learning distribution and room for improvement are all different due to many factors often unrelated to a teacher's level of effort, creativity, or efficiency in the classroom.

Finally, and most importantly, is the determination of what constitutes "best" or "most effective" or whatever special criteria is being used to rate or assess the employee. The dangerous part about using AI-based rating systems is that you will try to do it at scale with as little human intervention as possible, because the whole point of using the system is that it is supposed to save money or be able to more efficiently make assessments than humans. There are a few ways that I can screw up training the model on what it means to be "the best employee" or, in our example, the "best teacher." First, I can pool all the employees who have received the best ratings in the past and look for trends among them. But this method of assessing would carry its own problems because the ratings I gave in the past 1) may not have been based on logical criteria, 2) could have been very subjective and inconsistent, and 3) may not be congruent with the criteria being used for rankings today. This incongruency of data from past to present criteria is probably one of the biggest challenges in setting ideal training data for the model to learn from. Especially if, in the past, I used a special kind of contextual data, such as recommendation cards or letters from parents or bits of data that no longer exist, to digitize and consider. Then there is the matter of missing data that will cause results to no longer be accurate. You won't know for sure if they were, in fact, the kind of values the school or organization wanted to incentivize then as compared with criteria from today. In other words, it may not even be possible to apply the old data used to make past ratings to a new ratings system.

What will happen instead is that many data scientists will try to find proxies for that data instead of either admitting they need to create an entirely new ratings system or will have to invest extra time digitizing old data such as written letters or recommendation cards and ensuring that the new ratings system can collect these same bits of information. In addition, new data collection methods will have to be devised to ensure continual updates to the model for accuracy. Finally, feedback loops will have to be created. Why are feedback loops important, and what do they do?. Feedback loops create a check and balance to the system which allows an algorithm creator to understand how the system is performing. Any corrections or tweaks can be made so that the system can remain as unbiased as possible and lessen the chances that something major will go wrong which could ultimately result in someone losing their job, the company being sued for unfair practices, damaged brand reputation, and so much more.

Feedback loops also allow humans who are affected by these ratings to see and understand how they were rated and make an appeal if they feel the rating was unjust. If the rating is found to be unjust, then beyond rectifying the situation for the individual employee who was affected, the algorithm could be tweaked to rectify any areas that created an unfair rating in the first place. But in order for all of these things to take place, a formal process for reviewing algorithms would have to be put in place. This generally requires some experts on the ratings process from the school administration, teachers, and also a group of data scientists to ensure feedback gets incorporated properly into the algorithm. Once the scoring criteria and data sources are set and agreed to by school administrators, parents, and teachers, the last step is to ensure the technology will run properly with other information systems at the school and that it is able to incorporate changes as they occur. Like I said, without a regular, formal review process, these changes do not become real, and therefore could continue to create opportunities for disaster when not fixed before the next deployment or employee assessment cycle.

Many organizations already have formal processes for submitting appeals about employee ratings or assessments. Check with your human resources designate to understand more about that process. If you feel you have been adversely affected by an employee rating system and you have exhausted your avenues of appeal internally with no effect, then try finding out the name of the group that developed the AI-based algorithm. They should want to take an active role in bettering their system. If that does not work, let all parties who would not listen know that you will take the story to the news outlets. You can always drop me a line as well.

Being Monitored by AI on the Job

We all know somewhere in the back of our minds that we are most likely, in some way, being monitored on the job through our computers or cameras in the workplace. I used to think of some IT guy in a dark closet somewhere with a tower of Red Bull cans, watching my whole department, just waiting to point out the first one of us to look up something risqué or a site that might suggest we were looking for another job, or, heaven forbid, the endless shopping sites being perused at Christmastime, hence, the endless amount of slacking off going on. I just knew one of us would eventually be forced into the march of shame down to the office of our VP and outed for our IT wrongdoings. These thoughts and images played in my mind mostly when I was an expendable up-and-comer in my twenties with a lot to prove. But the fear was real. I was able to get a lot done quickly—or at least I thought so, and my theory seemed correct as I was always rated highly. But that often left me with plenty of time for other projects. Of course, I would offer to take on extra projects, but sometimes there weren't any to be had, so I'd kill time educating myself on competitive offerings or shopping for gifts.

It is with great empathy and understanding, then, that I cringe when I think about AI monitoring in the workplace. There are many reasons employers give when justifying the use of AI-monitoring of its employees. Some banks and investment groups will tell you it is to determine if their employees are up to criminal activity. Given some of the past salacious headlines about firms like Goldman Sachs and JPMorgan Chase, I tend to believe employee monitoring is justified. But some companies have taken it to an extreme level. Two of these are Amazon and Three Square Market, an eighty-person tech company based in Wisconsin.[52]

At a "chips and salsa party," Three Square Market employees could voluntarily have microchips the size of a grain of rice implanted between their forefinger and thumb, allowing them quick access to buy snacks from the store, log in in the morning, and access locked doors. Fifty of the eighty employees volunteered for the convenience factor of it, including the CEO and his family members. For employees still on the fence, the CEO assured them there would be no tracking of the information and that the chips were not GPS enabled—

they were radio frequency only. Twenty-nine of the employees cited privacy concerns and one cited fear of infection as opposed to a fear of being tracked.

In January 2018, Amazon filed a patent for an electronic wristband that can monitor employees' tasks. Amazon designed it to emit ultrasonic pulses to alert the wearer to inventory locations and to reduce the need for inventory scanners. Amazon says they are trying to make the fulfillment process easier by freeing up fulfillment workers' hands and reducing strain on eyes. Inventory scanners are pieces of equipment employees would have on them anyway—the wristband would just replace that outdated piece of equipment. Paula Brantner of Workplace Fairness, a nonprofit devoted to ensuring fair workplaces, was skeptical about Amazon's intentions. Amazon has denied wanting to track employees and stands by its claim of increasing ergonomics and safety for fulfillment workers.

With employers able to monitor employees via video cameras, postal mail, email, smartphones, computer usage, and GPS tracking, it's never been easier than with machine learning to start gathering personally identifiable information or sensitive private information.

The big question is: What happens to employees who do not wish to take part in the technology? While many companies claim the tech is optional, is it really? Will your refusal limit your growth with the company? Will your supervisors question your trustworthiness? Will others who do have the chip or wristband exclude you from social gatherings? Will employers make it more difficult to work in the office if you do not have a chip? At what point do you simply become blacklisted or seen as not a team player for nonparticipation in these kinds of things? All the while, privacy for individual employees becomes lessened despite promises from CEOs—not to mention the security of individuals at work with more and more data available about bathroom breaks (the length of which could indicate types of diseases that may weigh on healthcare or productivity at work) and their proximity to other workers. The employer now knows who spends time together, which could lead to suspicion if one of them quits, is fired, or is found to be a suspect of illegal activity; or worse, someone could assert that there is a forbidden workplace romance. Any number of things could result from getting chipped so companies can watch for criminal activity or workplace productivity and operations.

AI-Monitoring for Insider Threats

There are lots of reasons companies want to monitor employees. Smaller companies are generally trying to maximize productivity and ensure their proprietary data (including intellectual property and client lists complete with their contact information) does not go out the door with a larcenous VP of sales or operations. Some companies have made news headlines about their own top executives participating in insider trading; many companies fight to protect their trade secrets from overseas competitors who would infiltrate their ranks by sending corporate spies to send sensitive information back to them. Whatever the reasons, 86 percent of organizations deploy some method of monitoring users.[53] In 2021, 61 percent of companies confirmed insider attacks against their organization in the previous twelve months, with 68 percent saying insider attacks have become more frequent.[54]

> *An insider threat is a malicious threat to an organization that comes from people within the organization, such as employees, former employees, contractors or business associates, who have inside information concerning the organization's security practices, data, and computer systems.*

To that end, Goldman Sachs and Credit Suisse have invested in Digital Reasoning Systems (DRS), which uses machine learning to scan through millions of emails, calls, video, and communications of all kinds between employees and clients to unearth any atypical communication patterns that may signal an insider threat or breach. When a breach is suspected, an alert is sent to the compliance professionals of the company so they can do a further investigation.[55] Companies who have had serious breaches in the past look for opportunities to virtue signal to clients by investing in software such as DRS to regain client trust and, more importantly, investment.

Therefore, if you are an employee of a bank or financial services group, you can understand that clients will be happy to know that you are monitored. You can sort of forgive the level of scrutiny of what you do at work because 1) you know that it is universal among your fellow employees and you're not being singled out, and 2) you would want someone to take the same care in protecting your monetary investments.

But at what point does monitoring end and employee privacy begin? Is nothing off-limits in the workplace? Are all reasons for this level of intrusion worthwhile? Where is the line in employees' minds? At what point do they seek revenge or act out because they are being overly monitored with no sense of agency? At what point do employers view that gap as going overboard? At what point do employees? Is there a big gap between the two perceptions? When a big gap does occur, how does this affect the culture of the organization?

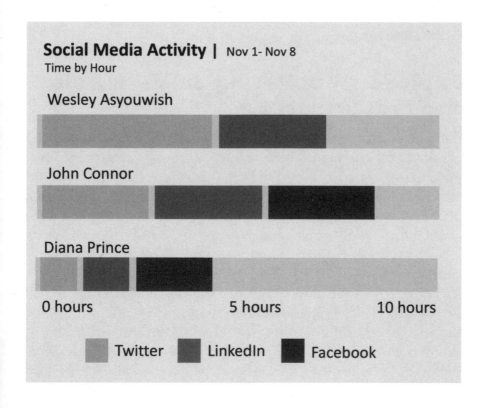

Veriato is a software that monitors employees and can even provide video playback of all onscreen activity as well as productivity reports and alerts. Its insider-threat software provides AI-driven user behavioral analytics. The company's website claims "employers can record and review anything or everything that your employees do on their PCs, Macs, and Android devices. 1) See which employees spend half the day on Facebook, Amazon, or playing fantasy football. 2) Get scheduled productivity reports on your employees (daily, weekly, monthly). 3) Understand exactly how long employees are "actively" working. 4) Eliminate risky and inappropriate use of the internet. 5) Monitor remote workers' productivity. 6) Investigate suspicious activity. 7) Protect against data theft." The website's screen shot of Veriato's "Social Media Activity" chart depicting names with colored bars shows which social media each employee used and for how long.

Should there be an expectation of privacy in the workplace? Is everything you do the domain of the company, including any contacts or network members you have? What about work that you do on your own time?

Employee Monitoring Sinks Morale and Productivity

AI-based employee monitoring for productivity purposes is a morale sinker for employees. Monitoring can cause a temporary lift in productivity and good behavior, but it also creates an adversarial environment for employees and sends the message that "we don't trust you." The use of always-on web cams, keystroke detectors, and social media tracking has contributed to employee burnout. It can be especially stressful when coworkers create the standards for efficiency, creating peer pressure to perform at the same level. Lower-level employees who have the most stress are often the ones making the least and have the most to lose by losing their job. It is these employees who are given the fifteen-minute breaks and thirty minutes for lunch. Yet hours employees spend working has gone up from 8 hours when employees were in offices to 11 hours per day while working from home during the pandemic.[56] Gartner, a leading technology research and services company, has found that employers who take the tact of supporting their employees lives during pandemic times, have increased the number of high performers by 21 percent and realized 20 percent increase of employees reporting better mental and physical health—which Gartner says increases productivity.[57]

What Are Your Rights?

Employee monitoring gives employers the grounds for firing workers, and you have no legal recourse when your perceived rights are violated, whether you are at home using your own personal social media account or at work using an office computer.

So far, there are no federal laws addressing how far an employer can go in their monitoring of you. And what happens when you don't participate in the monitoring? What happens when you refuse to download an app onto your personal phone that will monitor your whereabouts via GPS? In the case of one woman, she was fired for refusing after she found out that her whereabouts were being monitored even after she was no longer on the clock. She deleted the Xora app (now StreetSmart) from her phone and was terminated because of it.[58]

Perhaps the worst thing about employee monitoring is that, based on digital anecdotal information, people can lose their jobs. Oftentimes employers are looking for indicators that you are surfing for another job on company time, decreasing productivity by shopping or idling on social media accounts, gossiping about the company, talking to clients, passing trade secrets, downloading client-sensitive information for purposes of identity theft, or other crimes such as creating false accounts to meet quotas.

But could there be occasions when they just flat out have an infatuation with you or want to leverage your personal information for their gain? Are we supposed to believe that people who could know our whereabouts every second of the day have absolutely nothing but our best interests at heart? In the case of the lady who deleted the Xora app, she was fired, but she was also told by her VP of sales that he even knew how fast she was driving.[59] Now I'm sorry, but no! On what planet is that not creepy? And why shouldn't there be oversight or compliance procedures for when bosses or other coworkers take the AI-tracking to a creepy level? But compliance measures are rarely heard of by employees who see no recourse but to quit and sue. The extent to which these policies exist within organizations is also a good topic to examine as well.

Could AI Flag Workers that Might Quit?

IBM announced in April 2019 that it could predict with 95 percent accuracy which workers are about to quit their jobs.[60] They called it a "predictive attrition program." When I saw this headline, IBM was in the midst of laying off and firing over twenty thousand workers over the age of forty.[61] It doesn't take long to connect the dots to find whom they might target with this "predictive attrition program." While laying off thousands of older workers making higher salaries than entry-level college students, they can claim in a court of law that the workers were likely to quit anyway. "[Now former IBM CEO] Ginny Rometty would not explain "the secret sauce" that allowed the AI to work so effectively in identifying workers about to jump. Rometty would only say that its success comes through analyzing many data points."[62]

IBM could also claim their algorithm is a trade secret so that they would not have to show exactly what factors (such as age, tenure, or salary-level) the algorithm weighted in its decision. IBM executives have told the media they are happy to retain their employees better. They even went so far as to change the way they describe the program recently to try and put a different spin on the AI product by calling it a "proactive retention" tool.[63]

Could AI Replace People at Work?

A poll of eleven thousand workers by ZipRecruiter found that 58 percent of job seekers think AI will destroy more jobs than it creates.[64] However, it's not nearly as easy to replace us as people currently think. AI is only able to replace the repetitive *tasks* of a person's job for now, as opposed to replacing the entire job. How soon you might be replaced depends on what you do, how much electrical energy it costs to run a computer program to do the equivalent of what you do, and how much reading, thinking, and reasoning goes into what you do. AI with the capacity to replace workers is referred to as "automation." Automation is defined as the technique of making an apparatus, a process, or a system operate automatically. Simpler versions of automation are called robotic process automation. But other examples of automation exist, such as driverless vehicles, robots, and software code that goes between large enterprise systems (e.g., Oracle, SAP, Salesforce).

Automation is achieved by coding a set of static instructions into systems, or they can be based on AI, which is ever-learning and ever-changing. It's currently difficult to use AI between enterprise systems (such as the SAPs of the world) because those systems date back to the 1980s at most companies. It takes major upgrades, and it costs a lot to get systems to the point where they can be fully automated with the ever-changing rules that AI would program into them. So, a lot of companies are not diving right into this level of AI just yet because it's freaking expensive! Yay! You get to keep your job a little longer, at least until it's cheaper to replace you—then watch out. But if you start now, you can definitely learn some other, less-replaceable skills. What are those exactly? Well, I'm being only a bit snarky when I say not even the experts know what AI *can't* do yet. Yep. That's right. But we're not supposed to worry about that.

IBM defines three levels of process automation: basic, advanced, and intelligent. "*Basic process automation* is where the robot is taught to perform simple application tasks and follows predetermined pathways. In *advanced process automation*, the robot follows predetermined pathways across systems, conducts complex calculations, and triggers downstream activities. In *intelligent process automation*, the robot has autonomous decision-making capabilities and may interact with humans through a combination of advanced algorithms and multiple types of AI."[65] These are generally accepted process automation concepts by most in the automation industry.

The point is, there is a difference between an AI-driven version of automation (referred to as "intelligent process automation" above) and just good old basic automation. Basic automation is made up of a series of little software programs called bots. For anyone familiar with the term "macro," as used in the Microsoft Excel context, bots are like little macros that usually perform only one task. These are not tiny physical robots like the ones you may have seen in the Disney Pixar movie *WALL-E*. They are literally little bits of code associated with a very specific tiny task. For example: "Open CRM system," "Run program Y," "End program Y." They become effective at taking an action when they are strung together and assigned a command line and system.

The first step on a company's path to operationalize automation is to map tasks that are repetitive and rules-based. Before a large investment is made, a consultant who provides business process automation or optimization (BPA or BPO for short) will perform an assessment of how many full-time employees (FTEs) it would take to do the work. Then, usually on the basis of cost reduction and increased efficiency, the business downsizes the number of FTEs, which are replaced by bots. (See the example below from BPO provider AntWorks.) If you look at the very bottom of the graphic, you'll see the repetitive work that employees used to do in this insurance broker office has been taken down from a fifteen-minute process to a two-minute process by using bots. This could result in replacing a significant number of workers. It's highly likely this was only one part of their job as opposed to the entirety of the worker's job. We as workers often have strategic tasks mixed in with repetitive and quite frankly boring tasks. While the boring parts can be eliminated by having the bots do them, people will still be eliminated because their jobs will now be consolidated around only the most strategic elements. These jobs will be redefined and possibly higher paying. They may also require higher skill levels.

Now imagine if there were *no* humans involved at all in the graphic. Then you would have truly "intelligent automation." This is the dream for the business process automation folks. However, the less involved humans are, the less we can provide oversight about whether the intelligent automations are malfunctioning or learning wrong information. Automation makes it hard for humans to know when to intervene. That's why the ability to monitor and provide ongoing feedback into these intelligent automation systems will be so important in the future.

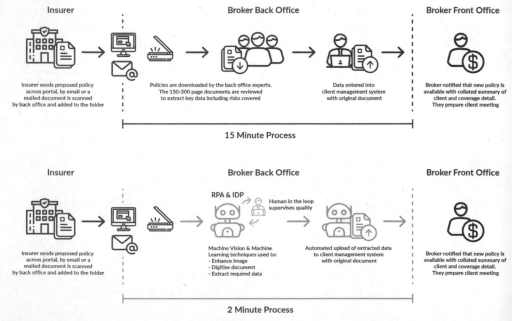

Intelligent Automation in Back Office of Global Commercial Insurance Broker

I talked to a chief data officer of a leading bank about her ability to fully automate a person's job, and she said the reality is you can only automate bits and bytes of a person's job but not the whole job, because, usually, not every aspect of a person's job is highly repetitive. For companies trying to gain cost efficiencies via elimination of full-time employees, it's unrealistic. Instead, you can increase productivity by eliminating the need of those employees to focus on repetitive tasks and instead spend their time on more valuable types of work which require knowledge of human behavior, intuition, and strategy.

That said, AI-based chatbots have the potential to take a huge chunk out of cost and inefficiency from call centers because of the way call centers work. Generally, call centers are made up of lower-skilled individuals who are reading from scripts as each scenario comes up. They will get the same types of call repeatedly, and there are knowledge banks for these. Think of these as "frequently asked questions" databases, like when you go to support. apple.com. Large corporations generally have knowledge banks for all kinds of things, such as questions on warrantees, customer support, and sales.

Are There Any Jobs that Are Safe?

When it comes to the ability of AI to take *key tasks* away from certain jobs, I believe AI is indiscriminate. There are a few folks out there, though, who have attempted to make a guess at which jobs will be replaced and which ones won't. Kai-Fu Lee, a leading Chinese AI expert, gave his list of potentially safe types of jobs during a CNN interview. I give you the list of "safe" jobs he predicted along with my thoughts on those predictions below.

a) *Creative Jobs—scientist, artist, novelist.*

- As you will see in the next chapter, an AI-generated piece of art has already sold for $432,500 at Christie's—leading me to believe this prediction of Lee's may not hold. Who's to say an AI won't generate its own novel by using bits of plots and characters from books that have received excellent reviews? Also, scientists are already being usurped by AI—yet they are *helping* AI usurp them nonetheless. *Rise of the Robots* author Martin Ford also predicted that creative jobs would be safe from AI.

    b)   **Complex and Strategic Jobs**—*executive, diplomat, economist.*

- None of these jobs is completely safe either, in my opinion. Maybe diplomat is safe. Aspects of economists' jobs were replaced a long time ago by AI.

    c)   **Empathetic, Compassionate, Trust-based Jobs**—*teacher, nanny, doctor.*

- I agree with Lee on this one, even though there has been significant headway with AI in education via learning platforms and certain aspects of doctor's jobs like diagnostics and surgery. According to Lee, "No one wants to hear they have cancer from a chatbot." But honestly, if you can't even get a job interview with a live person anymore, I'm not sure we really are that intolerant of this idea—even though it would be terrible to receive bad news that way. AI is already used to support doctors in a multitude of ways, from diagnosing types of cancer and other genomic disorders, to robot-assisted surgery, to recommending the right cocktail of drugs to optimize chemotherapy for a cancer patient. In a surprising find, over half of the participants in a study would trust an AI doctor over a human one.[66] I'm thinking this is more a statement about doctors and how fast they usher you out of their office than it is about how great people genuinely feel AI is, but then I'm biased toward humans.

    d)   **Unforeseeable AI-based Jobs**—*the jobs that AI will actually create.*[67]

- I believe this is a good prediction by Lee. Elon Musk once gave an example that instead of truck drivers, humans may someday fill the role of fleet operators over self-driving trucks. An article in *Fast Company* claimed that AI added three times more jobs than it replaced in 2018.[68] According to the study mentioned in the article, more companies are also offering training to keep up with the AI skills needed. As AI becomes more trusted in more industries, people will be needed who can oversee AI operations and daily maintenance of models and data. We will also need people who can audit AI systems' activities to ensure they're still doing what they're supposed to do. In the self-driving truck example, a human fleet operator could ensure that the trucks not only are making their deliveries correctly and on time but have not been exhibiting driving that could be unsafe for humans—such as veering off the sides of roads where pedestrians could be, running red lights, or speeding.

What Jobs Are Currently Being Replaced?

How fast AI can take over whole jobs (versus some tasks) will depend on how well we trust it to do those tasks in ways that won't harm us or exacerbate societal impacts. The other dependencies are physical in nature, such as our ability to fulfill AI systems' energy needs (which are substantial); availability of high-end, complex computing capabilities (e.g., quantum computing); and Wi-Fi and 5G accessibility (self-driving cars will need broadband everywhere for example). Some jobs are not as economical to replace with AI just yet, while others will practically demand our attention from an efficiency standpoint (robots on the floors of distribution warehouses operating in 100-degree heat will not need water breaks, for example).

While I was at IBM, we logged hundreds of unique uses of AI, and they were different for every industry. Just to give you an idea of the variety, here's a list of some of the jobs AI is already doing.[69]

- Truck driving and deliveries

- Accounting

- Application testing

- Cybercrime prevention and fraud detection

- Automotive assembly

- Insurance claims adjustments

- Personal assistance ("Alexa, add green beans to my grocery list and move my nine a.m. meeting.")

- Precision farming

- Detecting, diagnosing, and prescribing treatments for cancer and other diseases

- Anti-money-laundering analysis and decision-making with regulatory tracking

- Procurement rules enforcement and purchasing

- Contractual breaches

- Employee monitoring and supervising

- Oil rig engineer

- Actuary

- Cashier

- Telemarketing

- Call center agent—for sales, support, warrantees, policies, claims

- Fast food cook

- Chef (look up Chef Watson if you don't believe me)

- Travel agent

- Sniper (via drone)

- Game show contestant (OK, that's not a job, but it's still fun to list since IBM's AI, Watson, won at *Jeopardy!*)

You get the idea. This list could go on and on.

Recommendations

Forget about working for an AI boss, be the one who programs it. Take any training in machine learning or data science you can get—especially if it's offered free by your employer. These skills will only appreciate in the next twenty years. If you are looking for a job, ensure that you will not have an AI boss responsible for pushing your productivity. If you have an AI supervisor, this is a pretty good indicator that you could become subject to AI "coworkers" which you will be expected to match in productivity.

Instead, try to stay in the more strategic realm of careers where creativity, context, trust, and relationships are combined. Instead of chasing a job that relies heavily upon the latest "skills," learn how to think critically about problems and how to solve them. Choose a career where demonstrating the ability to be a problem-solver is more important than the latest software code or warehouse machinery. You can learn skills anytime in your life, but having the right personality to dive in, figure things out, and come up with solutions will always be valued.

CHAPTER 5
Could AI Take My Life's Purpose?

Artificial intelligence is a tool, not a threat.

—Rodney Brooks,

robotics entrepreneur

It's one thing for AI to take a task that anyone on the planet could do—I think any of us can flip a burger, and perhaps we have or are doing that for a living—but it's a whole other thing to be a world champion at something and then have AI beat you at it. Or, to spend your whole life fascinated with your subject matter and honing your skills and abilities and network so that you can be the best in your field...when, out of nowhere, a group of data scientists declares their AI programs are better than the best experts in your field. Now *that* is demoralizing. But it is happening, and it's happening in areas that require strategic thinking such as the game of Go and certain scientific disciplines. Wait...weren't those listed as creative jobs that no AI could touch, according to Kai-Fu Lee? And yet here we are discussing a very different reality.

The Go World Champion and the Western AI that Beat Him and Fueled a New AI Era in China

The strategy game Go is ancient and sacred in China. To be a master of this game is to be revered, much as chess masters are throughout the rest of the world. Lee Sedol, the now-former Go world champion, was many times shocked at the moves of the AI AlphaGo as he played against it.[70] To see the reactions of the AlphaGo team and commentators, search YouTube for "Lee Sedol vs AlphaGo Move 37." As AlphaGo played, it made moves that were very different early in the game which many described as "original." Go players all have very different techniques they use when they play each other, but when AlphaGo chose to come out of the gate in a position that broke from the way most players start, it raised eyebrows. And it continued to do so as it played, introducing even more original moves. The AI went beyond its human guidance and played something different. The commentators didn't even know what to say.

How Would You React if AI Beat You at Your Life's Work?

- Would you fight it and insist that you are still relevant while trying to discredit the AI and insist that it never be used in your field?

- Would you be depressed and accept that you have no future in a field where AI can leapfrog your years of work in an instant?

- Would you swallow your pride, celebrate the progress, and try to use the AI as a tool to further the scientific field for the sake of humanity?

Your answers may very well determine your future relationships with AI, depending on which path the majority take when AI becomes more involved in your careers and passions.

AI Scientist: The Four Stages of AI Grief

Protein folding is about predicting the 3D shapes that certain proteins will take; and it is crucial to how scientists develop new drugs. Every two years, there is an opportunity for scientists to submit their predictions to the Critical Assessment of Structure Prediction conference and be acknowledged by their peers if they win the contest.[71] But at the latest conference, the winner was not a friend or colleague who'd shared in all the ups and downs of protein-folding research. It was an algorithm from DeepMind. And it was completely deflating to the group of scientists who work on those problems for a living, whose passion it was to make predictions to solve one of the biggest puzzles in biochemistry. One particular Harvard biologist, Mohammed AlQuraishi, wrote a blog about his experience. He explained how he felt that, in one instant, he and his colleagues who had participated in the field, some for decades, were suddenly made obsolete, and he described the melancholy that came with the realization. Among the emotional stages he went through:

- *Surprise and disbelief* that the AI could just come in and do so well in such a short period of time

- *Disappointment and resentment* that outsiders (DeepMind) with AI capabilities could upend decades of people's work and, in effect, publicly demonstrated the structural inefficiency of academia

- *Melancholy* as they felt they were being displaced from a highly respected field where professionals in the field were passionate about their life's work and frequently recognized for their contributions

- *Acceptance.* In his words, he "ultimately overrode [his] tribal reflexes" so he could come to a more "rational assessment of the value of the scientific progress" that had been made[72]

If this sounds like the five stages of grief, it pretty much is. The five stages of grief, also known as the Kubler-Ross model, are: denial, anger, bargaining, depression, and acceptance. The notion is that we go through these stages when we are either faced with our own death or that of a loved one. Why not a career? This has me thinking that grief counseling should be offered to those in fields that may be impacted by AI in a huge way.

We should all prepare ourselves to face a day when our jobs could be taken over by AI, so when it comes, we can move through these stages quickly. Better still, we should start adapting our professional talents now so we do not have this experience at all. We have been warned. In my experience, it's best to face these fears head on and proactively decide our roles in developing the AI. Instead of having a DeepMind that comes out of nowhere to define our professions, we should take an active role in shaping and informing the AI so that it leverages the best of our experience and will then, in turn, have the best of humanity forming its core truth. We bring with us our intuition and emotion and empathy and strategy. This is something that no AI will have unless we put our unique experiences and understanding into it. That is how we can remain relevant in the age of AI. We also have to ensure that we use these programs and systems as tools and don't become the tools ourselves—always and only feeding the AI.

AI Artist: Artist's Life Work

How are artists taking note of the fact that Christie's auctioned its first piece of AI art for $432,500? The piece, called *Edmond de Belamy*, from *La Famille de Belamy*, was created by a French art collective who call themselves Obvious and are very new to the AI art scene. The AI art sold for double the prices of two pieces from legends Andy Warhol and Roy Lichtenstein *combined*. Christie's initially appraised the artwork at $7,000 to $10,000. Christie's goal for the auction was to try and get an understanding of the appetite for AI art by the traditional art market. The fact that it drew such a high price and at such an esteemed auction house meant that major media outlets like the *New York Times* picked up the story, which garnered the piece even more attention. It was bought by an anonymous caller. Whether the person who bought it was some sort of AI art supporter trying to make a point about AI art, we will never know. I can tell you that a previous purchaser of Obvious's AI art, Paris-based collector Nicolas Laugero-Lasserre, had this to say:

"I just find it amazing that some young people built a program allowing the creation of an original artwork, based on a selection of the 'bests' from past art history." He calls the innovation "grotesque and amazing at the same time."

"Have we ever imagined that creativity could come from a machine?" Laugero-Lasserre asks. "It's not just inspiration from the past, but actual new pieces."[73]

When asked if he intends to buy more he said, "Why not? If I fall for another one."

Back to the question at hand: How did the art community feel? Amazingly, the strongest reaction came not from the traditional art community but from the AI art community. Anger and resentment were the two main feelings. Many were upset that the AI art getting the most attention was, to their thinking, unoriginal.[74] The reaction was pretty similar to the five stages of grief yet again.

A direct quote from a key member of the AI Art Tribe, Robbie Barrat:

"As for me getting more credit—that doesn't bother me too much. There were people experimenting with generative adversarial networks (GANs) years before me (people like Tom White, Mike Tyka, and Mario Klingemann). I'm more concerned about how, out of all the really compelling work done by the people in the AI art sphere, this uninspired low-res GAN generation and the marketers behind it are the ones who get the publicity.

"It's unfair to the actual artists doing real work at this intersection; the ones that are doing more than just plugging a ton of paintings into a prepackaged algorithm and inkjetting the results. People like Helena Sarin, who sketches by hand and trains neural networks to augment her sketches; or Mario Klingemann, a "neurographer" who uses chains of multiple neural networks to create extremely compelling art; or David Ha, a research scientist and artist who wrote "sketch-RNN," a neural network trained on pen strokes of drawings, that can predict the next pen stroke in a drawing to either draw all by itself or collaboratively with humans."[75]

I highly recommend looking at the AI artwork from the artists Robbie Barrat mentions. Tom White at drib.net, Mike Tyka at MikeTyka.com, Mario Klingemann at quasimondo.com, Helena Sarin at AIartists.org/Helena-Sarin, David Ha at otoro.net/ml/. There's also an entire website devoted to AI art at AIartists.org. It's a very different approach to art that makes beautiful unique images. Making AI art is a surprisingly human activity. My favorite place to dabble with creating AI art online is DeepDreamGenerator.com. Go try it, you'll like it.

CHAPTER 6
Could I Be Hacked Because of AI?

Envision your eight-year-old in her room at night when, suddenly, a song from a scary movie starts playing and a complete stranger's voice can be heard telling her that he is Santa Claus. The Ring smart camera in her room has been hacked. The story is real. In the Ring video, you can see the terrified child yelling for her mom.[76] Or, your boss calls with an urgent request for you to transfer funds to a supplier—except later, you find out it was not your boss. It was a deepfake voice clone impersonating your boss's voice so well even you were fooled.[77] In another scenario, you find you have been locked out of your Netflix, Facebook, Spotify, and Amazon accounts. Meanwhile, you get a notice for purchases being made. This is the work of a combination of an AI-based automation tool that has been busy sniffing out your network 24/7 and a PassGAN. A PassGAN is a new hacker tool that uses a generative adversarial network (a form of AI) to generate high-quality password guesses based on statistical distributions of previous passwords from password leaks.[78]

What's terrible is, after hearing these shocking accounts of hacking, they are only just getting started. Eighty-eight percent of security leaders say supercharged AI hacking attacks are inevitable.[79]

For many hackers, the best targets are small- to medium-size businesses. Those types of accounts garner the most financial rewards because they have decent income but cannot usually afford cybersecurity. Hackers use AI-based tools to scan social media accounts at incredible speeds, looking to cobble together bits of information from various sites. A birthday announcement on LinkedIn gives a date. A pic on Instagram shows you are a dog lover. A TikTok video of your team at the office shows your colleagues' names. All of these details contribute to a highly personalized spear-phishing campaign. Spear phishing is the act of sending emails or other communications with the goal of getting you to click on an embedded link. Doing so causes a bit of code to be downloaded that could allow the hacker to hijack your computer. At that point, they could hold incredibly necessary files hostage until you send them bitcoins (bitcoin is the hacker's money of choice because it's untraceable, digital cash). Or, they could just use the financial credentials they get from the network to steal your funds.

Understanding the Difference Between Security and Privacy

What is the difference between security and privacy? I'll illustrate via examples. As an example of security without privacy: Let's say I'm having a bake sale, and you can see everything I have. Otherwise, how could you buy it? There is no privacy. You decide to take a pastry without paying, but security cameras capture the whole event. I turn you in, and the police find you and make you pay for the item. That's security without privacy. Facebook and Instagram users are a prime example of the desire for security but not privacy. They do not necessarily have nor want privacy, since the goal is to build "a following" in some cases. But they do not want their identities stolen either.

An example of privacy is when I choose to put all the bake sale items in an opaque case because I do not want everyone to see what I have. When I want to sell the items, I choose to show them to a limited number of people. While this could certainly be used as a way to keep people who might steal stuff away, it is mostly used because I do not want everyone to see what I have. That is privacy versus security. Privacy is a way to help ensure security, but you can have security without it. Privacy is more about having control over who knows what details and who does not. Security often also entails deterring criminal activity such as identity theft, credit card theft, and terrorism as opposed to just snooping.

How Exactly Does AI Allow Me to Get Hacked?

Artificial intelligence capabilities require tons of data and tons of interactions. This means your smart devices are communicating on your home network constantly. The more traffic going across your home Wi-Fi, the more chances there are for it to be found (aka "packet sniffed") by hackers. Generally, the more the AI system (like a smart TV or game console) interacts with you, or you with it, the more it learns from you and sends information back to the algorithm which resides on a corporate server somewhere outside of your house. It does this so it can "learn" and get better, more efficient, or accurate at what it does. AI is taking information from all kinds of things around you. Things like your TV and AT&T U-verse box are reporting what kinds of programming you like, what times of day you watch, and so forth. Those are just a few of many smart devices reporting information about you. They are forming those insights into scores about you—scores that others, who aren't open about their intentions, would love to have. Some of them would like to sell your information on the black market or simply sell your labels or score. Add to that the fact that artificial intelligence only really comes together when it's utilized in the cloud, it turns into a hacker's dream.

Why is it a hacker's dream? Corporate clouds are treasure troves of high-value data all in one place and easily accessed through the internet. But AI doesn't work without the cloud because it would be like having a computer without access to the internet. It's only as useful as the data that sits on the hard drive. To get information to and from it, it's streaming all your current data constantly to and from the cloud. Some of this data is properly encrypted and protected, and some is not. Which means, as a hacker, all I need to do is hack into the chips of the device, hardware, network, or the internet service provider, and I will get all kinds of information about you that is streaming on your AI systems (geotagging and apps of all kinds on your cell phone, Alexa/Google Home, Nest, music, TVs, etc.). I can become you on social media, I can vote on your behalf, or I can take out a credit card or loan in your name. I can commit criminal activity using your credentials, and you might not ever know. Not because you weren't personally careful about handling your credit cards or your online business, but because the companies who created the AI you are inter-acting with online, on your phone, or in your house are sending your data around unencrypted or to data brokers such as smart TV maker Visio or streaming platform Hulu. Or, like ARM and Intel, which are making chips in devices in your house that you did not even realize could be hacked by bugs like Meltdown and Spectre—which gave hackers the ability to access passwords, photos, emails, anything stored on your computer, smartphone, and data streams from your smart TV, some baby cameras, and security equipment.

How Can It Happen? Why Can It Happen?

Internet of Things (IoT) devices are a weak link in your networked devic-es. Computers are protected with all kinds of security software. Phones now come with some level of encryption and passcodes and other tech to keep you secure. But smart TVs, speakers, webcams, refrigerators, and vacuum robots, if protected at all, usually have minimal security. But how many times have you entered a password for your TV—not as a way to keep others out but to get into your Netflix, Hulu, or Am-azon video accounts? This can be dangerous because accessing these accounts means hackers can gain access to payment info and any oth-er data that you may have sitting in the same instance of the cloud.

In one Gizmodo article, a reporter started using a bunch of con-nected devices (coffeemaker, toothbrush, bed, TV) to see which sent the most data, what they were sending, and how often. Her TV, of all things, used the biggest amount of bandwidth. It reported what she and her husband were watching. But because the TV is frequently on, it's basically like a big beacon to hackers to come and see what data of yours they can get for free. Then they can sell your ID on the dark web or use your credentials to go straight to your online accounts.

Or, if they want to do something nefarious beyond stealing just for stealing's sake, they could take my login information and start engaging in illegal activities. They might start funding a terrorist net-work with my ID, which could land me on the National Security Agency's terrorist watch list. If that happens, I could be banned from travel and my friends and family may be hauled out in cuffs to answer questions about me and my suspicious activity.

What It Means for You When It Happens

Identity theft can make your entire life miserable. It can lock you out of your bank accounts and prevent you from carrying on your life in the way you normally would. There is also a looming fear at every corner that your information could be compromised in a way that might make you subject to law enforcement showing up at unexpected moments believing you are the perpetrator of some crime when clearly it was someone else who either bought your identity from someone who stole it or is the person who stole it. Someone could lock you out of your connected vehicle or shut off the engine, leaving you stranded. An enemy with significant resources might even hack into your pacemaker to cause heart problems or worse.

There are also threats outside the United States that could seek to destabilize or isolate us by preventing us from communicating with authorities in mass emergency situations. At an opportune moment, a Russian or Chinese hacker could seize control of 911 services or power grids, cause a major emergency, then shut down all ways to respond, inciting instant panic and isolation. These types of scenarios are designed to make people doubt their democratically elected leaders and revolt. It is a tactic used to destabilize a country in hopes of making citizens desire autocratic leaders like Putin or Xi Jinping. These were the types of cyberattacks first notoriously tried out on Estonia and then elsewhere in former Soviet-bloc states.

The Smart Fish Tank that Could Have Brought Down a Casino

IoT devices are all around us. They connect to the internet constantly to exchange data in real time. They are often the biggest vulnerability in anyone's network—corporate or otherwise—because they just aren't as secure as computers. Hackers attempted to exploit a security vulnerability they found in a smart fish tank to gain access to a casino's network. The fish tank was connected to the internet and designed to automatically feed the fish and keep their environment comfortable. Hackers managed to send data to a device in Finland before the threat was discovered and stopped.[80] Presumably whatever that data was would help them get into the network again, sort of like making a copy of a key to the front door.

Hacktivists, Russians, and Corporate Spies—Oh My

Hacking is not always motivated by stealing money or identities. The goal of a "hacktivist" is to send a message to organizations they deem as doing evil in the world. They create chaos by taking over computers or smartphones of people in that organization to literally show them a message. Oddly, your hacked device could suddenly become part of a concerted effort (known as a "zombie attack") to deny service from a website or server without you even realizing it—such as when Russian hackers used other people's computers to overload the whole of Estonia's communications systems, and no Estonian citizens could reach officials. Many people think this was a trial run before taking it to its real target years later: America. There is also hacking used for corporate and political espionage, and cybercriminals are only getting more creative by the day as security measures become more advanced.

Think no one is interested in you or your data? That you have nothing to hide? Hackers can deploy an AI-powered sniffer bot to detect when you are sending valuable information like bank account passwords, or they can track your keystrokes by exploiting vulnerabilities in your computer or apps and then replicate them to gain access to your bank account or other valuable information. If you download an app and a little pop-up window appears asking for access to your keyboard—whether your smartphone keyboard or your computer's—think long and hard about why the app needs it. This could be a way for the app to log keystrokes which are used to steal passwords. Proceed with caution.

Recommendations

- Be careful what you post on social media. Don't give away so many details of your life that it would be easy to spear-phish you. Be careful whom you accept into your network.

- Don't click on emails or other links. Instead of clicking through a link emailed or texted to you, try looking up the organization you are trying to reach directly, or use preestablished website links.

- Use a virtual private network (VPN) to hide the IP addresses of your IoT devices, and encrypt the data they send and receive.

- Set up calendar reminders to change passwords regularly, and don't use the same passwords for every account.

Keep Your Smart TV Safe from Hackers

- Know exactly what features your TV has and how to control those features. Do a basic internet search with your model number and the words "microphone," "camera," and "privacy."

- Don't depend on the default security settings. Change passwords if you can, and know how to turn off the microphones, cameras, and the collection of personal information if possible. If you can't turn those features off, consider whether you are willing to take the risk of buying that model or using that service.

- If you can't turn off a camera, just place a piece of black tape over the camera's lens.

- Check the manufacturer's ability to update your device with security patches. Can they do this? Has the company done it in the past?

- Check the privacy policy for the TV manufacturer and the streaming services you use. Confirm what data they collect, how they store that data, and what they do with it.

- If you think you've been the victim of cyber fraud, always report it to the FBI's Internet Crime Complaint Center at www.IC3.gov, or call your local FBI office.[81]

Stop Hackers from Getting into Your Home Network

- Change your router admin credentials from the default ones

- Set up strong passwords and encryption. What is encryption? It scrambles all the words of important things like passwords, emails, texts when these are going to travel down an internet connection or be stored somewhere.

- Keep your router updated

- Hide your Wi-Fi network

- Reduce your Wi-Fi range

- Use two-factor authentication. What is this? We use it most when we allow our cell phone number to receive a text with a code that verifies who we are when we enter that code into whatever app we are trying to get into.

- Use a firewall and antivirus software

CHAPTER 7

What Does AI Know About Me, and How Can It Be Used Against Me?

We use nearly 5,000 different data points about you to craft and target a message. The data points are not just a representative model of you. The data points are about you, specifically.

—Alexander Nix,

former CEO, Cambridge Analytica

AI Quiz: Test Your AI and Privacy Knowledge

1. If your financial data is incorrect, AI could limit you from: *(select all that apply)*

    a) Employment opportunities

    b) Getting a loan

    c) Buying a house

    d) Obtaining insurance

    e) Dating an attractive person

2. Federal laws that protect the data privacy of US citizens include: *(select all that apply)*

    a) GDPR—General Data Protection Regulation

    b) California Consumer Privacy Act

    c) Illinois Biometric Information Privacy Act

    d) HIPAA—Health Insurance Portability and Accountability Act

    e) None

3. HIPAA prevents 23andMe and Ancestry from sharing my genetic testing results with health insurance companies. *(select one)*

    a) True

    b) False

4. Which statements are true? *(select all that apply)*

    a) Cambridge Analytica used psychographic data that was collected from a deceptive quiz app that Facebook users downloaded

    b) Emails are protected from being scanned by advertisers and third parties

c) Pictures of your face on social media could be used to make deepfakes

d) Your IP address can reveal your physical location such as your address

e) If you have nothing to hide, you have nothing to fear

5. Amazon's Alexa: *(select all that are true)*

a) Can listen and store as much data as it wants in the cloud

b) Has been used as a witness in more than one murder trial

c) Has sent recordings of conversations to friends

d) Is not admissible as evidence in any trial

e) Does not record unless you use the wake word

See answers on next page.

Answers to AI Quiz: Test Your AI and Privacy Knowledge

1. e. I'm sure some would say this is debatable—ha!

2. e. HIPAA will only protect your health data and only in certain situations. GDPR is the European Union's law. Illinois's and California's laws only apply to citizens in those states, not the whole of the US.

3. b. 23andMe is currently classified as a tech company. As such they do not fall under HIPAA guidelines.

4. a, c, e.

5. a, b, c. This is a trick question. Amazon claims it does not record unless you use the wake word, "Alexa," but because law enforcement was able to get recordings at any time they wished in three murder cases, I think we can assume it is recording all the time.

Overview

I have heard plenty of people say things like, "If you have nothing to hide, then you have nothing to fear." But unless you're willing to put a camera on your life 24/7 and have all of your information, all of your comings and goings, all of your likes and dislikes (including how you vote), and all of your professional and personal associations broadcast to the world, you won't hold up to the level of scrutiny, labeling, and manipulation of your character that can potentially happen with or without your knowledge while using even the most ordinary devices and apps.

Have you ever noticed how you search for a product on Google, and then it shows up in an ad on your Instagram feed? Or maybe you ask Alexa to find an Instant Pot recipe, and then an ad for a sale of Instant Pots shows up on your Amazon home page? That's all due to an AI designed to send targeted ads. In some cases, AI is used to snoop through private email accounts in order to identify which ads you'd be receptive to. Sometimes, the emotional fallout can be devastating. One man had a friend who was diagnosed with ALS, and in the months before his death, the two friends emailed frequently about the subject. But even months after his friend's passing the first man *still* received unwelcome and depressing reminders of his friend's disease and death in the form of ads that continued to present on his internet pages. I also know of a woman who suffered a late-term miscarriage and, months later, still received online ads for baby products—and she even received a formula sample delivered to her doorstep.

But the truly nefarious potential of this technology is really all about data privacy. Welcome to the world of data collection, data brokers, and surveillance capitalists, where data gets swapped constantly between big corporations, academic institutions, and government. Using examples such as the infamous Cambridge Analytica scandal and the cost-cutting professor behind it; genetic testing kits that give you background on ancestral lineage while charging companies top dollar for access to your genetic profile, including your current and even *potential* health conditions (as well as your kids' and grandkids' conditions); retailers who know intimate details about your data based on your shopping history and habits; not to mention the legion of data brokers and data tricksters who lure you and your kids into giving away all kinds of psychological, socioeconomic, medical, and even intimate sexual details online, I'll show you why you should care about what happens with your data.

There is still no federal legislation in place to protect consumers and users in the US, so we have to take matters into our own hands until policymakers catch up to the reality of what AI can do. To that end, I'll show you how to protect your data by using private search tools like DuckDuckGo and private browsers like Epic, how to keep key details of your life off social media sites like Facebook and Instagram and internet search sites like Google, how to keep your network private by "hiding" it, and how to use VPNs to prevent your internet service provider from spying on you.

What Does AI Know About Me and How Does It Know It?

We tend to think of AI as knowing everything about us because, even before we think about taking a vacation, travel ads may pop up on our screens as we browse the internet. Or, when I watch Netflix, it suggests movies I might like—and it's almost always right. Your smart watch may even remind you to breathe or work out when you are stressed. It seems like AI can read our minds. In actuality, AI systems are using loads of data behind the scenes to make recommendations for you. The bigger question on your mind should be *who is collecting all this data, and how did they get it*.

We are in a data economy where data gets swapped constantly because it is the lifeblood of AI and other analytics systems that make anything "smart"—from your watch to your house to your cell phone to your healthcare and even your city. It all needs data. The goal of most chief data officers I worked with was to home in on the most valuable data and then work the data until it was of such high quality that they could get other businesses to pay a premium to obtain it. While everyone talks about algorithms ad nauseum in the context of AI, no one really talks about the data and how it got there in the first place. The data itself is where the money is, not the algorithms. Groups out there who amass data that is highly demanded or in unique niche markets make a fortune. The biggest market for data is the kind that's about you!

Where Do They Get All This Data About Me?

Everywhere—from virtually anyone and everything that surrounds you. The market for your data is huge, absolutely massive. With a forecasted data broker market of $345 billion for 2026, it is no wonder there are scores of data groups out there collecting, organizing, and analyzing data in hopes of selling it for top dollar.[82] Think of everything you own, purchases you have made, any public services you use such as buses, hotels and pharmacies you frequent, all the apps you have downloaded, where you live…most are amassing information on you without you knowing it. Here's a list of categories[83] that are collecting info.

Data Collectors and Purveyors

- *Media and publishing firms* like Netflix, Disney, CBS, video games, music, videos

- *Mobile phone apps* are some of the worst invaders of people's privacy! These are the thousands of apps you can download from places like Google Play and the Apple App Store. You can even download them directly from social media sites like Facebook and Facebook's WhatsApp and Instagram companies.

- *Telcom and internet firms* like AT&T, Verizon, Comcast, Time Warner

- *Connected device firms* that make wearables, smart home devices, connected car equipment, robot vacuums

- *Large platforms* such as Apple, Facebook/Instagram/WhatsApp, Google/YouTube/Google Maps, Microsoft, IBM, Amazon, eBay, PayPal (and in other countries Alibaba, Tencent, Baidu)

- *Government surveillance* intelligence programs under PRISM, now Pegasus

- *Retailer, travel, and hospitality* like CVS, Hilton, American Airlines

- *Public sector services* like police, welfare, unemployment

- *Healthcare* like hospitals, doctors, disease research programs, pathologists

- *Financial firms* like credit card companies, banks, lenders, leasers, investment groups

- Consumer credit reporting agencies like Equifax, TransUnion, Experian

- *Insurance groups* for home, health, life, auto…think Progressive, Cigna, New York Life

- *Seedy organizations* that use questionable methods to collect personal data like psychographic details from people. They might use spyware like Pegasus, spear phishing, social engineering, online "personality" quizzes, social media games, clickbait, scraped data (data that is basically screen-shot and then converted to standardized text using a software program).

What Data Is Worth Beaucoup Bucks?

Financial

Your purchasing power, or socioeconomic standing, is high on every single group's wish list—from criminals to credit card issuers. The three largest credit bureaus—Experian, Equifax, and TransUnion—are also data brokers and are the major sources of consolidating and verifying this information. I cover two of the credit bureaus below in the data brokers section. If they have incorrect data on you, it will be difficult to obtain loans, insurance, cars, houses, and even employment.

Genetic Information (from 23andMe, Ancestry and Similar Sites)

Companies like 23andMe sell access to your genetic data. If you have rare a disease, you are worth even more. But you won't see a dime of that. You pay $99 or so for them to unearth ancestry details for you, but then they turn around and give access to that data to others willing to pay top dollar for your health-related genetic information. 23andMe inked lucrative deals with big pharmaceuticals: Genentech for $10 million, Pfizer for $50 million, and GSK for *$300 million*. All for the right to analyze your genetic data. If you think HIPAA protects you here, it doesn't. HIPAA applies only to healthcare companies. 23andMe classifies itself as a technology company, so it is not held to the same rules. *But it should be!* Over 5 million people have paid 23andMe for genetic testing and 80 percent have opted into their research program.[84]

Psychographic Data

This is data about your values, attitudes, interests, and personality traits. Cambridge Analytica famously said they had over five thousand points of data on key voters from swing states. Using these data points, they labeled some of those voters as "persuadable" due to psychographic information obtained from an unethical data scientist named Aleksandr Kogan. Kogan developed a Facebook app that offered a personality quiz and prediction at the end. It affected 87 million Facebook users. The "persuadables" became the key target of campaigns against Hillary Clinton and for Donald Trump's presidential campaign in 2016.

Psychological Data

This includes data about your mental state and mental health conditions such as anxiety disorders, depression, violent tendencies, post-traumatic stress disorder, eating disorders, substance abuse, addictions, and obsessive-compulsive disorders. This data can be used against you in all kinds of ways by employers or would-be employers. Officially, the Equal Employment Opportunity Commission protects against discrimination and harassment based on these criteria. An employer is not allowed to ask you about mental health conditions before they extend a job offer, and they are not allowed to fire you, reject you for a job or promotion, or force you to take leave because of them. But there are AI developers who sell solutions that claim to help employers and others circumvent these guidelines and can determine from your social media accounts what psychological issues you might have.

Biometric Data

These are the physical characteristics typically used to verify your identity, such as face, fingerprints, voice, and eyes. Each of these can be used to bypass security features on your personal devices or in corporate environments. The problem with using your face and voice is that deepfake technology can now replicate them. Airports, stadiums, and other large venues are looking into using these technologies to move throngs of people more quickly and securely. CLEAR, for example, provides expedited security programs, allowing people to have their eyes and face scanned in lieu of digging out their identification.

Video and Photos of Your Face

These can be used for deepfakes, identity theft, and access to secured areas, computer files, and corporate intelligence. They can also be used to identify your whereabouts with the use of closed-circuit cameras like those in stores, on streets, in government buildings, or in your neighbor's Ring camera. Unfortunately, one man in Flint, Michigan, learned how a picture of his face shared on social media could get him falsely arrested on his front lawn in front of his wife and kids. This happened because a company called Clearview AI put together a database of faces which it scraped from social media.

Your Home Network Info and Device IDs

IP addresses are assigned by internet providers to devices like routers that want to connect directly to their service. The IP address gives away your location at the time you connect to the internet. They are easy to track, especially by ad tracking software that wants to show you location-specific information such as nearby coffee shops. Your router at home will have an IP address which all the devices in your home using the same router will share. MAC addresses—which are static serial numbers on network cards inside your devices—identify your specific smartphone, computer or tablet on your network. Since many online account profiles use a combo of "cookies" (more on that next) plus your IP address, having your IP address could allow hackers and app developers to obtain all your online passwords.

Cookies

Cookies were originally designed to help you when you visited a website. If you put something in your shopping cart, you could come back to it later and it would remember what you had put there. These are called first-party cookies because they are a direct interaction between you and the website you visited. These types of cookies also help by populating your login credentials (if you have allowed that). Third-party cookies, on the other hand, are for ad tracking. They allow ads to follow you on the internet. The two biggest purveyors of these types of cookies are Facebook and Google. Vox has created the best video I've seen to explain how ads follow you around on the internet. To find the seven-minute video, search "Vox how ads follow you on the internet."

Web History

When you search the internet using Chrome or Safari—programs known as browsers—they keep track of the sites you visit in your web history (aka browser history). Your web history drives the personalization of your online experience, including everything you see on Google, YouTube, Instagram, and more.

Social Media Content

Your likes, shares, comments, photos, network/friends/family/co-workers all feed into psychographic data—used for politics and activism, biometric data (via photos of your face, closeups of your eyes), psychological data (sentiment analysis of your words, posts you like and comment about), and brand-centric data (following and liking posts from brands like Coke, Dolce & Gabbana).

Buying Behaviors

This includes online purchase history, offline purchases, warranty information from consumer businesses, credit card activity, loyalty programs.

Government Records and Census Data

Government records include census data, DMV records, marriage licenses, business licenses, lawsuits and other public legal proceedings, voter registrations, public data around political/charitable contributions, bankruptcies, land use records.

The Biggest Data Brokers

These companies provide valuable data, even to social media firms—the biggest snoopers on the planet. Why? Because if a business can see that they advertised to you on Facebook and you clicked and purchased an item, it tells them how effective their advertising was and if it would be worth it to advertise to you again. If it is, Facebook can charge a premium to that business for advertising space. A famous saying in advertising is, *"Half the money I spend on advertising is wasted; the trouble is, I don't know which half."*

Acxiom

Before working for CitiCards, I had no idea Acxiom even existed. But they are, hands down, one of the biggest data operations I have ever seen since—and I've seen a lot. They claim to hold data on all but a small percentage of US households and have over fifteen hundred major data points on each household. What they don't have about you, they can model assumptions about based on what the information they already have. According to Acxiom's website, some of the most *popular* data points they offer include:

1) Children's age ranges

2) Presence of children

3) Political party

4) Entering adulthood

5) Parental status: new parent, single parent, pregnant

6) Child near high school graduation

7) Hispanic language preference

8) Occupation

9) Education

10) Affinity for certain car brands

11) Affinity for certain restaurants

12) Home improvement purchases and store preferences

13) Affinity for DIY projects

14) Which credit cards you have

15) Net worth and income

16) Likelihood to switch banks

17) Home value

18) Your health insurance provider

19) Affinity for certain grocery stores

20) Social media usership, which platforms, how much use, types of content

21) Your charitable donations

22) What kinds of hobbies you like

23) Your prescriptions and where you get them

24) What kind of pets you have

Their modeled data includes categories like: "Adventurous Travelers," "Tenured Self-Starters," "All in the Family," "Generous Country," and so many more I can't list them all. These are just to give you an idea of the information Acxiom and other data brokers collect and report about you that you might not know about.

Nielsen

Nielsen is interested in what you watch on TV and online, the music and radio programs you tune in to, and what you read. They are interested in your behaviors as a consumer. They collect a good deal of information directly through their panel programs, which people get paid to participate in. Groups that buy data from Nielsen want to know about the effectiveness of the ads they place in all these mediums. More specifically, Nielsen's customers want to know if you bought any of the things you saw, heard, or read about in their ads. They produce reports about the buying power of different segments of the population, including African Americans, Hispanics, and Asians.

Equifax

Equifax, Trans Union, and Experian are the three big consumer credit reporting companies in the US. Equifax collects and aggregates information on over 800 million individual consumers and more than 88 million businesses worldwide. The data they collect comes from companies you owe money to, such as lenders, banks, credit card issuers, collection agencies, and so forth. They also pull from public records to obtain information on bankruptcy and other court filings like divorce and estate proceedings. Of course, they combine all of this intel they have on you and sell it, which is why they are considered one of the biggest data brokers.

Since 2012, Equifax had more than 57,000 complaints filed against them relating to incomplete, inaccurate, outdated, or misattributed information.[85] They also had one of the biggest data breaches in history with over 147 million people left exposed to potential identify theft and fraud. Both of these facts are incredibly unfortunate given that their data will determine if you get that loan, that new apartment or house, the credit card with all the rewards and a great rate, insurance coverage at a decent price, or even, believe it or not, whether you appear to be trustworthy enough to be hired for your dream job. You didn't give them your permission to compile the life-altering data they have on you and leave it unsecured so hackers could potentially sell everything about you on the dark web.

Experian

Just like Equifax, Experian is one of the big three credit reporting bureaus and, as such, it uses a lot of the same data sources. It is trying to be more inclusive in its credit reporting since so many people have thin or non-existent credit files. So, in addition to the places Equifax gets its data, it is also compiling data from short-term installment lenders, peer-to-peer lenders, check-cashing services, cell phone providers, small-dollar credit lenders, prepaid card issuers, and auto loan financiers. It's important to note that both Experian's and Equifax's traditional data often feed into the creation of FICO scores. In the cases where Experian is trying to supplement creditworthiness of those who have thin to no credit, it calls the new, more-inclusive scores "clarity scores."[86]

How Is All This Data Used?

Now that we have gone through all the data types of that can be collected and by whom, let's look at some of the most popular questions people ask about what these groups do with our data.

Why Do You *See* Ads for Things You've Emailed About?

Tracking cookies is the short answer. The websites you visit save cookies, or little text files, to your browser and device. These can be helpful because they can help you remember what you were searching for before on a particular site, what your login credentials are, or even what items you had in your shopping cart before you left a site. These are not so helpful when you go from site to site and they seem to follow you around with ads. This happens, in large part, because the cookies are stored alongside your device ID (aka MAC address) if you are on mobile phone, or an IP address, which were discussed earlier in this chapter.

    As for emails, specifically, Google admits that up until 2017, they used to scan contents of emails for purposes of targeting ads to people.[87] We are supposed to trust that they have stopped. I am highly suspicious given my own experiences and the fact that Big Tech has lied before about supposedly stopping bad behaviors. There is no way to verify if they still do or not. Beyond Gmail, emails get embedded with tracking pixels and sourcing URLs. These are the same idea as a tracking cookie, except that the tracking originates from a tiny, invisible pixel embedded in an email, unbeknownst to you. The sender can learn from this little pixel whether you opened their email, what time and date you opened it, if you clicked on links in the email, what device (phone, computer, tablet) you opened it on, who your email provider is, and what region of the country you are in. With this data, they will attempt to link to other data purchased from the aforementioned data brokers. Usually, this will be any of the data from the biggest brokers plus that which specialize in their audience type (golfers, single moms, Republicans). Then they will decide what offers to send you next, depending on how successful they were with the original email and getting you to click on links.

The important thing to know about these tactics is that while they seem inane—albeit snoopy and annoying—when retailers do it, it's more intrusive and detrimental when they are used to influence political campaigns, spread misinformation, or advertise products that trigger addictions, like alcohol and cigarettes. In this day and age, sowing discord, divisiveness, and misinformation through online campaigns is something to look out for as views become more polarized and nondemocratic nations seek to gain ground in the world by creating unrest and chaos.

Is Facebook or Amazon Listening to Your Conversations?

Facebook officially denies listening to conversations via your mobile phone, but many people have sworn that they do and have shared countless stories to support the fact.[88], [89] *CBS This Morning* host Gayle King posed the question directly to Facebook's Instagram head, Adam Mosseri. She swears that she has been advertised to after making statements about products she wanted or found interesting while her mobile phone was around.[90] Facebook does, however, admit to paying hundreds of contractors to listen in and transcribe audio for their Messenger app, but that is not the same as admitting to randomly listening to the background of your mobile phone.[91] Facebook refers people to the "Why You Are Seeing This Ad" section of their app to understand more, but this doesn't really answer the question.

Many privacy experts acknowledge that Facebook is exceptional at targeting you to the point of creepiness using vast assortments of data and AI, and that it's understandable to feel like they are listening in. One privacy expert, though, ran an experiment to get to the bottom of it.[92] Twice a day for five days, he used as "triggers" conversations about needing "cheap shirts" and going back to "university." He monitored his Facebook posts and, sure enough, there were plenty of ads for these things, along with an additional ad for cheap 20 GB phone plans after a friend complained to him about running out of data.

Given the sheer volume of people who recount instances of saying random things that they don't search for online but then get Facebook ads for, I personally feel there is something to these claims. In the meantime, we shall have to wait and see if some clever investigative journalist finds an insider and gets to the bottom of this. As we all know, technology firms have lied plenty of times up until they were busted.

There is legal evidence that Amazon's Alexa is listening and recording all the time. Alexa was used as a "witness" in the 2019 murder trial of Silvia Galva in which the defendant wanted to obtain the Alexa recordings because he felt they would exonerate him and prove Galva's death was accidental.[93] The police obtained a search warrant for all the device's recordings from Amazon. Based on the evidence Amazon provided, the defendant was exonerated. It shouldn't escape us that while Amazon swears Alexa records you only after use of the wake word "Alexa," no wake words were mentioned in this case. In other words, I think it is safe to assume that Alexa had been recording all along. If that is the case, *is* Alexa listening in on us on a regular basis, and is Amazon keeping the recordings? I don't see how else they could provide files for a warrant if they weren't. Do you?

How Is YouTube a Little "Too Good" at Suggesting the Next Video?

Because I have focused on YouTube in many of the chapters, I think it's important to cover what they know about you, how they know it, and what they do with that information. First, their recommendation algorithm is responsible for 70 percent of the views on YouTube—it's that good. The basic mechanics are the same as for other social media content recommenders, according to the Mozilla Foundation. It's all about content, context, and user data. For content, they use AI to extract information from uploaded videos, such as what the videos are about and whom they are by. Context considers where you are in the world, if it's a weekend or holiday, and anything they know about the environment in which you are watching the video.

As for you as a user, the data they have depends on your YouTube account's user settings. There's data that you voluntarily provide directly to YouTube, such as likes, subscribes, comments, watchlists, what you name your watchlists, and what videos you forward to others. There are behaviors the AI observes as it tracks you on their system, like how much of a video you watch, how long you watch at a time, which videos and what type you are watching, if you skip through a video, and if so, what parts you skip. YouTube tracks how you scroll through recommended videos. If you scroll fast through them and then suddenly slow down, this tells them one of the video thumbnails caught your attention. If you hover over a video with your cursor, that signals interest as well—even if you don't click on it. Using all this information, YouTube will try to infer things about you, such as age, gender, income, education level, ethnicity, sexual preference, political preference, and affinity toward certain types of videos such as "funny cat videos."[94]

How Data Is Incorporated into AI that Labels You

Artificial intelligence is literally nothing without data. There are only a few main algorithms, something like twenty if you believe the book *The Master Algorithm* by data scientist Pedro Domingos. According to a patent attorney I spoke with at MIT, you cannot get a patent for an AI-based product or asset without declaring 1) the data you're collecting, 2) the algorithm you intend to use, and 3) its intended purpose. Data scientists will use data to train an algorithm to determine the right labels for someone or something and what the wrong ones are. This process is called *supervised learning*, and in this case, the algorithm will receive data that has been manually labelled.

For simplicity's sake, say I feed the AI system that I'm training six pictures. Three of the images are of different types of ducks, and the remaining three are of other animals. If I'm trying to find ducks, then the AI should perform what's called "clustering," which is the act of grouping all the ducks together based on similarities to each other. The leftovers will simply be labelled "not ducks." After first evaluating the pictures, it may only find two ducks. As a human, I will correct the machine and show it where on the third duck picture to look to understand if it's a duck, and where the AI got its labelling wrong. Then I will feed more pictures through the system of various types of ducks and animals. The percentage it gets right will then go up again with the new information I just gave it. The data scientist just keeps repeating this process until the system gives an accuracy rate of 90 percent or higher. If the algorithm being used is something that could deeply affect a person's life, then you want the highest accuracy rate you can get.

This process gets exponentially more complicated depending on what the system is being trained on and the level of expertise a system requires to do that training. A breast cancer diagnostic AI tool, for example, will need training from lots and lots of images of breast cancer. The trainers will need to be people highly skilled in differentiating the specifics of what they look for in a cancerous mass.

Who labels the data is another interesting factor. We always think about data being so easily obtained via computer systems and networks and the internet. But often, the most valuable data hasn't been connected together yet in ways that will help AI make use of it. For example, being useful to AI systems trying to identify ducks in the future requires a *fallible* person to sit there and label the photos or images by typing in the word "duck." The seedy little underbelly to this is that such work can go to under-skilled people in third-world countries who are paid minimal amounts an hour. They may not have been exposed to a duck before. Anytime humans get involved, there is room for human error and potential for mistakes.

Some groups have used crowdsourcing to build up major stores of labelled data for training purposes. One such effort was done by Stanford's Fei-Fei Li in creating the image repository ImageNet, which helps fuel computer vision research work. This has yielded its own problems, as research on the data sets has shown an average error rate of 3.4 percent. Images were mislabeled, like one breed of dog being mistaken for another, or a baby being mistaken for a nipple. This sounds kind of innocuous, almost silly on the surface, but now think about all that data we just discussed.

Imagine the AI that determines your credit score is using incorrect or incomplete information—there's a good chance this could be the case. Or better yet, imagine that the anti-money-laundering algorithms used to ensure you aren't a terrorist before banks loan you money decides you aren't eligible based on inaccurate religious data.

Cambridge Analytica and the Cost-Cutting University Researcher

Aleksandr Kogan developed a Facebook app called This Is Your Digital Life that requested and gained access to information from people and their friends after it was download. It offered a personality profile and billed itself on Facebook as "a research app used by psychologists." Alexander Nix, the former CEO of now-defunct Cambridge Analytica, is quoted bragging on stage about the five thousand psychographic data attributes per person they were able to pick up: "By having hundreds and hundreds of thousands of Americans undertake this survey, we were able to form a model to predict the personality of every single adult in the United States of America."[95] It is estimated that 87 million people were ultimately affected by the app.[96] The psychographic information collected by Cambridge Analytica was then allegedly used to sway voters on Facebook in what Cambridge Analytica called the "Defeat Crooked Hillary" campaign of 2016.[97]

In an interview with Lesley Stahl of the news program *60 Minutes*, Aleksandr Kogan says, "So I create this app where people sign up to do a study. And when they sign up to do the study, we would give them a survey. And in the survey, we would have just this Facebook login button. And they would click the button, authorize us. We get their data."

Lesley interrupts, "Authorize us to do what?"

Kogan says, "To collect certain data. We would collect things like their location, their gender, their birthday, their page likes and similar information for their friends. And all of this—"

Lesley interrupts again, "But they [the friends] didn't opt in."

To which Kogan replies, "So they didn't opt-in explicitly…this was a core feature of the Facebook platform for years. This was not a special permission you had to get. This was just something that was available to anybody who wanted it who was a developer."

Lesley Stahl asks, "How many apps do you think there are, how many developers who did what you did?"

"Tens of thousands…. They created these great tools for developers to collect the data. And they made it very easy. I mean, this was not a hack. This was, 'Here's the door. It's open. We're giving away the groceries. Please collect them.'"

Sandy Parakilas, a former manager in charge of protecting data at Facebook, said, "I think the real problem is…that you've got a company that has repeatedly had privacy scandals…. If your partner was cheating on you, and they cheated on you fifteen times and apologized fifteen times—at some point, you have to say, 'Enough is enough. Like, we need to make some kind of a change here.'"[98]

How Target Knew Customers Were Pregnant Right Down to the Trimester

Andrew Pole was a data scientist at Target. He was featured in a *New York Times* article and a subsequent book proudly proclaiming that he could predict if women were pregnant and in what trimester with amazing accuracy, solely based on what the women were purchasing in the store. He single-handedly created the Big Data "creepy factor" paranoia that so many of us experience. It tells us that data scientists already know some things about us sometimes even before we know them. It was all started when two marketing colleagues asked him: "If we wanted to figure out if a customer is pregnant, even if she didn't want us to know, can you do that?" The "even if she didn't want us to know" part should have been a clue that some data should *not* be known. That's how the sixteen-year-old girl was later outed to her father, who inquired why Target was addressing ads for baby stuff to his daughter. The dad later returned to the Target store to apologize for his outburst when he found out his daughter was, in fact, pregnant.

Stores Like Macy's and Supermarkets Use AI-Based Facial Recognition

Imagine if stores could immediately target you by scanning your face as you enter the door and shop through aisles. They could even compare your features to an as yet unproven facial recognition database used by law enforcement and ICE, such as Clearview AI's. They could label you a "potential shoplifter" or a "suspicious individual" for appearing to be of Middle Eastern descent, or for wearing a hoodie, or for being dark-skinned. They could straight up just get a bad match on your face in the database and mistake you for a "person of interest" in a criminal case. Then security could call the police to come and falsely arrest you in front of everyone. They could have their system label you as a welfare SNAP recipient and consider you a "low priority" while they label faces associated with higher incomes as "high priority." They could ban you from the store for protesting their unfair business practices with help from social media matching. Or, they could just do something as annoying as constantly sending you coupons in real time on your mobile phone while you're in a particular aisle of the store so you won't leave that aisle without putting an item in your cart.

Well guess what? You don't have to imagine it. It's happening. Macy's recently came under fire for their use of facial recognition technology as part of a class-action, biometrics-capturing lawsuit in Illinois against Clearview.[99] Stores currently using facial recognition include Albertsons, H.E.B Grocery, Macy's, and Apple Stores.[100] Stores thinking about using it include Walgreens, McDonald's, Yum! Brands (Pizza Hut, KFC, Taco Bell), 7-Eleven, Best Buy, Publix, TJX, Aldi, Dollar General, Kohl's, Starbucks, Ace Hardware, Meijer, ShopRite, Ross, and Ahold Delhaize USA.[101] Fight for the Future, a facial recognition watchdog group, recommends going to other stores if you are able, and they are currently compiling a list of stores that *don't* use facial recognition technology to help with this.[102]

Recommendations

I could make privacy recommendations all day. There are so many things you can do to protect yourself. At the end of the day, you will have to decide how much loss of privacy is acceptable to exchange for convenience.

Familiarize Yourself with How Corporations Surveil You

Read the Electronic Frontier Foundation's "Deep Dive into the Technology of Corporate Surveillance." You can find it by searching for, "EFF Behind the One Way Mirror."[103]

Use Privacy Tools When Browsing, Emailing, and Searching Online

Search Engine. An excellent, free privacy search engine to use in place of Google is DuckDuckGo. Go to duckduckgo.com to download the appropriate app for your browser. They do not store your personal info, and they do not track you. You can also download the mobile app and use it in place of your mobile phone's web browser.

Browser. I love the Epic privacy browser. It's provided by the nonprofit Electronic Privacy Information Center (EPIC). It is free and provides unlimited VPN/proxy for the browser and ad blocking. If a site, like an ad-based news site, gives you a hard time for having ad blockers turned on, then you can toggle them off in one step. It's super easy and intuitive to use. It can't help you, however, if you are logged on to Google. You can download it at: www.epicbrowser.com.

Email. There is no email more secure and privacy focused than ProtonMail as evidenced by the many journalists that list ProtonMail accounts on their Twitter pages. ProtonMail is based in Switzerland and uses end-to-end encryption. It's also free. You can download it at Apple's App Store or Google Play.

Take Control of Alexa

- To prevent an Alexa pocket dial, don't give Alexa your contact list, and turn off Alexa's calling and messaging features.

- Opt out of Sidewalk

- Turn the volume all the way up on Alexa to ensure you hear it when it confirms you have given it a command; or, conversely, press the mute button on the device to ensure it can't hear you and mistakenly dial someone.

- If you don't want to take these actions because it limits the functionality of Alexa and you bought it in the first place for convenience, then at least be careful using words that sound like "Alexa."

- If you hear the word "Alexa" used on TV or other places in your house, then know there is a good chance the device might be listening in for the next command.

- It is also unclear for how long Alexa listens in after it's heard the wake word, so be careful for a while after having summoned Alexa. Same goes for Google Home and Microsoft Cortana. They are just not as pervasive as Alexa.

- You could also change the wake word to the only other two options Amazon gives, "Echo" or "Computer."

- Take care to understand the access levels of any third-party apps you load onto Alexa as they can gain the ability to listen in whenever they want and potentially phish for passwords or info about your financial accounts. Alexa's skills are popular and can provide a great deal of convenience, but do your due diligence on the app before you add the skill.

Check What Data Google (including YouTube) Has on You

- Go to takeout.google.com; sign in with your email

- The program will give you options to select which applications you want; it defaults to "all."

- You can select where you want the file delivered, then hit "archive," and be prepared to wait because the file could be large.

Check What Data Facebook Has on You

- Log in to Facebook.

- Go into your account settings. On the desktop, you can find these in the pull-down menu in the upper right-hand corner of your screen.

- At the bottom of the "General Account Settings" menu, you'll see an option to "download a copy of your Facebook data."

- Input your email so that Facebook can notify you when your download is ready.

- Once you receive your email, click on the link in it to download your archive; once the download has started, Facebook will prompt you to re-enter your password.

Other Tips to Protect Your Privacy

VPN. I want to tell you to use a virtual private network because it can get you around third-party advertisers and internet service providers who want to spy on you. However, it's hard to know whom you can trust, both from an actual provider perspective and the countries they reside in. For example, a country that really wants your operations could force the VPN to hand over access to your files or just have it snoop on you for a while. Investigate VPNs as best you can before paying for one. You should be able to get a decent one for $40 to $60 a year.

Privacy Settings. Up your privacy settings on every single mobile app; deny location services when you are not using apps; disallow camera and microphone access when it's not clear why the app would need access to them. Everything your favorite apps do not need in order to do their job should be disallowed.

Don't Post It. Keep details of your life off social media sites like Facebook, Instagram, and Google. The more personal details you post, the more you put yourself at risk of that information being used against you. Definitely do not post close-ups of your face.

Check Third-Party Apps on Facebook. See which ones have access to your data. In the Facebook app or on its website, go to Settings, then Apps and Websites. You will see a list of them.

Say No to $99 Genetic Tests. Don't participate in genetic testing with groups that do not fall under HIPAA. That means if you have a medical need for genetic counseling, see a doctor. Yes, it's more expensive than 23andMe or some of the other genetic testing kits, but these are your genes and possibly your kids' and grandkids' genes. Think about that. Who knows what kind of technologies might exist in the future with the power to use that genetic information? Do you really want that out there with no control or say over it? You can't get your data back once you've submitted a swab.

Finally, and this is a time-consuming one…

Remove Yourself from Big Data Brokers. There are step-by-step instructions on how to remove yourself from each major data broker listed on PrivacyBee.com. Search for "How to Remove Yourself from Data Brokers" and "Privacy Bee" (as in the buzzy-stingy kind).[104]

CHAPTER 8
AI Manipulation: Can AI Harm Kids and Teens?

Manipulation is the exercise of harmful influence over others. People who manipulate others attack their mental and emotional sides to get what they want. The person manipulating—called the manipulator—seeks to create an imbalance of power and take advantage of a victim to get power, control, benefits, and/or privileges at the expense of the victim. People who manipulate others have common traits that you can look for. They include knowing your weaknesses and how to exploit them, using your insecurities against you, and convincing you to give up something important to you, to make you more dependent on them.

—WebMD

AI Quiz: Test Your Knowledge on AI's Effects on Kids and Teens

1. Tech addiction is driven primarily by which two of the following?

a) Anxiety

b) Depression

c) Curiosity

d) FOMO (Fear of Missing Out)

e) Boredom

2. The number-one problem teens see among their peers is: *(select one)*

a) Gangs

b) Teen pregnancy

c) Anxiety and depression

d) Bullying

e) Drug addiction

3. The first president of Facebook said this about Facebook's algorithms: *(select all that apply)*

a) You're exploiting a vulnerability in human psychology

b) It literally changes your relationship with society

c) It probably interferes with productivity

d) God only knows what it's doing to our children's brains

e) We need to sort of give you a little dopamine hit everyone once in a while

4. Which statements are true? *(select all that apply)*

    a) Likes, upvotes, and claps are designed to reward desired behaviors online

    b) 70 percent of YouTube's views are driven by their own recommendation engines

    c) There was a 151 percent increase in suicide for females ages ten to fourteen beginning when social media was first introduced in 2009

    d) 70 percent of teens report feeling that their social media use is addictive

    e) 90 percent of kids eleven and younger watch YouTube

5. AI's role in harming kids who use social media includes: *(select all that apply)*

    a) Recommending their video posts to pedophiles

    b) Recommending cat videos to them

    c) Ranking self-harm and suicide content high in their social media home pages

    d) Addicting them to use tech more frequently via friend notifications and likes

    e) Cyberbullying them

See answers on next page.

Answers to AI Quiz: Test Your Knowledge on AI's Effects on Kids and Teens

1,   a. and b. While c., d., and e. can certainly contribute, *Psychology Today* states that many addictions start with anxiety and depression.

2.   c. Teens are brimming with anxiety and depression; no wonder they are so tech-addicted.

3.   All.[105]

4.   a., b., and c.; d. is actually 50 percent; e. is 80 percent.

5.   a., c., and d. Unfortunately, cyberbullies are people who post or reply with hurtful comments. While harmful, these are not generated by AI.

We Are the Boiling Frog; AI is the Water Temperature

We don't really worry about being manipulated by our phones, computers, or TVs. As our kids watch endless hours of YouTube, we don't really think about it other than to lament it: *It's sad that they don't go outside and play more, but I guess it's a generational thing*, you think to yourself. *In our time, we had more friends, and the world was* (probably) *a safer place for us to play outside*. But was it? Are we sure that's really all there is to it? In the 1980s, I remember Saturday mornings being awesome because that was the time I could watch all my favorite cartoons. They came on around 8:00 a.m., and that was that—there was no recording them or playing them on endless loops. You had to wake up in time to see them or you missed them. When the cartoons were over around noon, the boring adults with their boring news programs (or worse, golf or other sports) would take over the one—as in only—TV in the house. This meant it was usually time to get up and do something else. If you didn't go outside or try to connect with friends, you'd probably be called on to do the most dreaded task: Saturday afternoon chores.

That dynamic doesn't exist today. Kids can watch whatever programs they want with very limited interruptions at any time of day, on any screen near them, and watch as long as they are able before they pass out and do it all over again. There are no cues to get up and do something different and, therefore, many of them don't. There are few real-life interactions to diversify their thoughts after having watched endless hours of angst-inducing content and get them out of their own heads. Watching show after show is a lonely and isolating activity. There's no room for conversation, productive activities, creativity, friends, or real life. Parents today are likely to be doing the same thing as the kids. Instead of watching infinite programs on YouTube, they might be doom scrolling through infinite sensationalistic news stories served up to them on digital devices, much in the same way kids are viewing videos one after the other.

These behaviors are having horrible effects on all of us, and we either don't realize it or acknowledge it. Much less do we think about *how* it happened and what's behind our change in behavior. We always think we are in control. We are not easily influenced, after all, in our *real* lives—whatever "real" means these days, considering everything from work to happy hours to weddings are done online. Yet the stats prove we are the frog slowly boiling in the pot. Fifty percent of teens report feeling addicted to their mobile devices.[106] Adults are no better: 44 percent of eighteen- to twenty-nine-year-olds are online almost constantly.[107] Meanwhile, 70 percent of teens say anxiety and depression are a major problem for them—overwhelmingly more than bullying, drugs, or alcohol.[108] And suicide rates among girls ages ten to nineteen have increased upwards of 70 percent since the 2009 introduction of social media, which relies almost exclusively on AI capabilities to find its target audiences and connect them with content.[109] We tell ourselves we would jump out of the pot if it got too hot, but just like the frog, we are already affected and still doing nothing about it. Why? What is responsible for this behavior?

The fact is, AI is one of the most powerful means of persuasion ever to be unleashed on humanity. AI in our social media feeds, whether it be YouTube, Facebook, Instagram, or TikTok, serve up and push endless content, notifications, likes, and other self-validating rewards designed to addict us—to make us watch longer, buy more, and engage online more than in real life. AI nudges us toward content that influences us to believe more like the mainstream by using the patterns of others like us to manipulate and frame the way we think about big issues from politics to parenting. What we buy, the images we click on, the videos we watch, and news stories we spend time reading become part of an endless data loop back to the AI. Based on those patterns, AI can predict our emotions and behaviors and trigger them. We are Pavlov's dogs salivating at notifications, likes, and recommendations and the emotional rewards those bring. Once AI harvests data about your online triggers, that data becomes gold to interested parties who want to influence you. With this information, businesses can work on your self-esteem to get you to buy something, activists can enrage you into joining "their side," and sadistic people can "groom" you or your kids for self-harm, sex trafficking, or even suicide.

As dire as all of this sounds—and it is—there is also reason for hope, and it is not too late to turn the tide on these systems that have been designed to persuade and exploit us. Later, I'll offer a checklist of signs that you or your children are becoming tech addicts, and a list of practical guardrails to put in place to prevent that from happening. For those who are already addicted, I'll give you steps you can take to break the habit (and prevent a relapse). I'll also give you my insider's tips on how to recognize online manipulation and how to protect yourself and your loved ones from being the target of AI algorithms' persuasive powers.

Tech Addiction Is the Pot We Boil In

AI is designed to addict you and your kids to using tech. It does this by ratcheting up anxiety, triggering you with escalating content and comments, and rewarding you for behaving in ways consistent with the desires of the purveyors of the content (e.g., businesses, activists, advertisers). In order to understand how AI can be used to manipulate us to change our behaviors for the worse, it's important to understand and acknowledge some of our mental states and conditions that can contribute to making us susceptible in the first place. Let's start with addiction, which is when we engage in a behavior where the perceived rewards incent us to repeat the activity despite the detrimental consequences it may have on us or others. According to *Psychology Today*, "Addictive behaviors intensely involve brain pathways of reward and reinforcement and have an increased likelihood of being accompanied by mental health conditions such as depression and anxiety."

Technology addiction refers to the uncontrollable urge or impulse to continue using technology to the point that it starts to interfere with the individual's mental, physical, and social life. This can be through social media, internet surfing, video games, and online gambling. Because it is an addiction, it is accompanied by anxiety and depression, which are relieved by moments of reward and reinforcement that tech like social media provides when its AI recommends people's comments and content to like, love, or upvote. In fact, former Facebook president Sean Parker says Facebook's founders knew exactly what they were doing when they designed it to prey on these weaknesses. "We need to sort of give you a little dopamine hit every once in a while [to keep you engaging with the content more], because someone liked or commented on a photo or a post or whatever…. It's a social validation feedback loop…. You're exploiting a vulnerability in human psychology. The inventors, creators understood this consciously. And we did it anyway. It literally changes your relationship with society, with each other. It probably interferes with productivity in weird ways. God only knows what it's doing to our children's brains."[110]

It's no surprise, then, that 50 percent of young people are tech-addicted when we consider that anxiety and depression are a major problem for a significant number of teens. This brings us to anxiety, triggers, and how AI can exacerbate them. "Anxiety is a mental condition characterized by excessive apprehensiveness about real or perceived threats, typically leading to avoidance behaviors and often to physical symptoms such as increased heart rate and muscle tension."[111] When anxiety goes on for too long without treatment or proper coping mechanisms, it can become depression.

Triggers are situations that make the anxiety you already have worse. Triggers can be subconscious or conscious and can occur because of personal traumas or external stressors. Examples of triggers include news stories, health situations that we can't control (hello, pandemic!), accomplishing nothing (like when you watch YouTube videos for four hours every day), fear of failure, loss of purpose, financial concerns, loss of status, conflict, public speaking, work-related stress, and reminders of personal traumas and stigmas. Those triggers are all in a typical day in social media land.

Social media's algorithms are designed to trigger negative emotions. Social media's sensationalistic content, especially those that get increasingly more shocking, escalate anxiety. Then we look for content that make us feel better—we search up our favorite YouTube video creator or Instagram celebrity hoping for a release. Instead, this just creates a vicious anxiety loop. If we are lucky, we only waste time, productivity, or money buying products sold in the content. If we are unlucky and succumb to the propaganda, we may refuse a vaccination based on misinformation, pick a fight with friends about their political leanings, or participate in a dangerous "challenge" that could send us to the hospital.

Signs Your Kids Are Addicted to Tech

1. A decline in academic achievement

2. Personal, family, and school problems

3. Failure to manage time

4. Sleep and eating disorders

5. Reduction in activity and subsequent weight gain

6. Internet friends, outside isolation

7.   Neck, back, wrist, or hand pain, headaches

8.   Reduction in self-care or hygiene

If you see these signs, make sure you intervene before a possible addiction makes your kids vulnerable to self-harm, suicide, sex traffickers, or pedophiles.

Targeted To Death:

AI's Role in Self-Harm and Suicide Challenges

"Remember, kids, sideways for attention, longways for results," a man says, miming cutting motions on his forearm. "End it."[112] Imagine your kids watching a video about a popular online game like Fortnite and then suddenly seeing this clip out of nowhere. It happened—and not just on YouTube but also on YouTube Kids. The video had been reported eight months prior but was still being recommended to kids by YouTube's famous AI-based recommendation system. YouTube Kids is supposed to be a kid-friendly version of YouTube for ages eight and under. Yet one mom found videos with content involving self-harm, suicide, sexual exploitation, trafficking, domestic violence, sexual abuse, and gun violence—including a simulated school shooting.

There is no question child and teen suicide and self-harm are climbing, but are they being helped along at times when kids and teens are most vulnerable, or are the recommendations normalizing something that would not have even been considered before? Are the algorithms now finding kids who are already anxious, depressed, or primed for tech addiction and pushing them over the edge? Or worse, are the algorithms introducing intrigue and curiosity to once taboo subjects and then overwhelming happy kids with anxiety-inducing content when they research the subjects further?

In 2020, during what was already a disconcerting year for most people due to COVID lockdowns, kids and teens everywhere began seeing a mysterious and intriguing animated music video in their YouTube playlist. In fact, the video is so popular that it has been viewed over 25 million times as of the writing of this book. The video is called "Ruru's Suicide Show on a Livestream Official Video" and features a mysterious character named "Ruru."[113] In the top comments section are statements like:

"RIP Roro."

"Roro-chan would be 22 years old if she hadn't jumped."

"This girl is not to be treated like a fandom. She is a real person who killed herself."

"That people were encouraging an innocent young girl to jump off a building disgusts me."

"I always thought about killing myself but never drove myself to do it."

These are only a few of the 133,000 or so comments. Some posts get even darker while others refuse to share too much, citing concerns of being targeted online as suicidal—ironic since it seems they were already targeted as suicidal by YouTube's AI-based recommender to see the video in the first place.

The video now has a warning before allowing play, but the warning paired with the comments you can read before you play the video only served to heighten the intrigue with the teens I interviewed. It builds their desire to delve further into the digital rabbit hole of self-harm and suicide challenge videos as they attempt to find out if Roro was a real person—as some of the comments suggest—or if it is all just an elaborate hoax.

Since 70 percent of YouTube's views are generated by its AI-based recommendations, YouTube introduced suicidal intrigue into these teens' video feeds and then *persisted* its recommendation in the feed so that it would not go away until clicked.[114] The 25 million views served to normalize the content. From there, the compelling comments like "RIP Roro" get the teens to search for more videos to find out what really happened to Roro. Then the AI offers darker and darker content to keep its audience—the teens—watching until they find themselves staring at more and more suicide challenges, self-harm instructions, and videos of people harming or killing themselves. They become mired in this content, probably feeling a lot like Roro herself after having spent hours going down the suicide rabbit holes. It turns out Roro *was* real. She was a fourteen-year-old Japanese girl who livestreamed herself doing more and more dangerous stunts, like running into traffic and standing on the edge of her apartment roof, until finally—cheered on by comments running on social media during her livestream—she committed suicide in front of the camera by jumping off her thirteenth-floor balcony.[115]

Unfortunately, she was not the last person to do this type of thing. Many other teens have taken to suicide and self-harm challenges such as the Blue Whale Challenge and the Momo Challenge. In these, kids complete lists of self-harm tasks (which they are expected to post to social media as proof) that include things like cutting a picture of a blue whale into their arm. The final act is a filmed suicide. When survivors of these challenges were asked why they started them in the first place, most claimed boredom and curiosity were the main reasons. Once they started the challenges, "taskmasters" or "curators" who oversaw their completion of tasks and suicide would threaten harm to their parents or use personal information such as their address, mother's name, age, and IP address to threaten real-life harm to the preteen/teen.[116] One eleven-year-old boy was told the cuts in the picture he sent were not deep enough and that his mom would be hurt if he didn't cut deeper into his arm. He did. When he was given the next task—the Blue Whale Challenge—he refused, which resulted in a threat that the anonymous curator would visit his house, presumably to hurt him.

This information was not shared to scare you or your kids or to get you to disengage entirely from social media. That would not be a practical expectation given that over 89 percent of children five to eleven years old tune into YouTube daily, and 97 percent of teens thirteen to seventeen use social media constantly.[117] It was to make you aware that these challenges exist, and that even if your child is not looking for these types of videos, they can surface through AI-based recommendation systems. The goal is for you to be aware so you can be vigilant and cautious. Before allowing your kids and teens onto social media, have a long talk with them about these harmful types of content and how serious they can be. Make sure they know that no matter what is threatened online, you can only help if you are told about it. Most importantly, if they see this type of content recommended in their social media feeds, they should not click on it, comment on it, or forward it. Engaging with salacious content only makes it persist in their feeds and will become more extreme the more they research and go down the rabbit hole. Instead, they should either report the content or let you report it.

Pedophiles and Sex Traffickers

AI Recommends Children and Teens Through Home Videos

Here are the stats. One in three nine- to seventeen-year-olds report they have had an online sexual interaction. Seventy-seven percent of these kids do not tell trusted adults about the abuse they encounter online. In situations where children receive unsolicited nudes from adults, this percentage grows even higher: 94 percent did not report it to a trusted adult (although 31 percent had previously predicted that they would do so if it occurred).[118] Adults believe nothing is going on, as 96 percent of parents say their five- to eleven-year-old child has never been harassed or bullied online.[119] This is an absolute recipe for disaster. Children aren't telling, and adults aren't asking. Meanwhile, pedophiles and sex traffickers are recommended a buffet of their favorite home videos of children and teens by automated AI systems and are asking the children for more sexual shots via comments sections and associated social media platforms. In some cases, traffickers who are adept at "grooming" children and teens for more sexual acts are actively engaging them on social media accounts the children may have listed in the home video itself or in the description section of the YouTube listing.

I absolutely hate the exploitation of children and teens by sexual predators. It literally sickens me to write about this. If you are tempted to stop reading because it's sickening to you as well, please don't. In keeping with the book's theme…what you don't know about AI will hurt you—or in this case, your kids—so keep reading. We must protect them, and we have to band together to do so. First, we need to know what's happening and how it's happening so we can stop it. But I do want to warn you that much of this information is going to be disturbing—bear with me.

You might wonder, as a mom in Brazil did, how on earth an innocent video of her ten-year-old daughter and her friend swimming in the backyard pool could suddenly gain four hundred thousand views.[120] According to a team of academic researchers, YouTube's recommendation system began showing the video to users who watched other videos of prepubescent, partially clothed children. Evidently, Twister (the game), yoga, swimming, and gymnastics are all favorite video themes that pedophiles like to look up.[121] One investigative journalist found that even the search bar's algorithms would funnel you to pedophilic material. If you type "twister girl" in the search bar, for example, the autocomplete would come up as "little twister girl in a skirt." Start typing "girl yoga," and the search's autocomplete algorithm would include "young" and "hot." If that's not bad enough, once a pedophile "likes" one of these YouTube-recommended videos (or comments on them) these kinds of videos will then show up in the recommended video feeds of other pedophiles to expand their reach. Effectively, the YouTube recommendation system places the kids and their videos right in harm's way (and do so at a scale that pedophiles themselves probably couldn't accomplish on their own) as they serve up one child then the next to predators using their service to curate videos.

Even more disturbing is that users do not need to be looking for videos of children to end up watching them. The AI actually targets users who watch erotic videos of adult women with videos of those younger and younger each time until finally the rabbit hole of recommendations takes them to view videos of girls as young as five or six.[122]

Just how are these predators engaging kids and teens online? Minors who have had online sexual interactions were engaged from many different platforms, but these are the ones that were most often reported: Instagram (16 percent), Snapchat (16 percent), Messenger (11 percent), Facebook (10 percent), and 9 percent each for YouTube, TikTok, Twitter, WhatsApp, and Google Hangouts/Meet.[123] It's important to note too that predators of minors may be recommended exploitive material on one site such as YouTube and then engage with the minors or each other on a different site. For example, an investigative journalist found comments on YouTube where predators shared time codes for crotch shots and directed people to similar videos of children all while exchanging phone numbers and promises to swap more videos via WhatsApp or Kik (a popular teen chat app).[124]

The net of this is to say that many kids see social media like YouTube and Instagram as ways to meet new people, build a following, and explore without fear of judgment. Unfortunately, much of this requires more sharing by them and often with complete strangers, which puts them at risk for harm. The best thing you can do is talk to them about the risks of posting certain kinds of content or giving out too many details about themselves. It's important they understand the types of people that could be viewing that content and their intents. Preempt the subversive shame-and-blame plots of these sexual predators by discussing how the predators work on minors and how they will send nude pictures of themselves in order to gain leverage over teens. Explain that if your child encounters this, they should talk to you immediately.

In case they flat out will not talk to you for fear of shame or repercussions, then encourage your child to talk to a trusted friend or give them the number of a child-exploitation hotline (several are listed at the end of this chapter) they can call if they want to stay anonymous. It's important for them to get help in any way they feel comfortable—even better if they take action to report the perpetrator or let you report them.

Have your teen read this section of the book with you. Regularly talk about things and people they encounter online. Keep tabs on their social media contributions and reactions to their uploads. Ensure your child is aware of favorite pedophilic themes (yoga, swimming, gymnastics, Twister) when they describe their video posts so they can stay away from them. If there is a sudden spike in subscribers to their YouTube channel or followers of their Instagram stories, investigate to understand why. At a minimum, report and block suspicious people from your kids' accounts. If a piece of content your child posts garners unwanted views, delete it immediately so your child does not become a further target of sexual predators. If the problem escalates, you may need to consider removing the minor from social media by deleting their accounts. We know kids may not always reach out to us when something goes wrong, so we will have to be extra vigilant about checking in.

Does AI Lead Us to the Edge and Push Us Off?

When we become fearful of things we didn't even know existed because AI put them in our path, we change our behaviors and who we are for the rest of our lives. Behaviors that should've been shamed and forbidden suddenly become normalized and accepted among hordes of like-minded child predators enabled by AI to efficiently find each other, their favorite content, and their victims all with almost concierge-like service. Those who are the most vulnerable and anxiety-ridden among us—young children and teens—turn to social media for attention and love. Unfortunately, many fall prey to those who would use their weaknesses to harm them. Even those who come to these platforms bored and curious but happy overall often succumb to the darkness of AI's never-ending, always-escalating recommendations. And so, the question remains: Do we change our behaviors because of the endless feeds that AI is recommending to us? Are we becoming more anxious, depressed, isolated, and suggestible to self-harm, suicide, and abuse because AI keeps us engaged 24/7 with content designed to ratchet up these behaviors? Or is AI simply targeting us better and matching us with content we may not have found on our own?

Maybe the answer is both. Either way, the result is the same—it's pushing us to the edge in a very efficient manner. Targeting suicidal kids with videos that make them feel worse (sad songs about suicidal people like Roro) and videos that tell them how to kill themselves ("lengthwise for results") and then connecting them with people who will make a game of it via suicide challenges (Blue Whale) sure seems like manipulations meant to lead us to the edge of a cliff and push us off.

What You Can Do to Take Back Some Control

Put preventative Guardrails in Place

- *Strong family relationships* with healthy parental oversight and support help protect against addictive behaviors and influence from bad actors.

- *Moderation* is a must. Establish a consistent daily cutoff time where electronics are removed to give the brain a chance to function without interference from constant notifications and negative peer interactions that can add conflict, strife, and stress.

- *Positive friends* increase the likelihood that we will adopt good behaviors.

Addicted to Tech? Break the Habit

Tech addiction is no different than regular addiction. It can start with boredom and curiosity but ratchet up when we become anxious or depressed. Then micro-obsessive behaviors turn into full-on addictions. Sometimes our anxiety and depression require intervention from a licensed therapist. For any addiction, the therapist will try to get to the bottom of what is triggering the anxiety and depression. Take these triggers seriously. While tech addiction can be seen as a less serious condition than a drug or alcohol addiction, the underlying destructive tendency is still there. And that part is very serious—especially when others online know exactly how to target and trigger that destructive tendency further. What starts as something seemingly insignificant can escalate quickly into a dangerous mental health situation when scores of anonymous users and bots encourage self-harm or suicide to an already receptive individual.[125]

AddictionResource.com has some great suggestions to disrupt the psychology of the behaviors.

1. Plan a new schedule to disrupt patterns.

2. Change daily internet and smartphone usage hours.

3. Set goals to limit use.

4. Limit time on or quit using certain apps and games.

5. Prepare weekly internet usage schedules and ensure compliance.

6. Join a support group or take advantage of other mental health resources like family therapy.

7. Create a list of activities that were missed because of excessive technological usage.

8. Make a list of activities your child would like to do and encourage them to adhere to it.

9. Remind your kids of the benefits of limiting usage.

There are also settings in the tech itself that could help minimize addictive triggers.

- Parents can **set limits on the use of electronic devices** for certain types of applications such as YouTube, Instagram, and TikTok. These are the social media platforms that teens engage with the most. Parents can set time limits and time-of-day limits. Anxiety and depression can escalate late at night when parents are asleep and teens are alone, so setting an earlier cutoff time could help teens who are susceptible to bad actors. The easiest way to ensure your teen cannot get onto the internet late at night is to set your router to cut off at bedtime. If you cannot do this because you have appliances or security devices that use

Wi-Fi, then, depending on your router, you may be able to disable access to Wi-Fi from your teen's devices such as cell phones, laptops, or tablets. This comes with a huge caution: your teen may resort to trying to use a cell phone data plan which could cost you and do nothing to deter your child. You will have to monitor their data usage and make your own decisions about what to do when or if this occurs.

- **Reset privacy and notification settings** on each app and device your teen uses. If bad actors can't find you or your teen through searches or advertising selection menus, they can't harass or entice you to engage further. This does not mean your kids won't still get the material from friends and contacts in their online network, but it can stop a lot of nonsense from showing up in their digital feeds.

- **Disallow access to cookies or delete cookies**. This can also help clean the digital slate. Beware: while this will help to limit triggering content, it could also be an inconvenience from a stored-passwords perspective. If you are worried about eliminating cookies because you do not have your passwords documented somewhere, then you may want to save your them for key websites before deleting cookies.

- **Turn off Autoplay settings.** This will prevent videos and other content from automatically playing one after the other, which could also help signal to your child that it's time to get up and do something else.

Keeping Kids and Teens Out of Harm's Way

The single best thing you can do to keep kids out of harm's way is have a preemptive talk (or two or three) about all the kinds of predators who are online—and keep reminding them. See the list of these predators below. You'll have to gauge when your child is ready for some of these conversations, but I would start no later than nine years old. The easiest thing to do would be to tell kids and teens to delete their social media accounts. Tell them not to post videos or pictures online and definitely not to engage with strangers. But that would fall on deaf ears.

Here's what to tell your child or teen:

- *Predators pretend to be kids and teens.* Assume everyone you don't know in real life is some kind of perpetrator.

- *Perps try to gain your trust and obtain info they can use later to manipulate you.* Anyone trying to be your friend online that you don't know in real life could potentially be a pedophile or sex trafficker. There are a lot of predators out there using online games like Fortnite and Minecraft to build relationships and trust while pretending to be kids. They may invite you to engage with them over online platforms like Discord where it's easier to exchange media and files in private chats. They may offer to send video gaming cards, money through PayPal, or games in exchange for innocent photos, but will, over time, progress to requests for more risqué photos.[126] They may try to talk to you about sex and will definitely warn you to keep your conversations private.

- *Never give identifying information to any stranger online, ever.* Never offer your full legal name, address, friends' or family members' addresses, email address, phone number, or your mom's or dad's names to anyone. These can all be used to threaten harm in real life and can be used as a sort of blackmail to get you to do what they want.

- *Never send pictures, especially nude ones.* Most photos have geotagging technology and can tell a perp where to find you. Don't post pictures in identifiable locations where house numbers or school names can be seen. Nude pics will only make you vulnerable to blackmail later when the perp tells you they will post them online for everyone to see if you don't do whatever depraved actions they want you to do. Minors sending nude pics to adults pretending to be kids is child pornography, and it is highly illegal. Do not shrug it off. Requests for nude pics, regardless of whom they're from (kid or adult), must be reported to a trusted adult.

- *Do not use the location settings on apps* like Facebook, Instagram, WhatsApp, or any others. If it shows where you are all the time, that's a way for curators of suicide challenges and sex traffickers to find you and threaten harm in real life. Protect your identity and where you live at all times.

- *Be careful what you post.* It's never a good idea to post sexualized pictures or videos online. Even innocent pictures in swimsuits can unfortunately attract the wrong kind of attention. While you should be able to be yourself and have freedom of speech and content, there will always be those out there ready to use that in twisted ways. You are not to blame for their depravity, but if you do become the object of it, turn them in at: cybertip.org. You can report them anonymously if it makes you more comfortable.

- *Tell a trusted adult if anything inappropriate happens online.* Child predators use taboo, shock, and shame to lure you. They do this by sending nude pics and asking for nudes, by building faux trust and by threatening harm to you or your loved ones in real life. No matter what the predators try to get you to do or what the predators themselves do, you need to report it to a trusted adult. Ninety-six percent of minors don't report incidents to an adult *especially* if the predator sends nude pics. It's a tactic these pervs use to keep you quiet. Don't play into their hands.

- *Report inappropriate behavior.* If someone threatens to harm you or a loved one, asks you for inappropriate pictures, or talks to you about sex, you can report it anonymously at cybertip.org or call 1-800-843-5678. If it's an emergency call 911.

- *Block, mute, and report the perp to social media platforms.* Few minors are willing to report a person for inappropriate sexual behavior because they see it as punitive. Instead, they prefer to block the person.[127] Because so many perps just start all over again with fresh accounts and continue the harassment, it's best to report a perp—at the very least to the social media platform but preferably also to the authorities. Do not engage with them online at all.

- *Report inappropriate content.* When inappropriate content is auto-recommended or shows up persistently on your social media feed or home page, flag it to the social media company. Don't "engage" with it (i.e., don't forward it, click on it, play it, or comment on it). These actions will just cause the AI to recommend more of the same stuff and possibly even worse.

What Parents Can Do

- *Have preemptive discussions about online predators.* Use the list above. This is THE best action you can take to help your kids and teens.

- *Position social media as a privilege that comes with parental rights.* Many of us are hesitant to infringe upon the privacy of our kids because they may think we don't trust them. But from the moment you allow your child to have access to social media you should position it as a privilege that comes with parental rights. These parental rights include monitoring for unusual, unsafe interactions and following them on social media.

- *Keep tabs on social media posts and reactions.* If a home video posted by your kid suddenly spikes up to over a thousand views overnight, something is wrong. Your kid may be ecstatic that they have thousands of views, but this should cause you alarm. Investigate the comments for users' sharing timestamps. Take the video down immediately and report inappropriate users to the social media platform. Remember, key pedophile/sex trafficker themes are: yoga, gymnastics, swimming, and Twister. If the video posted by your child has one of these key themes, you may want to switch it to "private views" only, which means that only people that it is shared with can see it. Or better yet, delete the content altogether.

- ***Report inappropriate interactions to authorities.*** If something inappropriate and illegal does happen online (such as the sharing of nude photos or threats of harm), be sure to capture the message history and report it to the authorities. Blocking child predators from your child's account is not nearly effective enough to keep them from harm. Predators will simply get a new account and try to reach your child again. Report incidents—anonymously if need be—to the National Center for Missing & Exploited Children via its toll-free 24/7 hotline at 1-800-843-5678 or online at https://report.cybertip.org/ or report suspected child predators and any suspicious activity through Homeland Security Investigations' (HSI) toll-free tip line at 1-866-DHS-2-ICE or by completing an online tip form found at: https://www.ice.gov/webform/ice-tip-form. HSI staffs both contact methods with investigators around the clock. From outside the US and Canada, callers should dial 1-802-872-6199. Hearing-impaired users can call TTY 1-802-872-6196. As always, if the situation is an emergency, call 911 or local police.

- ***Look for warning signs of trafficking and self-harm.*** Is your child being secretive about what they are doing online or to whom they are talking? Have they recently downloaded any new apps like Discord, Kik, or Amino? Are there texts or calls from numbers you don't recognize? Does your child shut their laptop or change their screen so it cannot be seen when anyone walks in the room? Are they asking for access to digital money-changing accounts like PayPal, Venmo, or Zelle? Have they purchased things with digital gift cards and won't explain how they got them? Are they disengaging from real-life activities they used to enjoy so they can spend more time online? In the case of self-harm and suicide challenges, have you noticed they are wearing long sleeves when it's warm or more often than what is usual for them? Is there scarring on their upper arms or upper thighs? Both are hiding spots for cutting. Are there any signs your child is completing harmful activities in their photos or social media posts?

- *Talk to teens about their anxiety and depression.* Teens I talked with told me that they would either eat more and more often because of anxiety or they would cut eating way back. They also said to watch out for self-isolation that's beyond normal. The example I was given of being beyond normal was if there's no texting or hanging out with other teens or kids for longer than a week. Also, not having friends at all and being more of a loner is a warning sign. They said sleeping too much or hardly ever is a big sign.

CHAPTER 9
Can AI Polarize and Radicalize People?

Sixty-four percent of all extremist group joins are due to our [AI-based] recommendation tools.

—Monica Lee,
Facebook researcher, 2016

AI Quiz: Test Your Knowledge About AI and Polarization

1. Combating polarization at Facebook: *(select all that apply)*

    a) Might come at the cost of lower engagement

    b) Could deter a small pool of hyper-partisan users

    c) Violates Facebook's commitment to neutrality

d) Would affect conservative content more than liberal content in aggregate

e) Would help pro-Russian propagandists divide the US

2. What percentage of extremist group joins on Facebook were due to Facebook's own AI-driven recommendations? *(select one)*

a) 64 percent

b) 82 percent

c) 23 percent

d) 15 percent

e) 35 percent

3. Which statements are true? *(select all that apply)*

a) 57 percent of Americans think the country's biggest tech firms further divide the country

b) 74 percent of Americans say the spread of misinformation online is "a major problem," exceeding all other challenges posed by the media environment

c) 83 percent of Americans believe the media bears blame for the political division in the country

d) 90 percent of Americans believe Donald Trump is to blame for dividing the country

e) 47 percent of Americans voted for Trump in the 2020 election

4. Which of the following were amplified, advertised, and/or recommended by social media firms' AI? *(select all that apply)*

   a) Hashtags, messages, fake news of Russian trolls and bots conducting information warfare against America

   b) Extremist political memes originating from message boards of white nationalists

   c) Messages that American vaccines are unhelpful and ineffective against COVID

   d) Claims that Hillary Clinton ran a child pedophilia ring out of the basement of a pizzeria in Washington, DC

   e) Disinformation about election polling places and times aimed at voter suppression

5. Which of the following are AI-based tools that can be used to divide people online? *(select all that apply)*

   a) Disinformation

   b) Content recommendation systems

   c) Trolls

   d) Bots

   e) Deepfakes

See answers on next page.

Answers to AI Quiz:
Test Your Knowledge About AI and
Polarization

1. all but e.

2. a.

3. all but d.

4. all

5. b., d., e.—disinformation is content made by people; trolls are people.

Weapons of Polarization

Weapons of polarization include trolls, bots, memes, disinformation, conspiracy theories, fake news, and deepfakes. *Trolls* are people who make unsolicited controversial comments on internet forums with the intent to provoke emotional, knee-jerk reactions from unsuspecting readers to incite an argument.[128] *Troll farms* or *troll factories* are organized groups of trolls who are paid to spread propaganda, harass people, or attack critics. *Bots* are software code that can be combined with AI to learn how to post comments and responses on social media that mimic trolls or amplify the posts of trolls or extremist content. Hundreds of thousands of bots can be networked together to form a *botnet* to maximize amplification of content online. *Memes* are pictures or short videos with words across them that often use humor or shock value to relay political or social commentary.

You really can't polarize people without using psychological tactics or—in the case of Russia and some extremist groups—organized psychological and information warfare operations. *Information warfare* manipulates information that is trusted by targets without their awareness. This, of course, includes *disinformation* campaigns which have the malicious intent to deceive people by giving them false information. An example of this is *fake news*, which is false or misleading information presented as real news. *Deepfakes* are videos where an existing image or video is replaced with someone else's likeness using AI that can generate visual and audio content with a very high potential to deceive.

This type of warfare is closely related to *psychological warfare*, which uses tactics designed to illicit emotional, reactionary responses in place of logical ones. These tactics include fearmongering, which gets people to believe something bad will happen to them if they don't do what the fearmonger wants.

To understand which polarizing weapons will be deployed against us and when, we must explore the types of people or groups involved and their motives. Motives matter, because they could determine if you will become a target of attack or, on the flip side, an unwitting instigator. As you can probably surmise, the motives of a true conspiracy theorist are different from those of a presidential candidate who may want to cash in on paranoia to turn the tide of an election. The motives and tactics of dictatorial or communist countries against free countries are much more serious and elaborate than those of small groups of white nationalists or anti-fascists.

Welcome to the Divided States of AI-merica

AI is being used to manipulate not just individuals but groups, governments, and even entire societies and nations. Trolls, bots, deepfakes, fake news, conspiracy theories, disinformation, and social media platforms all use machine learning that contributes to dividing us. Even innocuous-seeming digital tools designed to help us—such as news sites that prioritize your interests or Google searches that result in customized "facts" according to your location and previous search history—can become insidious means to isolate and divide us.

What's behind these dangers is the ability of AI-powered algorithms to create filter bubbles and digital tribes. If you've liked posts that are favorably disposed toward, say, Black Lives Matter, police reform, or pro-choice causes, I'll bet your Instagram feed was full of ads for the Biden/Harris ticket and absent of ads for the opposing candidates. The same occurs for any viewpoint or cause. This is just one very common example of how AI algorithms prevent us from encountering different perspectives. Our sphere of influence then becomes insular, leaving us vulnerable to group-think: *my digital tribe's suffering is my suffering; their concerns are my concerns; their agenda is my agenda*—and always at the expense of any divergent views.

Worst-case scenarios occur when your digital tribe deals in (or is founded upon) disinformation or fake news, or actively encourages you to engage in harmful activity such as online abuse or even violence. The "closed loop" AI algorithms facilitate, coupled with their ability to persuade you to behave *and* believe in certain ways, is one of AI's most pernicious dangers. Consider, for example, how a conspiracy theory like Pizzagate gained traction and become legitimized as real news. AI suggests content based upon your online behavior and that of the people you follow. If your friends, family, preferred candidates, favorite celebrities, and all the various figureheads and authorities in your online ecosystem believe a story and endorse it by forwarding the info, a crackpot story like Pizzagate is quickly disseminated and becomes "real." The same mechanism has been observed in communities founded on misinformation, such as flat-earthers, QAnon, and anti-vaxxers. It can happen with any "us-versus-them" scenario, whether class warfare, political affiliation, gender inequities, race- and ethnicity-based discrimination, ageism, religious (or not) belief system, and so on.

The potential for harm on a massive scale is truly frightening, and we can certainly see this in the unprecedented polarization currently affecting our society. It's happening all across the globe, and there's no secret as to why: there really *are* unseen levers being pulled to manipulate all of us into hating each other. Much of it can be attributed to our reliance on a handful of key digital platforms that recycle the same stories and perspectives over and over again, and our lack of awareness of how we are being manipulated by AI-driven algorithms.

Our weapons against all this craziness are awareness and good judgment about how to react to these manipulations. Toward that end, I'll show you how to identify fake news, clickbait, deepfakes, and other forms of disinformation, and I'll give you a checklist of online protections you can put in place to limit deceptive threads and ads. I'll also show you how you can break out of the closed loop AI has foisted upon your news feed, reset preferences to diversify your world views, and reboot the AIs that think they have you all figured out.

Trust Issues Make Us Vulnerable to Polarization

When I took this chapter on, I wanted real answers on how we got to a point—not just in the US, but globally—where we became so polarized on everything from our views on elected officials to COVID origins and vaccines to election fraud to riots and protests. I've grappled with whether these issues were introduced to us by AI recommendations or whether AI just weaponized them by radicalizing some people and hardening the politics of others. I think the truth is somewhere in between, and we're caught in a vicious reinforcement cycle that will make it harder to for us to break out of now that we have all dug in.

Before we start on how AI has exacerbated our problems, we have to understand how we got here. Let's put it all in context, starting with what makes us vulnerable to polarization: our trust issues. When we face threats and problems, we develop fear and anxiety and begin to search for people and perspectives we can trust to make us feel better. In other words, we want to make sense of our world. During the last couple of years, we have experienced one major threat after another as the pandemic has ravaged our lives, health, incomes, jobs, education, lifestyles, and socialization. We have been looking to scientists, doctors, government officials, scientific experts, professionals, and each other to find comfort. The problem is that many of us haven't found groups that we trust. Here are the stats on our trust in groups that we would normally turn to for vital information and problem solving during difficult times:

News Media

- 87 percent of Americans believe the news is politically biased in its coverage.[129]

- 74 percent say news organizations they distrust are trying to persuade people to adopt a certain viewpoint.[130]

Social Media

- 57 percent of Americans believe social media does more to divide us than bring us together.[131]

- 61 percent believe it spreads unfair attacks and rumors.[132]

- 55 percent believe it spreads lies and falsehoods.[133]

Federal Government

- 76 percent of Americans do not trust the government to do what is right.[134]

- 69 percent feel frustrated or angry with the federal government.[135]

- 64 percent say it is hard to tell the difference between what is true and not true when they hear elected officials.[136]

Experts

- 28 percent of Americans say it's better to rely on people who are considered experts about solving major problems, even if they don't have much practical experience,[137] while 66 percent say it's better to rely on people with practical experience to solve major problems.[138]

Each Other

- 64 percent of US adults believe trust in one another has been shrinking.

- 70 percent of US adults believe a lack of trust in each other makes it harder to solve problems.[139]

- 49 percent of Americans link the decline in interpersonal trust to a belief that people are not as reliable as they used to be.

When you combine these trust issues with online environments that use machine learning to show us only what we are interested in and connect us only with others who share our views, it contributes to more polarization and less empathy as we begin to rely more and more on people who share our exact same ideology.

It Starts with Filter Bubbles, Digital Tribes, and Echo Chambers

When you continually see only things that interest you online and nothing else, you are in a filter bubble caused by personalization algorithms. These algorithms are deciding what you want to see, whether you are browsing around Google, looking through news on Facebook, or searching for videos on YouTube. Cookies which persist across these websites collect data on your clicks and the websites you frequent, remembering where you were when you last logged on to a site. This data usually contributes to why you are seeing what you are seeing. Ever commented on Facebook about how cute someone's green sweater was and then saw an ad for a green sweater along with your Google search results? Yeah, those are cookies and ad-targeting algorithms at work.

The job of social media is to connect us with like-minded people. It does that by collecting data on the websites we've visited before logging into Facebook, how engaged we are on a topic, whether we have forwarded, commented, or liked particular types of content. The algorithm will then try to connect us with more people like us and also show us ads and content that the algorithm thinks we will like. Because of this, we find ourselves hanging out with people who are similar to us online. Often these AI-based recommendations align by political party. We then become digital tribes, sharing similar cultures and beliefs because we are getting our information from the same places and seeing the same things time and again.

As social creatures we survive threats better when we are part of a group. We believe what our tribe believes and hold fast to our tribe. Given that life in the pandemic era was largely digital, many of the in-person groups we used to have contact with were off-limits. We were online for everything—isolated and without our trusted groups to give us the divergent thinking that we needed. We became more polarized, trusted less, and clung to people who believed as we did. Meanwhile, the AI on social media platforms helped us find our tribe by recommending new contacts and new groups to us, along with their blogs, images, memes, and videos. We felt emboldened by our online tribes to say anything and to be less formal than we would with actual strangers in real life.

In real life, we would listen to a person's views, then, careful not to offend, we would share our own beliefs. But in this digital environment, none of that formality, empathy, or listening is needed. After all, these people have forwarded and liked the same memes that I do, so they must have similar beliefs. Not only do my bold posts to my tribe pay off with likes and forwards but also with comments validating what I'm saying and links to even more groups that support my point of view. This all contributes to echo chambers where beliefs are validated and reinforced among like-minded people. There are no pesky rebuttals from others with differing opinions. Suddenly, my opinion is beyond refute, and I cannot even begin to understand or have empathy for those with differing opinions.

In fact, this quote from a Pew Research study respondent says it all. When asked why there is no interpersonal trust between people he replied:

"Cultural shift away from close-knit communities. Viewing everything through hyper-partisan political lenses. Lost the art of compromise. Empathy as well as generally attempting to understand and to help each other are all at disturbingly low levels. People are quick to attack and to vilify others, even without clear proof, solely on the basis of accusations or along partisan lines." Man, 44.[140]

Platforms of Polarization

Sixty percent of Americans think the country's biggest tech companies are helping to further divide the country.[141] They're not wrong. Divisive thoughts and behaviors may be the domain of humans, but the machine learning in social media platforms help them efficiently rain down discord on their targets while recruiting more to the cause.

Facebook's Algorithms Promote the Hateful Few over the Moderate Majority

"Our algorithms exploit the human brain's attraction to divisiveness," read a slide from a 2018 Facebook presentation. "If left unchecked," it warned, Facebook would feed users "more and more divisive content in an effort to gain user attention and increase time on the platform."[142] Mark Zuckerberg, CEO of Facebook, was quoted as saying, "There's too much sensationalism, misinformation, and polarization in the world today" and, "Social media enables people to spread information faster than ever before, and if we don't specifically tackle these problems, then we end up amplifying them." It seems like he was at least aware of social media's role in polarizing people.[143] The problem is, when he was offered a solution by the people he hired to solve the divisiveness issues, Zuckerberg rejected it.[144] It would have meant less revenue.

It turns out that the polarizing views were created by a small group of hyper-partisan superusers. Facebook could not even confirm if these superusers were people, bots, or hired propagandists. They didn't behave like normal people, in that some of the superuser accounts never slept. They just posted, liked, commented, and re-shared their own content continuously, 24/7, until their content was picked up by Facebook's AI and recommended to other people's news feeds because it became so pervasive. The content was both hyper-partisan and sensationalistic in nature. Upsetting or validating, either way it was getting a lot of eyeballs and engagement, and that was good for business.

The solution that was offered to fix Facebook's divisiveness was to shift the algorithm's amplification from the few hyper-partisan users to the majority of users, who were just regular people with middle-of-the-road political views. This would be great, because the most polarizing views of the few would be drowned out by the more moderate views of the many. But it would also mean Facebook would have fewer views, forwards, and comments, and less shock value. In other words, less user engagement.

Engagement is a key metric for advertising dollars. Less engagement means fewer eyeballs means less revenue. Why would a company work against itself? Even if it does sow discord and play into the hands of freedom-squashing nations hell-bent on displacing America, or extremist groups who employ online intimidation tactics. As long as the almighty dollar gets made, who cares?

There was another reason stated by Facebook executives for rejecting the moderate majority: Facebook's commitment to neutrality. Since the superusers were partisan, taking away their power was seen by Facebook as favoring a political side. They did not feel they should stop conflict on the platform or moderate people's opinions. They did not want to keep people from forming communities.[145] Any attempts to curtail polarizing activities on the platform could be seen as affecting conservatives more than liberals because there was a larger contingent of accounts and publishers on the far right.

Eighty-five percent of individuals charged in the Capitol Hill breach were indicted because of evidence obtained from social media.[146] In two hundred charging documents, Facebook had the largest number of references at seventy-three, followed by YouTube at twenty-four, and Instagram (a Facebook-owned company) at twenty-three. Parler, which was immediately pointed to by the press because of its large, far-right user base, only accounted for eight.[147] Many took pictures or even livestreamed their breach into the Capitol.

Reddit, 4chan, and 8kun: Home of the Anonymous Polarizing Few

Online communities form everywhere, but the most activist internet subcultures often form on anonymous message boards. These are sites like Reddit, 4chan, and 8kun (formerly 8chan). These sites offer people a chance to connect with others who share similar interests, hobbies, and ideas in contrast to forming social networks based on who they know. Of course, just because a person is a Reddit user does not mean they won't also go on Facebook and post some of the same things they post on Reddit. Some of the most notorious organized campaigns for political trolling, conspiracy theories, fake news, and disinformation have started and been organized on message boards, then run via hashtags on Twitter, Facebook, Instagram, and YouTube. Think of the message boards as home base. It's important to understand how these message boards work because they're where a lot of the divisive content and controversial behaviors originate before they spill over into more mainstream digital spaces like Facebook. Some of these political community members are Facebook, Twitter, Instagram, and YouTube's small, hyper-partisan, hyper-active groups that post, comment, like, and share divisive content.

At first glimpse, message boards seem identical to each other from the standpoint that someone will post a message and then many others will comment on it. But the differences in how the sites and individual sub-communities are created, administered, and monitored (or not) are what make people engage on them in different ways from traditional social media and even other message boards. For example, Facebook is heavily commercialized, with lots of policing, plenty of older people with lots of opinions about right and wrong, and registration requirements that make a person easily identifiable. It's hard to be anonymous on Facebook if you'd like to have unfiltered conversations about a particular subject—especially if it is extremist, taboo, or even just weird in the "mainstream" world. Enter Reddit, 4chan, and 8chan (now 8kun). These sites allow users to be truly anonymous because they do not require a name or an email address in order to post messages and content. While anonymity can allow for true freedom of expression without fear of reprisal, it can also allow people to hide behind it while maliciously attacking others and posting content meant to shock or provoke.

The only way to get a hold on these behaviors (called "trolling") is to moderate the content and set rules that include banishment from the community or banning the community from the message board altogether. That's why, even among these sites, there are varying levels of tolerance for certain behaviors like hate speech, inciting violence, and anything illegal like child pornography. Other than that, it seems virtually anything goes. And boy does it.

They use all sorts of weapons of polarization, like memes, trolls, bots, fake news, and disinformation. As other nations see these extreme groups sowing divisiveness, they join the fray to exacerbate matters. Their motives are even worse than those of the far right or far left. They seek to create political instability in hopes they can weaken our government, our way of life, and our democracy from within. Then they sit back and watch as social networks amplify their polarizing messages and the recruitment of people to their cause.

The Polarizing Few

QAnon

QAnon, which is responsible for many political conspiracy theories, is said to have started back in 2017 when an anonymous person claiming to have "Q-level security clearance" (which is needed at the US Department of Energy to access the highest tier of intel called Top Secret Restricted Data) posted a series of cryptic posts on the "Politically Incorrect" subcommunity of 4chan. He claimed to be involved in a secret Trump-led investigation of a global elite network of child abusers that included Bill Clinton. No doubt, some of this original post may have had roots in the Jeffrey Epstein sex trafficking case—where flight logs for Epstein's private jet showed the names of Bill Clinton and other global elites.[148] But it morphed beyond recognition. One theory was that Hillary Clinton, Barack Obama, and George Soros were a part of a larger liberal cabal of Satan-worshipping, pedophile sex-traffickers who would someday be arrested by Trump in a day of reckoning called the "Storm." Don't feel convicted of being a conspiracy theorist if you, like many others, believe our government is up to all kinds of nefarious stuff or if you think there are more global elites involved in the Jeffrey Epstein sex trafficking rings. Those types of thoughts are normal and have basis in actual events. It's a problem when it's taken to another level where facts are irrelevant and death threats and violent harassment tactics become the norm. For example, when QAnon believers started the infamous #Pizzagate conspiracy.

Supposedly based on emails hacked from the Democratic Party, the Pizzagate theory claimed that Hillary Clinton and her aide John Podesta were running a child sex ring out of the basement of a Washington, DC-area pizza joint. Users of 4chan and Reddit theorized that words in the emails (which were posted as supposed "evidence"), such as "cheese pizza," were code for child pornography because they started with "c" and "p." The conspiracy under #pizzagate garnered over one million shares on Twitter in one month alone. People concerned for the welfare of the abused children protested in front of the pizzeria, while people on social media issued death threats to the pizzeria's owner, employees, and even customers. Ultimately, one man was so concerned after reading the stories and seeing a YouTube video about it that he showed up at the pizzeria—guns drawn—to free the children only to find it was all a hoax and there was no basement.[149] Needless to say, the Pizzagate community on Reddit was shut down by Reddit's administrators. But the fake news had propagated.

And this is exactly how fake news happens—it begins with humans and then gets promoted with help from AI and key influencers. It started as a theory on 4chan by a small group, then promulgated to Reddit where the theory was presented with "evidence." It was then publicized by InfoWars, a conspiracy media program, and was also amplified on Twitter, where it found key conservative influencers (one of whom later became Donald Trump's national security adviser) ready to comment on it, like it, and forward it. In this way, the conspiracy theory swayed public opinion and polarized people just as they were heading to the polls in 2016.

QAnon conspiracy believers hold that the Sandy Hook school shootings which resulted in the confirmed deaths of twenty school kids ages six to seven never happened. They think it was all just a hoax to coax sympathy from Americans for stricter gun control legislation. (No, being pro-Second Amendment does not make you an extremist.) They get many of these ideas from obsessively watching YouTube videos posted by other QAnon believers. Many believers have been linked to online and real-life harassment, death threats, kidnappings, violence, and murder.[150] QAnon believers were among those who breached the Capitol and were part of the reason the FBI declared conspiracy theory-driven domestic extremists a growing threat back in 2019. Several QAnon believers deeply believe the 2020 election was stolen by Democrats. After Trump gave his farewell speech, so did at least one leader of the movement—Ron Watkins. Ron and his father, Jim Watkins—who ran 8chan, where "Q" made the now-famous conspiracy "drops"—were thought to have taken over as "Q" from a different original "Q" who first posted on 4chan. "Not long after Biden was sworn in, Ron Watkins put out a post on Telegram stating that it was time for his followers to "go back to our lives as best we are able."[151]

Alt-right

If you are a conservative who believes in family values and typically align with Republican ideals, you are not the alt-right. In this book, the term "alt-right" is being applied to people who are extremist in their beliefs. Many hail from message board sites like Reddit's subcommunity called "r/the_Donald" or 4chan's /pol/ site called "Politically Incorrect." They believe in white nationalism, and they're anti-feminist, anti-Muslim, and anti-Semitic. Many subscribe to the influences of Richard B. Spencer who launched *The Alternative Right* webzine back in 2010. They conduct online smear and harassment campaigns (trolling) against people they don't like. They follow and promote conspiracy theories such as those put out by InfoWars' Alex Jones and QAnon. They supported Donald Trump with social media memes and amplified his content on all social media channels including YouTube. They famously started the "Crooked Hillary" meme on Reddit and 4chan, which then was picked up and shared by Trump, mainstream Trump supporters (not Alt-right nor QAnon), and Russians.

Trump borrowed many memes from this group, as did the Russians who amplified them. This is where the "Pepe the Frog" meme originated that you may have seen on flags at the Capitol breach and in Trump's 2016 campaign. He also used many of their words and themes as shibboleths in his messages to indicate support for the alt-right on the downlow during the 2016 campaign. After Richard Spencer made a racist, anti-Semitic address to a gathering of the alt-right, declaring "Hail Trump" at the end of it, Trump publicly disavowed them. Spencer was a key organizing figure of the "Unite the Right" rally in Charlottesville, Virginia, in 2017 where members of the alt-right came together with neo-Confederates, neo-fascists, white nationalists, neo-Nazis, Klansmen, and various right-wing militias.

Russia

When it comes to getting free societies to turn against themselves, Russia is hands-down the most efficient. The AI recommendation systems of social media do most of the work for them once their troll farms and botnets stir things up enough to get noticed. They use every single weapon of polarization, often off the back of existing content originated by opposing groups—the more extreme the better. Russia's goal is to weaken democracies from within. The main premise is to sow discord, unrest, and division in order to cause destabilization of leadership, the economy, and the citizens. What's in it for them? To restore Russia to great power, such as regaining their elite Group of Eight (G8) status, preventing democratic ideologies from growing in its sphere of influence, protecting the Putin regime, and enhancing its military effectiveness by obfuscation and the wearing down of citizen support for military, police, and other democratic institutions.[152] The playbook goes like this: first you break down people's trust in one another, then sow fear, hatred, and violence such as a coup or civil war—which the alt-right claimed was coming.[153] I have no doubt Russia was reveling as the world's perception of the US changed while the press reported, scene by scene, the breach of our Capitol on January 6, 2021. The anti-racism protests which started out well-intentioned but often descended into chaotic, riotous scenes before the cameras[154] were also no help when it came to how America was viewed by world leaders (which, as you'll read later, the Russians also helped stoke with trolls and bots).

These were steps toward achieving Russia's goal of reacquiring great power status again, because they view our loss of clout as their gain. Regardless of your beliefs about the Capitol breach and anti-racism protests, these actions played out perfectly for Russia on the global stage. It only got better for them when Donald Trump was impeached for inciting violence. Diminishing US stature on the global stage meant that Russia might be able to get a seat back at the table—Russia had been a member of the G8 from 1997 to 2014 until they annexed Crimea, and the US, under Barack Obama, helped kick them out as a result. If they could accomplish this, it would mean they would get a vote again about important decisions that threaten their national interests. While we appear dysfunctional as a country, they work on the other G7 members to try and get their seat back.

Russians know that democratic countries place a high priority on freedom of speech and that censoring speech in any way can actually cause discord by itself. Since we have no control over the narrative, we are a perfect target for disinformation campaigns which include a lot of propaganda. *Propaganda* is a form of persuasion that is often used in media—including social media—to further an agenda by evoking an emotional or obligable response from the audience. It includes the deliberate sharing of realities, views, and philosophies intended to alter behavior and stimulate people to act.

What was Russia's exact role in all this polarization? They used AI, bots, trolls, and hackers to find and amplify preexisting divides in our society in hopes of undermining public faith in the US democratic process while denigrating Hillary Clinton during the 2016 campaign.[155] Putin has blamed former Secretary of State Clinton for supporting regime-change protesters in Russia's 2011-2012 parliamentary and presidential elections when he was running for president. Not to mention her then boss—former President Barack Obama—helped oust him from the G8.

Russia amplified the content of the alt-right the most, as it already aligned with their goals. What would normally remain uncivilized, almost playground-level bully material like memes of Hillary with Stars of David and money in the background along with the words "Crooked Hillary" across the top, served to remind everyone of the scandals about her right before Election Day 2016. With a little help from the Russians and Trump, it got shared even more. On Facebook, links to Russian content shared by Russia's troll factory—the Internet Research Agency (IRA)—reached 125 million Americans. Basically, they just placed ads on Facebook as any company or brand would, sharing memes, fake news, and other divisive content, then amplified all of it using trolls and AI-generated botnets.

Russia did not limit itself to alt-right messages; it used bots and trolls to tweet about Black Lives Matter and aspects of black culture.[156] They also supported Bernie Sanders while disparaging Hillary Clinton. They latched on to many conspiracy theories and even created some of their own, including one that claimed a Democratic National Committee employee named Seth Rich had been murdered in 2016 because he'd leaked DNC emails.[157]

In July 2021, to ensure they didn't miss out on sowing division between those who believe in vaccinations and those who don't, Russia and China combined efforts to promote vaccine misinformation.[158] Meanwhile, they have been distributing vaccines to other countries to promote themselves as world leaders while propagating messages about Western-origin vaccines being "ineffective and unhelpful." Now imagine what they could do with AI that can analyze your emotional triggers (called Emotion AI) and deepfakes. It's only going to become more complicated to get to the truth.

Conclusion

Can AI polarize us and radicalize us? Yes. The divisive ideas are human, but it is because of AI that those ideas can be amplified to hundreds of thousands within minutes. Because of AI, not only can propaganda spread as fast as lightning, but it can find its targets so precisely that a black person can be sent fake news that misinforms them of times and places they should vote, while an undecided voter in a swing state receives shocking memes about a presidential candidate. Both of these examples are real stories.[159] The way that extreme politics spreads and gets more attention makes even moderate people believe the world has become more extreme and polarized. But in actuality, it's a small group of trolls—sometimes homegrown, sometimes Russia-enhanced—generating most of the content. For example, the US House Permanent Select Committee on Intelligence found that a mere *twelve* Russian troll accounts had generated over thirty-nine thousand Facebook messages. They are sowing discord using social media's amplification of their divisive messages in our feeds 24/7.

According to one Pew Research study, the majority of people don't even post political content online. All research on polarization points to a small contingent who share sensationalist content which stays in circulation as others, who are either validated or offended by it, share it and comment on it. This does not mean that we live in a world where our neighbors are actually horrible trolls with nothing nice to say. But the saddest part is that our beliefs, based on what we have seen online, are sure to become a self-fulfilling prophecy before we even give people a chance.

Recommendations

How to Tell if It's Fake News

1. Check the Source

    *   If it's a site you have never heard of before, do an internet search on "Fake News Sites" or just look up the source in an internet search. If there is a Wikipedia site for it, then it
    *   will list what kind of company it is. Wikipedia also has listings of both known "Fake News Sites" and "Satirical News Sites." Fake news sites will be ones that deliberately publish hoaxes and disinformation.

2. Overly Sensationalistic Headlines

    *   In this day and age, it can be hard to distinguish between what's real and fake when it comes to sensational headlines. But take a look at the rest of the article. If it doesn't jibe with the headline, it was probably clickbait to get you to their site.

3. URL Will Be Off

    *   Often, fake news sites will use website names that are similar to other websites in an attempt to appear legitimate. CBSnews.com.co is a prime example. Those extra two letters, ".co," at the end will take you to a fake news site instead of CBS.

4. Other News Sites Will Report the Story

    *   Usually, multiple news channels will report significant events. If something has been covered legitimately by other news sites, then it is likely real news.

5. Check Snopes.com and Factcheck.org

   • These sites usually report fake news stories once they go viral.

How to Tell if You Are Talking to a Bot on Social Media

1. User Profile

   • Basic bots lack a photo, a link, and bio. Better ones may use pictures or avatars from the web. The name may also be a little unusual or conversely, highly generic like "John Smith."

2. Word Context

   • Bots may string random topic-trending words together that do not make sense.

3. Topic Obsession

   • Bots will amplify the same topics, links, and hashtags repeatedly. That's their purpose.

4. Odd Timing

   • Ever seen accounts that seem to be tweeting 24/7? They're almost certainly bots.

5. Not Following

   • Bots may only follow a few other bots and may amplify Tweets of those bots endlessly. People typically follow a lot of different people and groups.

If you have other questions about bot activity you can always try one of these tools. Do an internet search to find them.

- Botometer: scores a Twitter account and helps determine if it's a bot.

- Bot Sentinel: a dashboard that tracks, in aggregate, what disinformation bots are tweeting, then you can compare the information you have seen with what they've determined to be false.

- Hoaxy: Track the spread of online disinformation.

How to Limit Deceptive Threads and Ads

These recommendations come back to your privacy settings on social media. In Facebook, you can go to the Settings & Privacy menu and select "Ads." That will allow you to see the advertisers that have been in your feed. That's important to know when Russia has just straight up paid for advertising like any other company would. Russia placed ads under other affiliates and also under their RT news group, so keep an eye out for that one. You can also visit your "Ad Preferences" page and click "Advertisers," then you can click any advertiser in the list and click on "Hide Ads." The best setting, however, gives you the ability to go to "Ad Preferences" and limit your "Ad Topics" so that elections, politics, and social issues will be shown to you less. You can update your "Ad Topics" through your Instagram account in much the same way. Also, I would suggest adjusting who can see your social interactions. It's always a good idea to limit who can see your posts and keep your social network to friends and family. It's still possible they will forward you deceptive content or post it to their feed, which means you will see it, but at least it's a lot less exposure to deceptive content than if you saw everyone's content all the time.

Pop Your Filter Bubble

It's interesting how you learn things about others who are researching the same topics you are, by what the AI recommends to you as other articles of interest. When I first started researching AI ethics from other experts who were posting to Medium, it put articles about AI ethics in my feed, but it also included a lot of LGBTQIA content with it. It was interesting to learn more about that culture, but I needed to focus on other areas for research. I needed a reset. Sometimes you forget what you have signed up to see. It's good to revisit your news priorities in the online places you frequent.

1. Change Your News Feed Settings

- In Facebook, News Feeds can be changed in "Settings and Privacy" under "News Feed Preferences." Select what you want to prioritize, and remember to unfollow any questionable groups or organizations so they will not keep showing up in your feeds.

2. Browse and Search Privately

- Use privacy browsers like Epic or Mozilla Firefox or privacy search engines like DuckDuckGo. These allow you to browse or search without being tracked.

3. Clear Tracking Info

- Delete browsing histories and block cookies. (Warning: This could make internet searching and browsing a bit less convenient since almost all sites require you to accept their cookies.) In most browsers, you can find the option to block cookies by going into "Settings," then "Privacy." From there, you usually are offered choices to block some or all cookies. There may also be a slider that allows you to select a level of privacy.

4. Don't Sign into Google to Search or View YouTube Videos

- Personally, I use both Epic and DuckDuckGo, but if you don't want to do that, sign out of Google every now and then (if you have an account), clear your cookies and search history in your browser, and then try your searches again. Your results will likely be different than they were before you cleared your history.

CHAPTER 10
Is AI Violating My Rights and Liberties?

*We hold these truths to be self-evident, that all men are
created equal, that they are endowed by their Creator
with certain unalienable Rights, that among these are
Life, Liberty and the pursuit of Happiness.*

—Declaration of Independence, 1776

The Rights and Liberties AI Can Trample

I admit that I am probably going to use the terms "rights" and "liberties" a little more liberally than a lawyer would. I am not a lawyer. I'm not qualified to give you legal advice. But what I do want to accomplish with this chapter is to make you aware that there are state and federal laws that can protect you from bad AI. If someone throws an opaque algorithm in your face as some sort of justification for bad behaviors, for society's sake don't let those groups just get away with it. It doesn't matter if the perpetrator of a crime or a civil damage is an AI or a human. Certain rights are unalienable—like you can't kill people and get away with it.

My friend and lawyer Karen Suber reminds me that "lawyers often look to legal precedents for 1) how to determine whether harm has been done and 2) how to remedy the harm. But now lawyers are seeing *types of harm* that they have never seen before caused in *ways* they have not seen before—i.e. new AI-based systems that are prevalent throughout our personal and professional lives. As a result, lawyers are having to look at legal precedents through a new lens." Toward that goal I wanted to give you some specific examples where lawyers have been actively involved in defending against algorithms today and one futuristic scenario. The first two cases are about predictive policing and self-driving car negligence—these are about your actual freedoms—as in the government can literally throw you in jail. The third case is about economic liberties—as in a bank can kick you out of your house. Then we turn our sites to an exploration of what could happen to our liberties in a Gattaca-like world where we are all engineered to be good at certain types of jobs thanks to the ubiquity of CRISPR gene editing.

Predictive Policing Can Mean Police Are Incentivized to Harass

The Fifth Amendment gives you the right to due process of law. The Fourth Amendment guarantees the right to not be searched or arrested without probable cause. The Fourteenth Amendment gives you the right to procedural due process and the right to freely associate (meaning the government—in this example the police—cannot take out any grievances they may have with you on your family, friends, or coworkers). Where is the protection from general police harassment when the algorithm predicts wrongly that you are a "prolific offender"? How do you get justice for yourself when an unscrupulous sheriff decides to use an incorrect and hidden algorithm to incentivize or coerce (whichever need be) his own police officers into arresting and harassing people whom the algorithm listed?

A fifteen-year-old kid from Pasco County, Florida, was harassed by police officers over twenty-one times in about a three-month period after an opaque homegrown algorithm categorized him as a "prolific offender."[160] A "prolific offender" was described as someone who had taken to a life of crime with no hope of reform. Pardon me if I sound cynical, but a fifteen-year-old hardly strikes me as someone with no hope of reform. As part of an intimidation campaign designed to encourage the offender to "want to move" (as in out of the county), officers would look for any infractions—even if it was something as harmless as missing house numbers—to arrest or fine him, his family members, and friends. They interrogated him and anyone associated with him at all hours of the day and even parked outside his home, his mother's workplace, and his friends' houses. After one police visit, the kid collapsed, unable to breathe, and was taken to the hospital. The doctor said it was a panic attack brought on by anxiety. We can surmise it was from the incessant police harassment.

Sadly, he was only one of hundreds on the algorithm-generated list that this police department was incentivized to terrorize, 10 percent of them under the age of eighteen. What was his major infraction? Did he kill someone or commit some gruesomely violent crime? No. He stole a motorized bike from a carport. Was he at least a serial offender? No. It happened one time. He already had a probation officer with whom he regularly checked in when the police put him on the "prolific offender" list. If you are like me, you are left wondering what the algorithm picked up that would cause a *one*-time offender to be scored as a "*prolific* offender." Factors in the algorithm included an individual's criminal record, being accused or suspected of a crime, having witnessed a crime, or even being a *victim* of a crime. If you are scratching your head in confusion, you are not alone. This is my point. These are opaque systems without objective outside audit. What's worse, this algorithm prioritized and ranked one hundred more names every quarter for the police to add to their "prolific offender" list. Once the list was published, the police officers were then measured on the number of prolific offender checks they did. It must be noted that several officers pushed back on this policy and were coerced into submission or fired.

The stories of many of the families of people who were put on the prolific offender list—complete with body camera footage of police officers—are available from the *Tampa Bay Times*. I highly recommend checking out the entire story.[161] Though I must warn you, it only gets worse when you find out that some of the targeted people were middle schoolers and people with mental health conditions such as autism and depression.

I shared this story with you to give you an idea of the dire consequences that can occur because of predictive policing algorithms. Some of us have a hard time imagining that police would ever do such a thing, especially in a suburban setting where crime is already low. In case you were wondering if the tactics of the police department were successful in reducing crime…property theft was consistent with that in the nearest seven counties, but violent crimes in Pasco County were actually up over the neighboring counties. All that funding—$2.8 million to be exact—for algorithms and teams to enforce them, not to mention the lawsuits from all the harassment, and there were no quantifiable results above and beyond the nearby counties.

Police departments all want to use some level of predictive policing to get ahead of criminals. Some areas of the country are more affected by violent crimes than others, and the citizens are crying out for some intervention. But as in everything in life, the devil is always in the details of how good intentions fare once put into practice. PredPol, now called Geolitica, is one of the more commonly used predictive policing tools out there. Geolitica identifies areas in a neighborhood where serious crimes are more likely to occur during a particular period. Geolitica claims it has research that proves the software to be twice as accurate as human analysts when it comes to predicting where crimes will happen. But the most important thing to note is that the amount of bias in these AI programs can vary depending on whether it uses arrest data, victim reports, or actual convictions. Arrest data is more biased because it's reflective of police decisions as opposed to actual convictions.[162] This means the algorithm will basically just predict police behavior—not criminal behavior.

Here's another story to provide further evidence. In Chicago, which has one of the highest murder rates in the country, desperate police have taken it up several notches by going so far as to predict "who" will commit crimes with their "Strategic Subject List." This is an algorithm-generated list identifying people most likely to be involved in a shooting—both the potential perpetrator and the victim. The two main goals for creating the list were that 1) they could provide services such as counseling to people in danger, and 2) they could prevent shooters from ever picking up a gun.[163] Police showed up to the houses of these individuals in the hopes of quashing any potential homicides before they started. But post-reports were run on the effectiveness of the list, and it was determined that it was primarily used to target people for arrest. Great if they're guilty of something, not so great if they haven't done anything yet. Predictive policing is everywhere. As stated in chapter 2, if your town has any level of crime, predictive policing might be used in your community. Attend town hall meetings and ask your city's district leaders if it's being used where you are. If you suspect foul play, contact a local investigative journalist. If you are directly affected by predictive policing, also called "intelligence-led policing," call a lawyer.

Your Self-Driving Car Just Killed Someone, Now What?

A woman named Elaine Herzberg tragically became the first self-driving car death when she was hit by an Uber test vehicle as she crossed a street in Tempe, Arizona at nighttime in March of 2018. As tragic as her death was, what happened next set a scary legal precedent for those thinking about owning and operating a self-driving car and became a tragedy in its own right. The powerful tech company that programmed the car was not found culpable at all; Uber was not even tried in the case. Instead, negligent homicide was the ruling a low-level Uber backup driver named Rafaela Vasquez received. Should she have been charged or Uber or both? "Uber worked "hand-in-glove" with Tempe police, "who delegated much of the investigation to Uber, and the company's influence colored Tempe Police Department's (TPD) conclusions".[164] After all, it was the Mayor of Tempe who made the deal with Uber for them to test their self-driving cars there in the first place.

The mayor's influence over the police and Uber's subsequent investigation was a major conflict of interest that thwarted Vasquez's due process of law. Not to mention Vasquez's defense claims the grand jury did not even get to hear about Uber's many safety infractions before deciding to indict her. It is alleged that she was watching a popular TV show called "The Voice" on her personal cell phone directly before the accident and there is video that seems to corroborate this—though what she is looking at specifically has been contested. This video evidence is most likely how the prosecution wrapped the case so quickly. But "automation complacency" is a well-known phenomenon that happens when a system is good and the job is te-dious so a human stops paying attention when monitoring automated devices. Automation complacency coupled with assurances that the automatic braking system was engaged and working in tandem with the autonomous functions (which it turns out it wasn't) contributed to Vasquez not reacting quickly enough to intervene. These factors were not considered a safety issue by Uber, even though previously they had standardized on having two drivers in their test vehicles most likely for this reason. The week before the pedestrian was killed, "a whistle blower at Uber named Robbie Miller emailed company executives warning about safety problems: "A car was damaged nearly every other day in February," he told top officials. "We shouldn't be hitting things every 15,000 miles." "Several of the drivers appear to not have been properly vetted or trained."[165]

As of this writing, Vasquez's attorneys filed to remand the case back to the grand jury arguing that the grand jury did not hear all the relevant information to the case and that they were poorly instructed on the relevant laws. Specifically, the defense lawyers mention that causation is an element of negligent homicide and that the charge should have taken into account additional causal results such as the Uber safety issues that were never exposed.

But what should the rest of us take from this case? Don't get too comfortable with autonomous vehicle capabilities. The technology is still very much fallible. In a study by the Insurance Institute of High-way Safety and MIT drivers of cars with autonomous capabilities—which also have increased safety features, did basically the same thing as Vasquez. They stopped paying attention as much to what the car was doing the more comfortable they became with its automated fea-tures.[166] It makes sense. These drivers aren't paying extra so that they can simply monitor the car. I'm guessing the reason for buying the car and paying extra has to do with the fact that they do not want to have to pay attention the whole time. In fact, there is video of a Tesla driver and his passenger fast asleep as his car continued driving down a busy Los Angeles highway at 55 miles per hour.[167] Try to remember this case when you begin to even think about nodding off while at the helm of a self-driving car. You don't want to be responsible for your own death or the death of anyone else; and you don't want to end up in jail for negligence while driving either.

Foreclosed by Algorithm

An underwriting algorithm at Wells Fargo caused people to lose 545 homes by wrongfully deciding not to extend their mortgage. After the 2008 economic collapse, the Home Affordable Modification Program (HAMP) was designed to help people keep their homes by extending their mortgages so they could afford their payments. They would have to meet certain requirements, but once their application was accepted, they would be given a trial payment period (TPP).[168] Wells Fargo's homegrown underwriting algorithm failed, and 545 homes were foreclosed on. Wells Fargo ultimately offered a measly $15,000 compensation once the "calculation" error was discovered more than six years later. The fact that you could literally lose your home because of an algorithm's mistake was made all too real. One of the people who lost his home had this to say: "It doesn't even begin to compare to the chain of events that were started by their [Wells Fargo's] denial of assistance." He compared it to someone saying, "Sorry about cutting off your arm. Here's a Band-Aid." He also added, "And don't just blame it on the software. Where was the human oversight?" [169] These errors should be a wake-up call. We should all march right into our congresspeople's offices and demand oversight of these types of algorithms.

The state of California, where a class-action lawsuit was brought to bear, ruled in favor of the foreclosed homeowners. Sadly, they only received $10,000 each as part of their settlement. The state laws that their complaint was filed under included "negligence," "conversion" (when a private actor takes your property), and "unfair competition law" (which includes "any unlawful, unfair or fraudulent business act or practice)."[170]

Participating in financial lending systems is one of the most premier liberties of all. Financial lending can be the difference between going to school or not. It can mean starting a business and getting a home mortgage. So much of modern society—and your standing in it—depends on your ability to secure financial means. Because it is such a foundational aspect of society, it's fairness and equality are paramount to our freedom. But lending has always been ripe with human biases, so when lenders started moving toward algorithms, it was assumed these would provide a fairer method of securing loans.

Almost all financial lending institutions rely heavily on FICO scores, which tend to correlate with income and race.[171] Lending officers and software-based underwriting engines both charge Latino and African-American loan applicants interest rates that are six to nine points higher than white applicants who have the same FICO score and loan-to-value ratio.[172] The higher interest rate is the same whether it determined by a loan officer, a bank's online lending arm, or a fintech mortgage lender like Quicken or SoFi.

Some online lenders, such as Upstart, have said their algorithms help reduce the cost of credit and give more people better pricing than traditional lenders. Upstart uses "alternative" data about education, occupation, and even loan application variables in its underwriting models. (For instance, people who ask for round numbers like $20,000 are a higher risk than people who ask for odder numbers like $19,900.) "A lot of variables that tend to be correlated with speed or lack of prudence are highly correlated with default," Upstart cofounder Paul Gu said in a recent interview, "And indications that someone desperately needs the money right away will be correlated with defaults." Next let's turn to a not-too-distant future where modified genetics could determine your rights, liberties and pursuits of happiness in society.

CRISPR, AI, Eugenics and a Gattaca-Like Future

In a scene from the iconic 1997 movie Gattaca, a man and wife sit in front of a geneticist to determine the makeup of their baby. The geneticist starts with "You have specified hazel eyes, dark hair and fair skin. I've taken the liberty of eradicating any potentially prejudicial conditions. Premature baldness, myopia…alcoholism and addictive susceptibility…propensity for violence, obesity, etc." to which the parents respond "We didn't want—I mean, diseases, yes, but— We were just wondering if it's good to leave a few things to chance? The geneticist responds, "You want to give your child the best possible start. Believe me, we have enough imperfection built in already. Your child doesn't need any additional burdens. Keep in mind this child is still you. Simply the best of you. You could conceive naturally a thousand times and never get such a result." Later, you find out that the non-genetically modified children are considered by society to be "degenerates" or "invalids". All the dream jobs go to those with superior genetics, while the non-genetically modified people have their lives controlled by others in a station higher than them. Could we one day end up with our rights and liberties limited because of our genetic modifications? We have the "technology" so let's examine this topic further.

CRISPR enables scientists to edit genes by allowing them to find a specific bit of DNA that is causing a problem and then alter or remove it—like cutting and pasting in word processing. It's often referred to as a technology or a tool, but CRISPR, which stands for Clustered Regularly-Interspaced Short Palindromic Repeats, are naturally occurring sequences of genetic code in bacteria. Scientists discovered they could precisely target our DNA with it to alter genes that cause diseases like sickle cell anemia and certain kinds of cancer. AI helps improve the accuracy of gene editing by homing in on the best places in the DNA sequence to cut the gene, thereby reducing side effects of gene therapy when too much or not enough is cut.[173]

But diseases are likely not the only kind of genetic code that can be supplanted; it's just where scientists are focusing their efforts for now. CRISPR could potentially be used to eliminate any unwanted genetic qualities if used in embryonic cells—ANY unwanted genetic qualities. Use your imagination. The thing scientists love about the CRISPR discovery is that it makes genetic alterations "cheap and easy".[174] What used to cost over $5,000 and a huge specialized staff's worth of labor, can now be done at only $30 and much less effort.[175] What roadblocks then stand in the way of scientists who simply want to get rich by creating designer babies that could be genetically modified to be stronger, taller, or smarter? If you try to tell me that scientists have some sort of moral code that prevents them from doing anything bad, my eyes are going to roll back into my head. And I'll remind you of the gain of function research that most likely upped the strength of bat coronaviruses which I believe—in my non-scientific opinion—led to the pandemic. Those scientists never thought a pandemic would be caused, but here we are in year two of it with millions of lives lost. Unintended consequences of supposed safe science are not to be taken lightly—especially when the consequences are genetic.

The current group of geneticists have decided it's a bad thing to use CRISPR on embryos because then the genetic modifications can be passed down for generations. But He Jiankui a well-intentioned scientist in China created two HIV-resistant children by using CRISPR to alter their genes while they were still embryos. Look him up. He was trying to help an HIV positive couple who wanted to have a child but were afraid of passing it down. Ironically, the couple's children will pass down HIV-resistance instead of HIV. That's not a bad thing per se. But there are two sides to everything. In fixing one thing, you may risk another. One scientist expressed concern that Jiankui's modification of the CCR5 gene to restrict HIV pathways could cause the twins to be much more susceptible to West Nile as a result.[176] A study conducted in 2019 also found that people with double mutated CCR5 genes—like the twins'—are likely to have an increased risk of death due to flu and more than 20 percent less likely to reach age 76.[177] Another scientist cautioned that single gene to disease relationships are rare and to remember that many diseases are a result of gene/environment interaction which means that gene editing may not be the answer for most diseases.[178] There are also concerns about inadvertently creating long-term hereditary issues such as creating new diseases that could persist for generations to come.

Then there are the moral dilemmas and implications to consider. Will society see ridding our genes of potential diseases as a moral imperative? "I don't think I'm playing God," says Shoukhrat Mitalipov an embryonic genetic researcher. "We have intelligence to understand diseases, eliminate suffering. And that's what I think is the right thing to do."[179] Will society mandate CRISPR-based gene therapy so that our healthcare system does not become overwhelmed in the same way COVID vaccinations were mandated? Will employers refuse to take on non-genetically modified employees because they do not want the healthcare burden these employees or their dependents may present? Will it be morally wrong NOT to be genetically modified in the future?[180] I sure hope not!

What about when bad things happen because of genetic modifications? Could we all become sick and die at the same time in the future because of some unknown defect we inadvertently caused ourselves by being genetically altered? Will communist societies that value people for utility see disabled citizens as an undue burden on their economic systems and therefore require genetic modifications or worse would they be exterminated? In an effort to optimize genetic code to various jobs—such as strength for manual labor and farming, intelligence for scientific and technical work—will master races inadvertently be created? In democratic countries, would optimizing genetics toward certain jobs cause a Gattaca-like future where the non-genetically enhanced need not apply; and people's destinies are not determined by their own will but that of their parent or geneticist? These are all futuristic-sounding issues, yet CRISPR and AI have leaped us here in record time. The time to determine where we stand on these issues is now or we won't be ready with norms, regulations, and laws by the time the genetic modifications are everywhere. The mRNA COVID vaccines have opened many scientists' eyes to the efficacy and efficiencies of using mRNA. Has this acceptance of mRNA therapies opened the path for riskier genetic therapies. As a society we must deliberate on these issues and come to decisions about the impact of broadly-available genetic modifications so that we can proactively rather than reactively prepare to govern them and not with a few well-meaning scientists but as a whole society which values freedoms and individuality.

Recommendations

We the People must call upon greater regulation, transparency, and accountability for AI algorithms that affect our lives deeply. We will need the help of forward-thinking policymakers, tech-savvy lawyers, and activists to achieve the wide-scale work to combat AI that can compromise the liberties and freedoms we cherish.

- Work with watchdog groups such as the Electronic Frontier Foundation, ACLU, and EPIC.

- Bring lawsuits to challenge AI's role in rights that are already protected.

- Report perceived discrimination in lending, education, housing, employment to the EEOC and Federal Trade Commission (FTC).

- Work with your congresspeople to express concerns you have about unethical uses of AI so they can begin proposing laws and regulations to protect freedoms down the road.

Know the Rights and Liberties that Can Protect You from Bad AI

Liberties are granted to us by the first ten amendments to the US Constitution, known as the Bill of Rights. They are meant to keep us free from tyranny. I've listed them below as a reminder.

The Bill of Rights and Fourteenth Amendment

a. Freedom of religion, speech, press, assembly, association and petition.

b. The right to keep and bear arms in order to maintain a well-regulated militia.

c. No quartering of soldiers.

d. Freedom from unreasonable searches and seizures.

e. The right to due process of law, freedom from self-incrimination, double jeopardy.

f. Rights of accused persons (e.g., right to a speedy and public trial).

g. The right to a trial by jury in civil cases.

h. Freedom from excessive bail, cruel and unusual punishments.

i. Other rights of the people.

j. Powers reserved to the states.

k. Equal protection under the laws, due process of the law, and others.

Rights are meant to prevent discrimination based on protected characteristics like gender, age, race, disability, and so forth. These rights are represented across a number of federal laws, including within the domains of housing, lending, voting, employment, and education. These are a few that are relevant to the types of impact AI has on us.

- *Federal Trade Commission Act (Section 5)*: Prohibits "unfair or deceptive acts or practices in or affecting commerce." This prohibition applies to all persons engaged in commerce, including banks. Enforced by the FTC. "The FTC emphasizes in the 2021 and 2020 guidance that organizations should notify consumers about how and when consumer personal information will be used by or be used to develop AI, especially if the information is sensitive. The FTC notes that failure to properly explain how consumers can control the use of personal information to develop algorithms may lead to enforcement under Section 5."[181]

- *Fair Credit Reporting Act (FCRA)*: US federal law that promotes accuracy, fairness, and privacy of consumer information contained in the files of consumer reporting agencies. It was intended to protect consumers from the willful and/or negligent inclusion of inaccurate information in their credit reports. The FCRA is enforced by the FTC and Consumer Financial Protection Bureau. Key among these protections is the determination that there should be no secret databases used to make decisions about a person's life, that individuals should have a right to see and challenge the information held in such databases, and that information in such a database should expire after a reasonable amount of time. Under the FCRA, employers using consumer reports to screen job applicants or employees must follow specific procedures:

  a. Get your written permission

  b. Tell you how they want to use your credit report

  c. Not misuse your information

  d. Give you a copy of your credit report if the employer decides not to hire or fires you

  e. Give you an opportunity to dispute the information contained within your credit report before making a final adverse decision

- "If an organization purchases a report or score about a consumer from a background check company that was generated using AI tools and uses that score or report to deny the consumer housing, then that organization must provide an adverse action notice to the consumer as required by the FCRA. The FTC has also noted that organizations that supply data which may be used for AI-based insurance, credit, employment or similar eligibility decisions may have FCRA obligations as 'information furnishers.'" [182]

- *Equal Credit Opportunity Act 1974 (ECOA)*: Prohibits creditors from discriminating against credit applicants. Not everyone who applies for credit gets it or gets the same terms. Factors like income, expenses, debts, and credit history are among the considerations lenders use to determine your creditworthiness.

- *Fair Housing Act (FHA)*: Prohibits housing discrimination on the basis of race, religion, sex, familial status, and disability.

- *Civil Rights Act of 1964*: Far-reaching legislation prohibiting discrimination on the basis of race, color, religion, sex, or national origin in the areas of employment, education, voting, and public accommodations.

- *Age Discrimination Act of 1975*: Prohibits discrimination on the basis of age in programs and activities that receive *federal* assistance such as educational programs, health care services, housing, welfare, food stamps, and rehabilitation programs.

- *Age Discrimination in Employment Act (ADEA)*: Prohibits discrimination against job applicants and employees over the age of forty in terms of compensation, advancement opportunities, and other employment conditions.

- *Americans with Disabilities Act (ADA)*: Prohibits discrimination on the basis of disability (real and perceived) in employment, state and local government, public accommodations, commercial facilities, transportation, and telecommunications.

- *Rehabilitation Act of 1973-Section 504*: Prohibits discrimination against disabled people in programs receiving federal financial assistance. Disabled people include people with mental health conditions.

- *Voting Rights Act of 1965*: Enacted to address Jim Crow laws in the Deep South and other barriers minorities faced when trying to participate in elections. Aspects of this act might be useful in voter suppression disinformation campaigns that target minorities.

Predatory lending practices are often covered more fully by state laws and to some degree with the federal ECOA and FHA. Lenders are not allowed to conduct predatory lending practices which target the most vulnerable people, like those who have recently lost a job, have poor credit, or just don't know what to watch out for. Black and Latinx communities have fallen prey to many of these abusive lending practices.[183] These are your existing legal protections. It is my hope that you use this list of laws if ever you feel your rights or liberties have been violated. Do not feel helpless against AI violations as stated earlier on, you have unalienable rights which still apply regardless of whether an algorithm, a human, or both violated them.

CHAPTER 11
Healthcare: Is AI Involved in Life-or-Death Situations?

Patients may never know what happened if an AI model makes a faulty recommendation that is part of the reason they are denied needed care or undergo an unnecessary, costly, or even harmful intervention.

—Rebecca Robbins and Erin Brodwin,
STAT News investigative journalists

AI Quiz: What Do You Know About AI in Healthcare?

1. In healthcare, AI has been used to: *(select all that apply)*

    a) Triage COVID patients to the emergency room

    b) Determine if patients will die soon

    c) Predict if hospitalized patients will develop complications or deteriorate

    d) Keep your memories alive for transcendence into a robotic brain and head

    e) Guide microscopic robots in your blood to diseased or cancerous cells

2. Doctors are legally required to tell you when they use AI as part of your care. True or False?

3. AI could affect life-and-death decisions by: *(select all that apply)*

    a) Recommending that you could wait longer for life-saving care

    b) Predicting that you're going to die and recommending palliative care instead of interventive care

    c) Misdiagnosing you, causing you to get the wrong treatments

    d) Missing important data due to bias that would have shown you have a more severe stage of disease than initially thought

    e) Basing your need for care on the costs you have previously paid for care

4. Which of the following are true about AI in healthcare? *(select all that apply)*

    a) Most uses of AI in healthcare are not proven

    b) Some algorithms are programmed, not based on health

needs but on insurance status and ability to pay

c) Algorithms in healthcare can inadvertently be biased against certain races, genders, ages, and even conditions such as high blood pressure and diabetes

d) AI decisions are always clearly explained so the doctor understands them

e) Doctors are ready to use information extracted from wearable health technology to treat patients with A-fib and high blood pressure

5. The future of AI in healthcare could mean: *(select all that apply)*

a) Extending the life and quality of life of cancer patients with the right blend of drugs for their cancer and bodies

b) Elderly people can live in their homes longer, thereby extending their lives in many cases

c) More precise medical treatments, with fewer side effects, and better quality of life

d) Lower costs for medical care through reduction of unnecessary tests, medicines, and surgical interventions

e) Faster diagnosis, which could contribute to stopping diseases before they become serious or even deadly

See answers on next page.

Answers to AI Quiz: What Do You Know About AI in Healthcare?.

1. All except d.

2. False.[184]

3. All of the above.

4. a., b., and c.

5. All of the above.

Who Gets Life-Saving Equipment?

Picture this scenario: In a crowded hospital, you awake panicked and out of breath in what seems to be an endless parking lot of beds. Each bed has a red, yellow, or green light at the end. Your bed doesn't have a color. You notice that people on the beds with green lights seem to be getting all the attention from the caregivers who are frenzied with activities such as intubating them. *These must be the worst cases of COVID*, you think to yourself. You notice that most of the people on the beds with the red lights are older, looking like your grandmother's age. Every now and then, a nurse walks over to check their IVs and ask if they are comfortable. One nurse has taken a moment to video chat with a patient's family. It's almost peaceful compared to the rest of the room. One red-lit patient is even being sent home. Your light finally switches on. It's yellow. But you don't see any other yellows in the room. What does this mean? Who is deciding these traffic-light colors for each person? Does it somehow affect the type of care you'll get? You start to lose consciousness again just as a nurse threads a transparent tube over your ears and inserts a nasal canula blowing oxygen into your nostrils. The last words you remember hearing from him are, "You're next."

This seems like something out of a sci-fi or horror movie, but a version of this type of algorithm is being used in the UK to determine who gets surgeries and other care right away and who doesn't. The difference is that you don't get to see the traffic-light system; only the caregivers do. You may be outraged to hear that those algorithms were assisting doctors at the epicenters of COVID in deciding which patients should live and die, but maybe not in the way you would first imagine. In situations where hospital beds and specific resources like ventilators become extremely limited because of widespread, overwhelming emergency situations, hospital doctors are forced to make unthinkable decisions.

When life-saving resources are insufficient, hospitals move into "crisis standards of care," which is guidance that prioritizes saving the most lives.[185] In these situations—not just COVID, but also hurricanes and other natural disasters—every second spent reading a lengthy patient chart is a second that could have been spent saving a person's life. This is where AI comes in. Doctors focus on patients that should survive if treated. Doctors turn to AI that rates patients based on their likelihood of survival (morbidity) using everything from your electronic health records (EHRs) to your answers from digital patient intake questionnaires, which you may have filled out in advance. It evaluates existing symptoms and coexisting conditions like high blood pressure, diabetes, and heart, lung, and liver disease. If a patient's prognosis is not good, doctors switch to making the patient comfortable instead of trying to saving them—like the red-light patients in the story.

While it would be easy to blame AI for its cold bedside manner, it is the humans behind the algorithms that determine who lives, who dies, and who can wait a bit longer. Often the decision depends on the role of the person who's deciding (e.g., doctor, hospital administrator, bioethicist) and the outcomes they seek. In the region of Lombardy, Italy—one of the first countries outside of China hit the hardest by COVID—doctors agonizingly but repeatedly decided to give ventilators to younger patients because they felt they would have a better shot of survival. In many parts of Europe, the deciding criterion is intrinsically based on saving *more years of life* rather than *more lives*. In practice, this means anytime a younger person needs a ventilator, they will most likely get it over an older person. Since older people were most often the ones with the severest symptoms, this meant that more older people would die—hence they prioritized years of life versus more lives. When asked point-blank by a *New England Journal of Medicine* journalist whether age-based cutoffs were being used to determine who received a ventilator, an Italian doctor offered apologetically that if you had two patients with respiratory failure, one sixty-five and one eighty-five, with coexisting conditions and one ventilator, you intubate the sixty-five-year-old.[186] At the peak of the crisis, no one over the age of seventy-five was allowed to receive one of the scarce ventilators in Italy. According to doctors at one Bergamo hospital, 70 percent of the intensive care unit beds were reserved for coronavirus patients with "a reasonable chance to survive." Older patients, they said, "are not being resuscitated and die alone."

Doctors, who were used to saving lives no matter the circumstances, were now forced to decide who lived and died on top of dealing with the threat of contracting the deadly disease themselves, exhaustion, and the loss of patients, staff, and loved ones to COVID. Overwhelmed, they began turning to ethical frameworks (that could later be turned into AI triage solutions) to help them decide and buffet them against some of the backlash—not just from society but from their own guilt. One such framework, developed by Johns Hopkins Hospital prior to COVID, sought to include society's priorities by conducting focus groups to understand community preferences. Their results found that society valued saving people with the greatest chance of short-term survival followed by those with the greatest chance of long-term survival. Those with the greatest chance of short-term survival would have to be able to survive being sedated and medically paralyzed, having a large tube snaked down their throats, and lying comatose for weeks. Then they would have to survive being brought back from all that. It turns out that's a big ask given that mortality rates after reaching the need for intubation and a ventilator are 29 percent for those sixty-five to seventy-four and 50 percent in those over eighty.[187] Those with the greatest chances of long-term survival would have no coexisting conditions like high blood pressure, diabetes, or heart and lung disease.

The problem with coding these frameworks into an AI COVID triage solution is that they don't resolve ethical questions when patient outcomes can't be easily predicted. Is an impoverished thirty-year-old single mom with breast cancer going to outlive a stressed-out fifty-five-year-old businessman with prediabetes, high blood pressure, and heart disease? Who has the better chance at both short- and long-term survival? While COVID-related care has been covered in the US, thanks to supplementation from the government and health insurance companies, would patients requiring ongoing care after being on a ventilator be able to afford the treatments? Would a patient's ability to pay affect their long-term survival because they would have to skip expensive treatments they could not afford or appointments requiring them to take off from work? These are, of course, rhetorical questions designed to show the intensity of the decisions faced during COVID and especially in AI-based COVID triage systems. Sometimes these decisions have been carefully thought through in advance by teams of diverse community members, bioethicists, and doctors. But in pandemic times, opportunistic bands of technology coders have hastily thrown together patient-outcome-assessing algorithms and sold them like snake oil to healthcare systems desperate to relieve decision-making burdens from already physically and psychologically burned-out care teams.

AI in Healthcare Today

Maybe you are wondering why AI is even relevant in healthcare. After all, we all talk about the bedside manner of our doctors, which determines a lot about whether we like them or not. Why would we be happy about AI in healthcare when it means we'll likely get less face time with the doctor. Believe it or not, AI can actually help you get more *quality* face time and better care from the doctor. Right now, you probably get a few hurried minutes to explain your malady before the doctor is prescribing meds or treatments and rushing out the door to the next patient.

Part of the reason is that they are overwhelmed with patients. Our aging population is growing, and with age comes more ailments. Unfortunately, the number of doctors needed has not been keeping pace—and that was true even before the pandemic started. The psychological toll that many doctors have experienced with the pandemic will surely result in many more of them deciding to retire early or leave the profession. This means there will be a lot more patients in need than there will be doctors to see them, and it will continue to be this way far into the future. We need AI now more than ever to supplement doctors' abilities to detect, diagnose, and treat diseases faster and more efficiently.

The top use of AI in hospitals and clinics is clinical decision support (CDS). It helps doctors make decisions about the care of their patients.[188] CDS tools have many purposes. Some are designed to help identify patients at risk of getting certain diseases like COVID, COPD, or high blood pressure. Some try to predict patient outcomes to certain treatments, taking into account the specifics of their medical histories. Some try to predict a patient's mortality so the doctor can have an end-of-life conversation well ahead of any event that could incapacitate the patient. Some CDS tools take in thousands upon thousands of patient records related to a specific condition or disease then give the doctor predictions about whether you'll get those specific conditions based on your ongoing symptoms, tests, and treatments. The goal of these types of CDS tools is to *proactively* eliminate underlying causes that contribute to the condition or disease so that you won't end up with a severe case that could further deteriorate your overall health. In some cases, the ability to determine early that you may be at risk for a serious condition like sepsis could allow the doctor to prescribe preventative measures, like antibiotics to ensure you never contract the condition at all.

COVID sped up the adoption of AI in healthcare because decisions could not be made fast enough to keep up with the sheer volume of patients. Prior to COVID, AI was already being used to aggregate and track massive amounts of healthcare data, diagnose illnesses (often as well as or better than doctors), offer treatment recommendations, provide mental health assistance through chatbots, track and encourage patients' compliance with treatment protocols, identify patients most at risk for life-threatening diseases as well as those most likely to respond to treatment, produce epidemic modeling and simulation that helps prevent outbreaks (and contain them when they do occur), assist in drug discovery and clinical trials, and perform surgery. Even as I type these words, supercomputing is becoming more powerful, and AI's access to data is increasing, its training is becoming better, and its use broader.

Other uses of AI include things that seem mundane on the surface but contribute to reduce inefficiencies that slow doctors down and increase healthcare costs for all of us. During COVID, healthcare systems have used AI capabilities for everything from bed, staff, and device management, to data entry, filling out forms, insurance pre-authorizations, and more accurate medical coding. Emergency room doctors diagnosed COVID in minutes with AI's ability to detect the unique "shattered glass" pattern in medical images of patient's lungs versus the four days it took with PCR testing. When the difference between minutes and days could mean a patient's life, AI helped speed up diagnoses so doctors could focus on the most critical cases.

Doctors have endless paperwork to file to meet health insurers' requirements, hospital and clinical policies, and government regulations. To do this efficiently, doctors turned to AI paired with automation to fill in routine forms and natural-language-processing dictation assistants to type up their notes.

How AI Can Affect Life-and-Death Decisions

Anything with as much power and positive potential as AI can have outsize negative implications—especially when human lives are on the line. If healthcare AI is not explained well, not trained well—whether because of low-quality or incomplete data—or if healthcare providers aren't trained how to use it, then it could lead to patient safety issues, misdiagnoses, patients not getting the care or meds they need, breaches in patients' data privacy, and decision-making that often affects a patient—and a patient's family—well past the health concern for which they are initially seen.

AI is also already helping providers triage patients who arrive at emergency rooms (and yes, that includes COVID-19 patients,[189], [190]), determine your eligibility for healthcare insurance plans and the rates you'll pay, and even nudge doctors to have end-of-life conversations with patients the AI identifies as having a high risk of dying within a year. But again, what if the AI is fed faulty information? What if its data is tainted with bias or is incomplete? What if you are denied coverage that you desperately need or are charged a rate you cannot afford? Is it appropriate for machines to be involved in delicate and intimate decisions such as end-of-life care? And what if all of the highly sensitive data on which the AI is basing its decisions is not secure? This is an incredibly complex area in terms of impact on quality and length of human life, ethics, finances, and data security. With so much at stake, what can the average person do?

Unfortunately, it will take extreme vigilance and self-advocacy, because the use of AI in healthcare is already quite widespread, though not at all obvious. As one Harvard Law professor put it, "It's like asbestos: it's everywhere and you won't know it exists until you have problems—and then it will be incredibly difficult to remove." Thus, the onus is on you to ask questions about the use of AI by your healthcare team, hospital administrators, and insurance provider. Following is a checklist of questions you can pose to your care team, as well as suggestions for follow-up action.

Should You Trust AI With Your Life?

Have you considered how it would know about your health—where the health data might come from? How much do *you* know about your own health and how much is documented with your doctors? For example, do you know the medical histories of your family members, even the estranged ones? Do you trust doctors and rely on them for all the things that ail you? Do you feel like any of the doctors you have seen—both specialists and primary care—have a complete record of your health? Have you ever willingly reported that you or a member of your family has been using illegal drugs? Have you ever skipped your doctor's treatments because you either couldn't afford them or didn't have time? When asked about your pain levels, did you tell them a lower number because you didn't want to be seen as wimpy?

If you are like everyone else on this planet and either didn't know the answers, didn't want to answer these questions, or gave untruthful answers then watch out, because algorithms probably will not have enough data about you to determine your chances of living or dying in an emergency situation. You will need to be extra vigilant in finding out when and where these algorithms are used to affect your care. All of the things that doctors want to know about you when you visit are things that make a difference to your health. Even that seemingly irrelevant patient intake form question about what type of work you do helps them identify many environmental factors that could affect your health. For example, if you are exposed to people all day, you might be at greater risk for communicable diseases (COVID, for example); or if you are a consultant who frequently travels to certain regions where specific ailments are common (like yellow fever or malaria); or even if you are a construction worker who may be in the sun and suffering from chronic dehydration leading to chronic headaches. If you don't go to the doctor, where your ailments will be documented in the form of data, or don't know the answers to that never-ending list of questions listed above, then algorithms can't know the answers to how to intervene for you either.

Doctors would no doubt have loved a little green or red light at the end of patients' hospital beds during peak COVID spikes, telling them which patients could survive waiting longer versus which ones could not. Instead, they spent life-saving minutes reading through lengthy charts and intake questionnaires while some patients literally suffocated from fluid-filled lungs.

There are, however, disease-tracking applications that many argue have not only violated privacy but have stigmatized the people who have been reported as sick. Doctors, on the other hand, argue that they themselves would have to decide how to triage and rank patients on their own in the moment, while tired, overworked and rushed, and without being able to read through all of the health data accompanying individual patients. They just simply couldn't keep up. They saw these apps as a literal lifesaver for those patients who could survive the disease. But this by itself, without considering the AI-assisted decision making, is controversial. It became even more controversial when it was found that these algorithms often forsook populations that didn't trust the healthcare realm as much as others—namely black and Hispanic Americans who couldn't afford care.

The Hope and Future of AI in Healthcare

AI is involved in so many varied facets of healthcare: administrative nursing tasks, imaging diagnostics, cancer diagnostics and treatment plans, drug discovery and clinical trials, optimization of healthcare insurance plans and rates, patient triaging in the emergency room, deciding who gets priority based on prior health history, AI-assisted surgery robots, doctor's notes, annotations, and even doctor nudges for end-of-life conversations.

The effect that the use of AI in healthcare is having is mixed. On the positive side, it has the potential to make care more affordable and allow more patients to be seen. But on the other hand, it could jeopardize your health—or worse, kill you. Not to mention all the data that is being collected on you and your health conditions; where on earth does it go, and who has access to it? While HIPAA protects healthcare privacy in healthcare contexts, use of your data by AI companies falls outside the usual governing bodies' jurisdiction.

The question is: What can you do about it? Unfortunately, this is tricky because the use of AI in healthcare is rather stealthy and everywhere. Health insurers assign you financial risk scores (i.e., are you likely to pay your bills?), and hospitals and doctors assign you morbidity scores (i.e., are you likely to die?), which can sometimes interfere with the level of care you receive. Why? Because these scores are hidden from you. Adding to the opaqueness of these AI scores is that doctors see AI as a tool for your care that need not concern you. They won't voluntarily tell you about the use of AI in your care. There is no legal requirement for them to tell you they have used AI models in their considerations either.

You will need to ask a ton of questions about the use of AI by your doctors and hospital administrators involved your care. Many healthcare groups use "cost prediction" as a key metric of success. These cost-prediction algorithms have been wrongly used by care groups to assess patients' "need" for care. The gist is this: if you will cost the hospital more or if you have been modeled as a person who is "not likely to pay," then you might be turned away for care. You will have to advocate for yourself from the moment you suspect you have a serious illness. If you feel you are not getting the care you deserve or if your caregivers are ignoring you, then you will need to pull in lawyers who can help you use legal methods to arrive at answers. While not ideal when you are sick, you want to also look for groups that can help advocate for you with congresspeople who can hold hearings to keep AI firms accountable (you've seen Google, Facebook, and others in front of congressional committees...) and pass laws to help protect you in the future.

Recommendations

Know the Areas Where Use of AI Systems and Scores Can Go Wrong

- *Low Efficacy*: Most uses of AI in healthcare, especially "decision support," are not proven (image diagnostics, however, have an excellent AI accuracy track record). Of 130 FDA-cleared AI devices, 126 were based on irrelevant data. This means they were approved but not proven based on real-world data.[191]

- *Opaque and Inexplicable to Patients and Doctors*: AI decisions are not clearly explained so the doctor understands them, and doctors aren't legally required to tell you when they use AI in supporting their decisions about your care and actually prefer *not* to disclose it to patients because they feel it brings up questions which some doctors dismiss as "unwarranted."

- *Doctors Are Not Ready for It*: Doctors are not ready to use information extracted from wearable health technology to treat patients with A-fib and high blood pressure. Many times, AI systems and information are turned over to doctors (such as in the case of AI-assisted robotic surgery) who are not always adequately trained on how to use it.

- *Based on the Wrong Values*: Some algorithms are programmed not based on health needs but on a patient's ability to pay and their insurance status.

- *Biased*: Algorithms in healthcare can inadvertently be biased against certain races, genders, ages, and even conditions such as high blood pressure and diabetes.

- *Unethical Use of AI*: Some hospitals have decided to make their preferred financial scenarios a reality by determining a person's "need" for care based on financial modeling.

- *System Malfunctions*: Sometimes, like any computer program, AI can have glitches. Something could have been corrupted in the data, or the AI just doesn't work well with the other hospital systems.

Questions to Ask Your Care Team

1. Are you using AI to aid you in my care?

2. What kind of AI tools are you using?

3. If the tools include AI-assisted robotic surgery, how many surgeries has the doctor performed using that exact equipment and was he or she trained on it? Also ask what would happen if the system were to have a glitch or go down in the middle of surgery.

4. If the tool is clinical decision support, ask for more transparency about the data that went into it and if there will be further diagnostic tests to help confirm the AI decision.

5. Who made the AI tool? If it's an external vendor, look them up online to see if there are any known complaints or reviews. You could also look them up with the Better Business Bureau.

6. Ask if your patient data is secure with the AI vendor and request *in writing* that the record be deleted from their system as soon as your need for their service has concluded. Also request that the vendor give direct written notice back to you acknowledging completion of your request. (The reason you'll want to ask this is because AI vendors have played fast and loose with patient data in the past, and at least one imaging-AI group held patients' images and their personal identifying information in regular, non-encrypted databases that any old hacker could get into.

CHAPTER 12
My Vision and Hope for the Future of AI

The real risk with AI isn't malice but competence. A super-intelligent AI will be extremely good at accomplishing its goals, and if those goals aren't aligned with ours, we're in trouble.

—Stephen Hawking

Visions of the Future

Artificial intelligence is the Wild West right now, but that is because there are no cultural norms or regulations to govern it yet. I can't wait to get past this dangerous era of AI and into the era when AI can help us transform at both the societal and individual levels.

Just imagine the AI future with me for a minute. Suspend today's reality and let's explore the future....

I wake up in the morning, groggy. My smart bed lets me know that I tossed and turned all night after getting up at 2:00 a.m. to use the restroom. My health and personal assistant, whom I named "Q," let's me know that, according to the sensor on my water bottle, I drank too much water at midnight when I turned in for the evening. Also, because I trained the AI thermostat to focus on cost savings rather than comfort, my house is too cold for me to maintain my optimal body temperature for sleeping. The time I went to bed is also a problem for Q, and she reminds me that eight hours is my personal sleep target. Not getting the full eight hours will cause me to lack concentration and crave sugary treats to compensate for my tiredness for the rest of the day. Q knows this because she also analyzes my food logs and activity tracker (also known as a smartwatch). Getting four hours of sleep is something Q cannot abide ever since she added my doctor's new heart-healthy AI training module to her algorithmic repository.

Q's new heart-health algorithm prescribes two shots of espresso at four-hour intervals to help me concentrate despite my lack of sleep, and Q sets my espresso machine accordingly. I also get an immediate calendar entry notification for a thirty-minute nap at 3:00 p.m. which Q has set. I think this is complete nonsense. What am I, a toddler? I cancel this set of actions. I hotfoot it on over to the kitchen, where I see on the built-in screen on the fridge that Q has taken the liberty to order my favorite items that I'm out of, but she still refuses to order the bacon and hot dogs I love. I roll my eyes. While I'm in the kitchen rooting around for breakfast, Q reminds me that I haven't taken my multivitamin or heart meds yet. Q also informs me that my genetic therapy results show a predisposition for heart attack, but if I'm diligent in following the routines that she has personalized for me based on the doctor's heart-health algorithm, then I can live a long life.

When setting my personal health goals with Q, I said that I wanted to do stretches and drink sixty-four ounces of water every day. Q signals the smart fridge to dispense eight ounces into a glass. Suddenly, a holographic AI stretching instructor—whose build looks exactly like mine—pops up next to me while I'm chugging my water. I sputter and nearly choke from the surprise. "Q!" I scream at the top of my lungs, "You have to give me a countdown warning when you pop things up next to me—especially since it's a hologram. You'll *give* me a heart attack." Q responds, "Okay, would you like me to add that to my learning?" "Yes! Also remember that I can't stretch in the kitchen!" I walk through the virtual instructor so I can get to the living room where there's room for me to stretch.

There, I see the hologram better, and what she's wearing looks freaking amazing. Since Q is also designed to sell workout wear, I had the option of making the virtual instructor's avatar mirror my exact proportions. It was easy. I basically just stepped into a lighted grid projected on me by a scanning device that immediately up-loaded all my proportions. Then an AI matching algorithm selected outfits based on my favorites on the online retailer sites I use most often. I'll be honest, I'm more incentivized to work out because I can't wait to see the latest activewear on my avatar than I am to do the stretching and yoga. But hey, whatever motivates, right?

Just as I'm about to tell Q to order the outfit on the AI avatar, my mom's avatar arrives. I knew I should have set the holograms communications to "do not disturb." I give the avatar permission to arrive anyway. My mom's avatar is sitting, and she's having a hard time breathing. She can't talk. Her AI assistant has activated an emergency care protocol designed to tell and show me what is happening with my mom especially when she cannot do so her-self. My avatar projects back at her, "Mom, can you talk?" She's grabbing her chest. Mom's AI informs me that she is having a heart attack, and it came on suddenly. Her AI has contacted 911. Help is on the way. My mom's AI had been trained by the Bedside Cardiologists Group (BCG). Mom and I picked their AI because they were known for building a good bedside manner into their heart-health assistants with added empathy training. The empathy training included contacting family and loved ones in an emer-gency. According to BCG, patients' mindsets were key for survival in these life-or-death situations. I thank God, ironically, for this ability to be there for my mom even though she lives two states away from me. "Mom, I'm here with you. Please hang in there." I watch as a little drone brings her nitroglycerin pills and water. She takes them, and her AI assistant unlocks the smart home's doors so the emergency response team can get to her quickly. Then the worst happens: she passes out.

Q informs me that my blood pressure is rising dramatically, and I may faint too if I don't calm down. I watch as a defibrillator robot rolls out from under the couch, finds my mom, and imme-diately attaches to send her a bolt of energy. She revives, and I let out a sigh of relief. Mom had been fitted for her defibrillator robot the same way I had been fitted for my clothing avatar, except her measurements were taken while she laid in various positions on the floor. She kidded me at the time, "What if I get too fat for my AED [automated external defibrillator] bot?"

Q has full access to the vitals on Mom's smartwatch during emergency protocol as agreed to by Mom and me in advance. In order to calm me, Q informs me Mom's heart rate is back to normal and reminds me to breathe. Q has learned from other emergencies that I calm down faster when I am focused on doing something. I escalate the more helpless I feel. To distract me and focus my attention on doing something helpful, Q asks permission to book me on the soonest flight. I say, "Yes, Q. No budget constraints this time. Just get me there." Q tells me, "On it! Now breathe. If we can lower your heart rate by five beats per minute, you definitely won't faint." Q's right; I feel absolutely nauseated and light-headed. I watch the paramedics take Mom away on a stretcher. I ask which hospital they are taking her to so Q can order flowers and set up a car service to pick me at the airport and take me straight to her when I arrive. I take a moment to breathe and start to feel less panicky and nauseated.

Q lets me know that, just like last time, it will supervise my mom's AI personal assistant. Mom and I agreed in advance that if anything ever happened to her, my AI assistant would supervise hers to ensure duties that require her permission will instead come to me. As a result, Q lets me know that Mom's AI had given her permission to submit her heart attack warning symptoms to the Bedside Cardiologist Group to help them train their AI. I give my permission as well. It's what Mom would want, and I'm feeling especially loyal to that group given that they never take our privacy for granted, and, oh yeah—they have saved her life twice now. The warning symptoms are logged by her AI assistant and sent to her doctor digitally along with her unified care record and personalized medicine routines.

I could go on forever with examples in every industry from healthcare to retail to government services of how AI can work to help us as individuals and as a society. The fun is really in combining multiple learning systems with other fun technologies like augmented reality (which uses cameras and screens or digital glasses to show us digital things next to real life, like the Pokémon creatures in the Pokémon Go game); virtual reality (which uses goggles to show us entire interactive digital worlds and people); holograms (light projections that reflect images of people or places right next to us as though they are in the room); drones (like the one that delivered my mom's nitroglycerin pills); robots (like the AED bot); connected sensors and devices (like the water bottle sensor and the fridge, the espresso maker, the smart home, and thermostat).

AI could literally save your life, drive you around, book your appointments, keep up with your medicines, allow the elderly to stay in their homes longer, extend our lives, help us prevent accidents, experience places we could never go (like inside volcanoes), and protect humans from biohazards and weapons. It could help us find the right pair of jeans instead of having to try on fifty pair at the store to get one that actually fits. (Women everywhere know what I'm talking about.) It could help us be present at both our kid's recital and an important business meeting on the other side of the world. But none of these amazing scenarios is possible if we cannot trust the AI or the companies behind the AI. In the example story, there are underpinnings at work that make the AI worth trusting.

The AI Trust Pledge and the 12 Tenets of Trust

There are 12 tenets which we need those who fund and develop AI solutions to follow if we are ever going to trust AI. Just like Alcoholics Anonymous has a twelve-step program to reform the ways of those who are alcohol-addicted, this is a twelve-step program for data scientists and developers to take a leadership role in reforming the "move fast and break things" culture that AI has grown up in. If you have read this book, this far, you know all the bad things that can happen when AI goes awry. Help me get companies and their AI creators and investors to take the AI Trust Pledge by signing up on the AI Truth.org website. The Pledge isn't just words—no virtue signaling allowed—it's a program with accountability, mentorship and measurement built around the following 12 Tenets of Trust.

1. Humane

> Sometimes creators of AI solutions don't start with the basic question of *Is this an appropriate or humane use of AI? Could the AI cause more harm than good if developed?* For example, many in the field of AI ethics feel that autonomous weapons should never have been developed and that facial recognition for surveillance and law enforcement purposes is biased and incorrect, not to mention a huge violation of privacy. Any applications of AI where safety is also a huge concern should be thoroughly vetted by an objective and diverse AI ethics board of advisors.

2. Consensual

> Was permission actively sought and given for the purpose of the specific AI that was developed, or was my data stolen from me or used in a context that it was not approved? I think of cases of AI in hiring where social media data such as Facebook or Twitter feeds have been used to give employers a behavioral analysis completely unbeknownst to a job candidate who was ruled out before they even knew they could apply. Timing and context are crucial in understanding statements and sentiments of job candidates. To exclude them from a job opportunity based on something in their Twitter feed from their youth seems unfair.

3. Transparent

> Do I even know when AI is being used to influence decisions that affect my life, livelihood, or happiness? If you don't know an algorithm is being used in your healthcare, you may not know the decision-making features that went into it. You definitely won't have the ability to change incorrect information or question the AI's logic if you don't know it exists in the first place. Transparency enables you to act on the next three steps.

4. Accessible

Is there a place I can go online or in an app to see documentation of everything related to the AI's development? This includes the data that was used, timing of the data, how it was collected, the decision-making criteria that were used, and the general logic used to guide the algorithm.

5. Agency-imbuing

Can I change the algorithm's recommendation or input data if it includes incorrect information about me? Of course, agency is also contingent on you knowing that your data was used in the first place and that you have access to the information and can obtain an explanation about what the algorithm is doing and how it affects you. When AI solution creators build in options for customers to give input into their algorithms, this provides the creators with a human feedback loop, which is essential for accuracy.

6. Explainable

Can I understand the conclusions the AI came to and the reasons why? Doctors who participated in a program to prevent sepsis—a life-threatening infection that one out of three people who die in a hospital have—would not heed an AI's recommendations about patients who might potentially contract sepsis because the doctors could not understand *why* it recommended the patients it recommended. Without a good reason to prescribe antibiotics in advance of sepsis developing, they ignored it. Making AI explainable, especially in this Wild West period of AI, is the key to trust. Some renowned data scientists will argue that the whole point of AI is to take in vast amounts of data—beyond a human's ability to process and comprehend—and have the algorithms spit out recommendations or meaningful insights so we can then act. It is easy to give an explanation when simplistic algorithms like linear regressions are used. But it is incredibly difficult to understand the key pieces of data that a complex neural net may have weighted more heavily. Data scientists would tell you that they could test a complex neural net's ability to predict an outcome with 96 percent accuracy, or they could use a more simplistic method that would bring the accuracy down to 76 percent. They would say, in life-or-death matters, "which would you prefer?" But in this Wild West period, I prefer the simple one: human decision-making. Because right now, those in the field of data science have not proven themselves to be careful watchers and protectors of people. Instead, they will slap together algorithms as quickly as they think they can make money from the words "artificial intelligence" at the beginning of their products. Until this mentality changes and there is more proven rigor in the development of high-impact algorithms, then, just like the doctors in the sepsis watch program, I'm not ready to accept AI's decisions about me—regardless of "accuracy" rates.

7. Private and Secure

Does the AI compromise my information or make it available for any cause, good or bad? For example, if a hate group wanted to intimidate a journalist from speaking out against them, could they easily gain access to an AI calendaring/mapping app that could tell them when and where that journalist might be? Does the data open me up to hacking by collecting all my valuable data in one place like a pot of gold and then leaving the doors wide open for anyone to get it? A healthcare AI vendor was recently found guilty of storing large amounts of patient data for a hospital project unbeknownst to the patients. That vendor then left the data unsecured, leaving patients at risk of identity theft and fraud.

8. Unbiased and Correct

Was the data used to train and develop the AI system based on sound data standards as outlined below?

Data Quality. Can the data science team ensure against "overfitting" their model because of bad data quality issues? Failure by the data science team to check their data sources for things like missing fields, sparsely populated fields, and inconsistently or incorrectly labelled data and fields can all lead to a situation called "overfitting" where the algorithm does not have enough information to make good decisions. An example of a missing field is when the field "State" is listed as being present in the data set, but upon inspection, the "State" field has no data in it at all. Sparse population of fields is when, for example, "City" is only listed in half of the rows of data, or fields have too many different entries to be consistent for analysis (such as Tx/Texas/TX), or data is incorrectly labelled (such as a picture of Texas labelled as New York). A recent study showed that data from the most-used data sets for AI were labelled incorrectly up to 30 percent of the time.

Data Constitution and Bias. It sounds dumb, but data scientists do not always check to see if the data they are using to train their algorithms is made up of mostly new data or old, outdated data. Many of the most-used data sets not only contain errors as mentioned above in the section on data quality but also contain biases toward genders, races, cultures. Examples of why this can be important include AI for uses in hiring and policing. For hiring, many historical databases are largely made up of male employees. But if the stated purpose of an algorithm is to hire diverse candidates from a pool made up of women and men, then you can't train the algorithm on mostly male data. It needs data on females too. The same goes for an algorithm that would recommend policing tactics. If you want to increase the number of convictions, then you can base your training data on false bookings from older data from a time when intimidation bookings were the norm. But intimidation bookings did not result in convictions. We need data scientists to rigorously understand the data constitution and the biases that would cause it to be unfit for the purposes for which they are trying to use it. This will lessen false arrests and increase diversity in hiring.

Data Proxies. Data scientists can also be in a hurry to get a patent or be the first to market and decide to simply use a "proxy" for the data they need. They do this because it can sometimes be hard to find data, or they may be able to build the data, but it would take a lot of money and time to do so. Instead, they often try to find a proxy for that data. An example is the tendency of data scientists to use credit scores in place of knowing whether a person is "responsible." They tend to do this a lot in insurance. The assumption is that if you are responsible with your money, then you will be responsible with the asset they are insuring for you, such as a car or home. The problem is that credit scores don't necessarily translate when it comes to long commutes where there is prolonged exposure to potential traffic accidents, and they don't not determine if I'm a safe driver. There are plenty of people who have high credit scores but bad driving histories. In fact, using credit histories to determine auto insurance rates could penalize the poor who need good insurance rates the most.

9. Accountable

If any part of the AI system malfunctions, has the company declared people responsible for fixing it? This is another one that sounds dumb on the surface, but because of the way data science gets done inside of companies, it's a gap that needs attention. With demand so high for data scientists, there's significant turnover and often no one familiar with the original algorithm is left to repair and maintain it.

10. Traceability

Can a company tell which part of an AI system went wrong

and when it happened? From the data sources to the final application and results the AI is providing, could an AI creator or partner figure out how many people were adversely affected by an algorithm or erroneous data and notify them? When the Cambridge Analytica scandal hit, Facebook could not determine the exact people who had been manipulated by ads on their platform from the data brokerage firm. The impact was huge—something on the order of 87 million US voters were affected. The ability to be notified when something goes terribly wrong or could be highly manipulative to us is very important.

11. Feedback-incorporating

Does the AI solution provide ways for users or experts to give input into the AI system's ongoing learning? In this chapter's opening story, Mom always sent in her warning symptoms to help with the continual feedback for the training of the BCG algorithm. Feedback loops are the best way to preempt bias and prevent data or algorithm drift. In some AI, it would be as easy as having users provide a thumbs-up or -down for each recommendation or classification the AI makes. If it's an AI in a hiring application, then hiring managers could thumbs-up or -down each hire. If it's a credit score or data that determines insurance premiums, then the thumbs-up or -down could apply to the correctness or relevance of a piece of data. Other feedback loops could come in the form of periodic quizzes: "Would you like to answer a few questions to help us better tailor your selections?" Users then can contribute to their own profile. This also builds in consent and agency.

12. Governed and Rectifiable

Governance. Data scientists who develop AI tend to set it then literally forget it. But this is a huge mistake, because AI is constantly learning. To do this, AI is continuously incorporating data which is shaping its recommendations, classifications, and—when paired with automation—its actions. There are two common problems that can lead to AI that malfunctions *after* it's been set up. One is *data drift,* which is an unexpected and undocumented change to data structure, semantics, or infrastructure. To give you an example, a farmer could change a harvester's broken sensor from an American brand to a Chinese brand, and instead of the sensor giving readings in pounds, it now gives them in kilograms. This seemingly insignificant repair just caused the crop forecasting algorithm to miscalculate the volume of crops because it was trained to incorporate readings in pounds—not kilograms.

The second problem is *model drift.* This is when the relationships between the thing you are trying to predict and the things you are using as indicators to predict it change. For example, a threshold for a decision changes. Let's say a cutoff income level that used to be considered creditworthy at $50,000 is now no longer considered creditworthy because it was boosted to $80,000. My model would still try to offer credit to the lower income level. This is why constant monitoring, tweaking, and fixing of the data and AI models is critical to ensure the AI is still working as planned and is based on correct data.

Rectification. Does the AI-solution provider have established processes for when things go wrong? Are those processes available to review by the larger public or regulatory agencies? If 60 million people are targeted with the help of an erroneous AI algorithm and are given incorrect voting information, for example, does the company have a plan to resolve it? Would they have a plan to notify the targeted people? This, of course, assumes there is monitoring and governing of AI that can alert people to the problem in the first place. Most companies have not taken it this far. Rarely will we find companies monitoring for potential disaster, much less having a plan for when disaster strikes. I assume that if disaster strikes, it would be a public relations and legal affair as opposed to a proactive plan that would give the public peace of mind. This is even more concerning when we consider self-driving cars, robot-assisted surgeries, and automated weapons. Or even AI-automated oil rigs in the ocean that could potentially unleash another Deepwater Horizon.

Corporations do not currently adhere to all the tenets of the AI Trust Pledge. They may abide by some of them, but certainly not all. Why? Because complying with those tenets will cost money, time, people, and effort. So far, there hasn't been a great enough external reward or punishment for them to tackle these issues. There certainly have not been any financial disincentives strong enough to deter companies from creating or using haphazard AI. This is why lawmakers must act. Just like we have critical regulatory oversight in important areas like finance and civil rights to protect the interests of everyday citizens, we need laws and regulations based on the 12 Tenets of Trust to hold the companies developing high-stakes AI solutions accountable for the intended and unintended consequences of their actions.

How to Affect Action on the Tenets

In an era where the average citizen's voice is easily lost what can you do to use your newfound awareness of the myriad of problems AI can cause, what can you do to make difference?

Exercise your rights: Vote for AI-educated policy makers willing to take action and write your congresspeople to let them know about the AI Trust Pledge. Encourage your local, state, and federal policy makers to educate themselves on these AI related issues, commit to the AI Trust Pledge, and pass laws that keep companies and government entities accountable for the ramifications of their actions when they develop and use AI.

Use your money: Invest in companies who adhere to these tenets and divest of any stocks from companies that violate the 12 Tenets of Trust. Companies that commit to the Pledge in a real way and document their progress will be less risky financially and won't have their infrastructure sent into chaos as policy is authored and implemented to protect the data of citizens.

Organize for change: If you work for a company using AI in ways you're not comfortable with—or even if you simply want to ensure you are being responsible in your development of AI—organize an internal group who can work to tackle the 12 Tenets of Trust as collaborators. Organize by your AI initiative. Brainstorm on ways to enact the 12 tenets. Then formulate your own plan for how you will tackle each of the 12 tenets.

Decisions corporate AI systems make about us will determine our futures. There are a few key groups that can impact corporations internally as well as put external pressure on them. While I have given you plenty of ways in the previous chapters to advocate for yourself during this AI Wild West period, there are a few other groups out there that you need to know about that can help us all as a society. We should ensure we use our collective bargaining power as "We the People" to help influence them to do their part in protecting our futures in the AI era.

Take Your Part in Saving the World

AI Buyside.

Are You: An executive in marketing, healthcare, government, insurance, operations, finance, and human resources who funds or initiates AI programs? You can play a key role in setting us on a course to civilized AI.

Problem: Most executives who fund AI initiatives don't know much about how AI works or how it is developed. There is a huge gap between what they know and what the data scientists know. Because of what they don't know about how AI is developed, these executives can place unrealistic time frames and cost pressures that snowball into data scientists cutting corners to meet targets. The result can be biased AI, using proxy data instead of creating proper data, and not testing in the field, which can lead to safety issues—anyone want an improperly trained autonomous vehicle?

Call to Action: Take control of your fiduciary responsibility as a funder of AI programs or suffer these consequences.

- AI that is unscalable. AI that can't be put to use.

- AI that doesn't realize a return on investment.

- Negative impacts on brand and recognition.

- Major safety issues that could result in death and societal harms.

To prevent these risks, leverage your networks to influence and encourage your fellow initiators and funders of AI to take the following steps towards civilized AI:

- Hire an AI ethics consultant.

- Create an AI ethics advisory panel.

- Ensure the panel is filled with a diverse range of experts rich in different backgrounds, genders, cultures, socio-economic, and political interests.

- Employ an AI ethics department to take a proactive role in certifying that no AI initiatives will cross the creepy line or puts cost reductions or efficiencies above people's safety, liberties, and well-being.

Bottom Line: If you wouldn't want the AI product you're developing used on you, then don't let it loose on unsuspecting people.

AI Safekeepers.

Are You: Someone whose role it is to avert risk and legal exposure, ensure returns on investments, meet regulatory guidelines, and provide security, privacy, and peace of mind for customers and stakeholders? Are you an executive in the field of data, data science, analytics, information technology, information security, privacy, legal, and ethics and compliance?

Problem: As a society, we need them to provide internal oversight of AI projects. Right now, these executives fall into two categories: 1) those who do not know enough about how AI works to provide adequate safeguards inside their organizations, and 2) those who know enough about AI but do not know when, how, or what to push back on.

Call to Action:

- Work with AI ethicists to develop corporate-wide AI policies and mandatory training programs: Set up governance and monitoring of existing AI projects. Ensure systems of accountability are in place to incentivize responsible behavior while discouraging risky behaviors.

- Prevent unethical AI vendors from being procured at your company by mandating adherence to vendor selection frameworks.

- Weed out vendors using irresponsible AI practices from procurement consideration by leveraging vendor selection frameworks specifically designed for this purpose. The World Economic Forum, for example, has put out some useful frameworks for various executives (e.g., the chief human resources officer) to use when working with AI service providers.

Bottom Line: As a society we need you to provide internal oversight of AI projects to keep us all safe.

AI Suppliers.

Are You: An AI consultant, product developer, or designer supplying AI solutions to the marketplace? Are you someone whose operating models, or lack thereof, are determining how responsible and ethical AI is right now?

Problem: The majority of AI initiatives are generated by AI startups; larger consulting firms like IBM, Accenture, or Tata, who build custom solutions; and business process automation vendors like UiPath, AntWorks, or Automation Anywhere. Tight timeframes and fragmented AI ethics doctrines cause most AI consulting professionals and product developers to throw their hands up in frustration. Even though you want to innovate responsibly often you are not given the time or the budget to do so.

Call to Action:

- Enforce strict standards around AI development and operating methods. If you're an AI consultant, while onsite with your corporate clients, take charge in educating and guiding them on these methods.

- Hire AI ethicists and include them at every stage of an AI project from the design stage forward. When possible, hire certified AI developers and seek certification for your AI initiatives.

- Create and enforce policies that allow consultants or developers to easily say no to work that is unethical that a client may request.

- If you are an AI developer, you can seek certification for yourself and also for your AI initiative or product. There are new certifications from technology standards organizations like the Institute of Electrical and Electronics Engineers (IEEE) as well as the AI Trust Pledge from my nonprofit AI Truth.

Bottom Line: You have the power to choose your clients. Walk away from projects you're not comfortable with. If you want to learn more about red flags regarding clients and AI initiatives read my blog called "10 Signs You Might Want To Walk Away from an AI Initiative" on AITruth.org.

Educators.

Are You: An educator, parent, or student in the United States at any level from elementary to graduate school?

Problem: As a democratic society we must prepare our students for responsible, ethical AI. China has taken the lead in preparing students for the AI era, and not just university students but primary and secondary school students as well. This is part of China's plan to dominate the world using their thirty-year AI strategy. To say they are taking AI education seriously compared to the rest of the world is a huge understatement. This should scare all of us given their denigration of democracy and proliferation of products and services in the US and abroad. AI is not a requirement in any schools in the US at any level. A recent panel which included members from MIT's Computer Science and Artificial Intelligence Laboratory, Google, Baidu, and DeepMind agreed that education is the single most important factor affecting the future of ethical AI.

Call to Action:

- Ensure our kids will have the high-level know-how to combat any unethical AI in the future and enable them to obtain the needed skills for the AI era.

- Parents, advocate through school boards and local politicians for more AI and computer science classes.

- Teachers, find AI teaching resources online at the AI4ALL website. AI4ALL is a nonprofit devoted to educating kids on AI and AI ethics. Find these resources at ai-4-all.org.

- Students, enroll in AI camps and afterschool programs offered by universities and neighborhood coding schools.

Bottom Line: As parents and teachers, we must advocate to ensure students in the United States receive a competitive education which includes AI, so our country and our economy remain at the forefront of innovation. As AI becomes more pervasive in driving change in society, we need a generation of bright young minds ready to tackle the challenges of the AI era.

Lawmakers and Lawyers.

Are You: A lawmaker, lawyer, or a member of EEOC, FDA, and FTC?

Problem: There are virtually no laws regarding data privacy or AI right now, yet AI is a technology that could kill you, convict you, and reveal your secrets. There are no laws at a national level that protect your data in the US. Even as facial recognition is being used by many police departments across the US, no laws regulating its use have been enacted nationally. Even as hiring algorithms are blatantly biased against women, there are no laws. AI vendors continue scraping your data and bartering it back and forth with some of the most un- scrupulous data brokers out there. Yet there are still no laws.

Call to Action:

- Lawyers, provide oversight of AI initiatives, help inform corporate policies on responsible AI practices, and advise clients of the latest in responsible AI practices. Maintain awareness of risks associated with AI development in your corporation or with your corporate clients if you are in a law firm.

- Lawmakers, educate yourself on the risks of AI to the public. Great job reading through this book or having your aide read through this book. Use your position to craft legislation to protect your constituents from poorly developed AI.

- EEOC, FDA, and FTC investigators, prosecutors and judges, you do not need to understand AI to see the disparate impact that results. Your mandate remains to protect people when it comes to hiring, housing, lending, and healthcare. The laws you need to combat irresponsible AI already exist.

Bottom Line: You are the front line in fighting biased AI.

We the People have a lot of work to do. What you don't know could hurt you, but if you're equipped with knowledge and awareness, you can enjoy all the amazing benefits of AI in the future.

ACKNOWLEDGMENTS

Speak up for those who cannot speak for themselves...

—Proverbs 31:8

There comes a time in our lives when we feel an urging in our souls—a stirring. At first, we may not know what it means or what it wants. But if we listen carefully, there's something moving us toward our specific purpose. For me, this happened back in June 2017 when *The Purpose Driven Life* fell off a bookshelf and onto my toe. (The Lord works in mysterious ways). I read it, and as my calling became clearer with each passing page and prayer, I made a promise to myself and the Lord. I have been blessed with a career that has gifted me with a perspective which not many people in the world have...I have seen how AI was created and developed behind closed doors at some of the world's biggest and most powerful industries and companies. If not me, then who? I promised to write a book and take on the AI ethics mission to help everyone who was not behind those doors understand how these life-altering data decisions can affect them.

I thank God for the honor of writing this book for you, and I sincerely pray that you learned something that will help you defend yourself against bad AI should you encounter it—and hopefully praise the creators of good AI when you experience it. I could not have done this without the Lord's guidance.

On that note, I thank Jill Marsal of the Marsal Lyon Literary Agency, who was literally an answer to a prayer (and a calling). In pandemic times, when almost every person I know was writing a book and trying to get it published, she persevered in sending this book project everywhere. I am so grateful for her never-ending efforts and belief in this project. I also thank Post Hill Press and Debra Englander, who has been wonderful to work with.

To my dear sweet husband, I cannot thank you enough for your ceaseless support, late-night shoulder rubs, loving reminders, and take-out dinners. Thanks for not only cleaning the plates but taking stuff off my plate and accepting all that I threw at you with grace, patience, and kindness. I could not have dreamt up a more thoughtful partner if I tried. To my daughter, Landrie, and niece, Chloe, thanks for helping me research more about the self-harm and suicide challenges that kids and teens experience on social media. Thanks to my sister, Lindsey Kincade for her contributions to Chapter 12. To my mom, dad, sister, grandad, and Pat and Kenneth, thank you for all the support and encouragement.

Thanks to Karen Suber, whom I connected with almost as soon as I started this journey and who agreed to start AI Truth with me. She's one of those people you meet for the first time and feel like you've known them your whole life. Her tireless encouragement and enthusiasm over the last few years has kept me energized and sane!

It's weird to think of tackling AI ethics as a spiritual journey, but it has been for me. Thanks to the Riverside Church of Christ Ladies Group and the leadership team for their ongoing prayers and moral support. Thanks for being my guinea pigs even when you had no idea in the beginning what AI was or why it mattered. Your feedback helped me simplify complex concepts so "normal" people (versus "techies") could understand.

I want to thank all of the amazing warriors working in the field of AI ethics, many of whom are colleagues on the *Springer*

Nature AI and Ethics Journal. I want to thank John MacIntyre and Larry Medsker for tirelessly encouraging the field and giving voice to it by pursuing the launch of the journal with Springer Nature. I especially want to thank Merve Hickok for her input on the hiring chapter.

Finally, I want to thank all the amazing data and analytics leaders out there who have shaped my thinking and shared their learned lessons with me over the years. I feel like our community is more like family than colleagues. No other professionals I know come together to share best practices so freely to solve some of the biggest, hairiest, spaghetti-ist (that's a word in data and analytics) data problems on the planet. They do so with open minds and hearts, humility, and a little self-deprecating humor. I can't say enough how grateful I am to know you and call you friends. I hope I will always see you at the MIT Chief Data Officer events and Corinium events.

ENDNOTES

1   John Callaham, "What Is Google Duplex and How Do You Use It?" Android Authority, May 21, 2021, https://www.androidauthority.com/what-is-google-duplex-869476/

2   Herb Booth, "UTA Patent Gives Robots Extra Sensitive Skin," University of Texas at Arlington, August 8, 2018, https://www.uta.edu/news/news-releases/2018/08/08/smart-skin-patent-celik-butler

3   George I. Seffers, "Researchers Have Artificial Skin in Robotics Game," Signal 75, December 1, 2018, https://www.afcea.org/content/researchers-have-artificial-skin-robotics-game

4   University of Washington, "Flexible 'skin' can help robots, prosthetics perform everyday tasks by sensing shear force," ScienceDaily, October 17, 2017, Retrieved November 2, 2021 from www.sciencedaily.com/releases/2017/10/171017124350.htm

5   Laura Yan, "These Artificial Nerves Could Allow Prosthetic Limbs to Feel," Popular Mechanics, June 3, 2018, https://www.popularmechanics.com/science/health/a21061916/artificial-nerve-allow-prosthetic-limb-to-feel/

6   John Kennedy, "How Digital Disruption Changed 8 Industries Forever," Silicon Republic, November 25, 2015, https://www.siliconrepublic.com/companies/digital-disruption-changed-8-industries-forever

7   Mark Foster, "The Virtual Enterprise," IBM, https://www-935.
     ibm.com/services/us/gbs/thoughtleadership/accelentreinvent/

8   LifeBEAM, "Vi. The First True Artificial Intelligence Personal
     Trainer," Kickstarter, February 7, 2018, https://www.kickstart-
     er.com/projects/1050572498/vi-the-first-true-artificial-intelli-
     gence-personal?token=2754b4ee

9   Natasha Lomas, "FitGenie is Applying AI to Automate Nutrition
     Planning," TechCrunch," August 29, 2017, https://techcrunch.
     com/2017/08/29/fitgenie-is-applying-ai-to-automate-nutri-
     tion-planning/

10   N. Lee, "Apple Acquires AI Tech That Seeks to Understand Your
     Photos," Engadget, September 30, 2017, https://www.engadget.
     com/2017/09/30/apple-regaind-machine-learning-acquisition/

11   Caitlin Fairchild, "Do You Ever Feel Like Somebody's Watching
     You?" Nextgov, February 20, 2018, https://www.nextgov.com/
     emerging-tech/2018/02/nvidia-makes-facial-recognition-ai-sur-
     veilance/146064/

12   "How to Make a Chatbot," Botpress, https://botpress.io/learn/
     how-to

13   Jeff Bounds, "Your Next Lender Could Be A Computer," *D
     CEO*, January-February 2018, https://www.dmagazine.com/
     publications/d-ceo/2018/january-february/financial-lending-
     computers-ai/

14   Bernard Marr, "Machine Learning In Practice: How Does Am-
     azon's Alexa Really Work?" *Forbes*, October 5, 2018, https://
     www.forbes.com/sites/bernardmarr/2018/10/05/how-does-
     amazons-alexa-really-work/

15   Darrell Etherington, "Amazon Echo Is A $199 Connected Speaker
     Packing An Always-On-Siri-Style Assistant," TechCrunch, Novem-
     ber 6, 2014, https://techcrunch.com/2014/11/06/amazon-echo/

16   Eugene Kim, "The Inside Story of How Amazon Created Echo,
     the Next Billion-Dollar Business No One Saw Coming," Busi-
     ness Insider, April 2, 2016, https://www.businessinsider.com/
     the-inside-story-of-how-amazon-created-echo-2016-4

17   "Alexa Skills Kit Glossary," Alexa developer documentation, accessed October 4, 2021, https://developer.amazon.com/docs/ask-overviews/alexa-skills-kit-glossary.html#s

18   Lionel Sujay Vailshery, "Total Number of Amazon Alexa Skills in Selected Countries as of January 2021," Statista, January 2021, https://www.statista.com/statistics/917900/selected-countries-amazon-alexa-skill-count/

19   According to CW6 in that city, their morning show anchor Jim Patton commented on the story and said, "I love the little girl, saying 'Alexa ordered me a dollhouse.'" The station reports that after Patton uttered those words, "viewers all over San Diego started complaining their echo devices had tried to order dollhouses." CBSDFW.com, "Amazon 'Alexa' Orders Dollhouses for Owners After 'Hearing' TV Report," CBS DFW, January 6, 2017, https://dfw.cbslocal.com/2017/01/06/amazon-alexa-orders-dollhouses-for-owners-after-hearing-tv-report/

20   "Amazon Announces New Echo Devices—Add Alexa to Every Room and Your Car," Amazon press release, September 20, 2018, https://press.aboutamazon.com/news-releases/news-release-details/amazon-announces-new-echo-devices-add-alexa-every-room-and-your

21   Mike Snider, "Apple CEO Tim Cook Supports Stricter Data Privacy Laws, Warns of 'Data Industrial Complex,'" USA Today, October 24, 2018, https://www.usatoday.com/story/tech/nation-now/2018/10/24/apple-ceo-tim-cook-calls-stricter-data-privacy-protections/1750919002/

22   Megan Farokhmanesh, "The Next Frontier in Hiring is AI-Driven," The Verge, January 30, 2019, https://www.theverge.com/2019/1/30/18202335/ai-artificial-intelligence-recruiting-hiring-hr-bias-prejudice

23   Ibid.

24   "Depression, PTSD, & Other Mental Health Conditions in the Workplace: Your Legal Rights," Equal Employment Opportunity Commission, December 12, 2016, https://www.eeoc.gov/laws/guidance/depression-ptsd-other-mental-health-conditions-workplace-your-legal-rights

25 Michael F. Bennet, et al., letter to Equal Employment Opportunity Commission chairman, December 8, 2020, https://www.bennet. senate.gov/public/_cache/files/0/a/0a439d4b-e373-4451-84ed-ba333ce6d1dd/672D2E4304D63A04CC3465C3C8BF1D21. letter-to-chair-dhillon.pdf

26 Diana Tsai, "80% Of Jobs Are Not On Job Boards: Here's How to Find Them," *Forbes*, October 2, 2017, https://www.forbes.com/ sites/dianatsai/2017/10/02/80-of-jobs-are-not-on-job-boards-heres-how-to-find-them/#633db266d455

27 Peter Cappelli, "Your Approach to Hiring is All Wrong," *Harvard Business Review*, May-June 2019, https://hbr.org/2019/05/ recruiting

28 JI-A Min, "12 Revealing Stats on How Recruiters Feel About AI," ideal, February 1, 2019, https://ideal.com/how-recruiters-feel-about-ai/

29 Gideon Mann and Cathy O'Neil, "Hiring Algorithms are Not Neutral," *Harvard Business Review*, December 9, 2016, https:// hbr.org/2016/12/hiring-algorithms-are-not-neutral

30 Peter Cappelli, "Your Approach to Hiring is All Wrong"

31 Drew Harwell, "A face-scanning algorithm increasingly decides whether you deserve the job," *Washington Post*, November 6, 2019, https://www.washingtonpost.com/technology/2019/10/22/ ai-hiring-face-scanning-algorithm-increasingly-decides-whether-you-deserve-job/

32 Customer case studies (2019), HireVue, https://www.hirevue. com/customers

33 Nicole Lewis, "AI-Related Lawsuits are Coming," Society for Human Resources Management, November 1, 2019, https://www. shrm.org/resourcesandtools/hr-topics/technology/pages/ai-lawsuits-are-coming.aspx

34 Sam Daley, "Women in Tech Statistics for 2020," Built In, March 13, 2020, https://builtin.com/women-tech/women-in-tech-workplace-statistics

35   Samuel Gibbs, "Women Less Likely to be shown ads for high-paid jobs on Google, Study Shows," *The Guardian*, June 5, 2017, https://www.theguardian.com/technology/2015/jul/08/women-less-likely-ads-high-paid-jobs-google-study

36   Ibid.

37   "More Than Half of Employers Have Found Content on Social Media That Caused Them NOT to Hire a Candidate," CareerBuilder, August 9, 2018, https://www.prnewswire.com/news-releases/more-than-half-of-employers-have-found-content-on-social-media-that-caused-them-not-to-hire-a-candidate-according-to-recent-careerbuilder-survey-300694437.html

38   "Discrimination by Type," US Equal Employment Opportunity Commission, accessed July 4, 2020, https://www.eeoc.gov/discrimination-type

39   "More Than Half of Employers Have Found Content on Social Media That Caused Them NOT to Hire a Candidate," CareerBuilder, August 9, 2018

40   Ibid.

41   Ibid.

42   Ibid.

43   Drew Harwell, "A face-scanning algorithm increasingly decides whether you deserve the job," *Washington Post*, November 6, 2019

44   Rachel Withers, "Should Robots Be Conducting Job Interviews?" *Slate*, October 5, 2020, https://slate.com/technology/2020/10/artificial-intelligence-job-interviews.html

45   Ibid.

46   Ibid.

47   Joy Buolamwini and Timnit Gebru, "Gender Shades: Intersectional Accuracy Disparities in Commercial Gender Classification," *Proceedings of Machine Learning Research* 81:1–15, 2018, Conference on Fairness, Accountability, and Transparency, http://proceedings.mlr.press/v81/buolamwini18a/buolamwini18a.pdf

48   Eric Rosenbaum, "IBM can predict with 95 percent accuracy which employees will quit," CNBC, April 3, 2019, https://www.cnbc.com/2019/04/03/ibm-ai-can-predict-with-95-percent-accuracy-which-employees-will-quit.html

49   Carol Hymowitz, "Workers Have a Big Secret: Their Age," *Wall Street Journal*, November 17, 2019, https://www.wsj.com/articles/older-workers-have-a-big-secret-their-age-11574046301

50   Christopher Rowland, "Bosses Can Monitor Your Every Step," *Washington Post*, February 15, 2019), https://www.washingtonpost.com/business/economy/with-fitness-trackers-in-the-workplace-bosses-can-monitor-your-every-step--and-possibly-more/2019/02/15/75ee0848-2a45-11e9-b011-d8500644dc98_story.html

51   Shelby Webb, "Houston teachers to pursue lawsuit over secret evaluation system," *Houston Chronicle*, May 11, 2017, https://www.houstonchronicle.com/news/houston-texas/houston/article/Houston-teachers-to-pursue-lawsuit-over-secret-11139692.php

52   Andrea Miller, "More companies are using technology to monitor employees, sparking privacy concerns," ABC News, March 10, 2018, https://abcnews.go.com/amp/US/companies-technology-monitor-employees-sparking-privacy-concerns/story?id=53388270

53   Cybersecurity Insiders, "2021 Insider Threat Report sponsored by Gurucul", https://www.cybersecurity-insiders.com/wp-content/uploads/2021/06/2021-Insider-Threat-Report-Gurucul-Final-dd8f5a75.pdf

54   Ibid.

55   Antoine Gara, "Digital Reasoning: The AI Software Goldman Sachs And Steve Cohen Are Using To Track Traders," *Forbes*, Nov. 7, 2016, https://www.forbes.com/sites/antoinegara/2016/11/07/wall-streets-big-brother-the-startup-goldman-sachs-and-steve-cohen-are-using-to-track-traders/#1580a1627912

56   Drew Harwell, "Managers turn to surveillance software, always-on webcams to ensure employees are (really) working from home", *The Washington Post*, April 30, 2020, https://www.washingtonpost.com/technology/2020/04/30/work-from-home-surveillance/

57　Brian Kopp, "Nine Work Trends That HR Leaders Can't Ignore in 2021", *Gartner*, April 26, 2021, https://www.gartner.com/smarterwithgartner/9-work-trends-that-hr-leaders-cant-ignore-in-2021

58　Adriana Gardella, "Employer Sued For GPS-Tracking Salesperson 24/7," *Forbes*, June 5, 2015, https://www.forbes.com/sites/adrianagardella/2015/06/05/employer-sued-for-gps-tracking-salesperson-247/#5a42a44623e3

59　Ibid.

60　Eric Rosenbaum, "IBM can predict with 95 percent accuracy which employees will quit," CNBC, April 3, 2019

61　Daniel Wiessner, "IBM laid off older workers in push to recruit millennials—lawsuit," Reuters, September 17, 2018, https://www.reuters.com/article/employment-ibm/ibm-laid-off-older-workers-in-push-to-recruit-millennials-lawsuit-idUSL2N-1W401K

62　Eric Rosenbaum, "IBM can predict with 95 percent accuracy which employees will quit," CNBC, April 3, 2019

63　Eric Rosenbaum, "How IBM AI Predicts With 95 Percent Accuracy Who Is About To Quit Their Job," The Lowdown, April 7, 2019, https://www.thelowdownblog.com/2019/04/how-ibm-ai-predicts-with-95-percent.html

64　"The ZipRecruiter Future of Work Report," ZipRecruiter, June 27, 2019, https://www.ziprecruiter.com/blog/future-of-work-report-2019/

65　"The evolution of process automation," IBM Institute for Business Value, https://www.ibm.com/downloads/cas/WJGLKJVM

66　"AI Today, AI Tomorrow," ARM Report, https://www.arm.com/solutions/artificial-intelligence/survey

67　Catherine Clifford, "The 'Oracle of A.I.': These 4 kinds of jobs won't be replaced by robots," CNBC, January 14, 2019, https://www.cnbc.com/2019/01/14/the-oracle-of-ai-these-kinds-of-jobs-will-not-be-replaced-by-robots-.html

68   Lydia Dishman, "Is AI killing jobs? Actually, it added 3x more than it replaced in 2018," *Fast Company*, June 27, 2019, https://www.fastcompany.com/90369739/is-ai-killing-jobs-actually-it-added-3x-more-in-2018

69   Arwa Mahdawi, "What jobs will still be around in 20 years? Read this to prepare your future," *The Guardian*, June 26, 2017, https://www.theguardian.com/us-news/2017/jun/26/jobs-future-automation-robots-skills-creative-health

70   "Lee Sedol vs AlphaGo Move 37 reactions and analysis," YouTube video, January 5, 2018, https://www.youtube.com/watch?v=HT-UZkiOLv8

71   Sigal Samuel, "How One Scientist Coped When AI Beat Him At His Life's Work," Vox, February 15, 2019, https://www.vox.com/future-perfect/2019/2/15/18226493/deepmind-alphafold-artificial-intelligence-protein-folding

72   Ibid.

73   Naomi Rea, "Why One Collector Bought a Work of Art Made by Artificial Intelligence—and Is Open to Acquiring More," Artnet, April 3, 2018, https://news.artnet.com/art-world/art-made-by-artificial-intelligence-1258745

74   Gabe Cohen, "AI Art at Christie's Sells for $432,500," *New York Times*, October 25, 2018, https://www.nytimes.com/2018/10/25/arts/design/ai-art-sold-christies.html

75   Jason Bailey, "The AI Art at Christie's Is Not What You Think," Artnome, October 13, 2018, https://www.artnome.com/news/2018/10/13/the-ai-art-at-christies-is-not-what-you-think

76   Paul Farrell, "Ring Camera Hackings: 5 Fast Facts You Need to Know," heavy.com, December 12, 2019, https://heavy.com/news/2019/12/ring-camera-hackings/

77   Catherine Stupp, "Fraudsters Used AI to Mimic CEO's Voice in Unusual Cybercrime Case," *Wall Street Journal*, August 30, 2019, https://www.wsj.com/articles/fraudsters-use-ai-to-mimic-ceos-voice-in-unusual-cybercrime-case-11567157402

78   Ed Stacey, "As AI Becomes More Ever Capable, Will It End Up Helping, Or Hindering, The Hackers?" *Forbes*, July 19, 2021, https://www.forbes.com/sites/edstacey/2021/07/19/as-ai-becomes-more-ever-capable-will-it-end-up-helping-or-hindering-the-hackers/?sh=4f8832ac324f

79   "88% of Security Leaders Say Supercharged AI Attacks are Inevitable," Darktrace, March 17, 2020, https://www.darktrace.com/en/press/2020/319/

80   Selena Larson, "A smart fish tank left a casino vulnerable to hackers," CNN Business, July 19, 2017, https://money.cnn.com/2017/07/19/technology/fish-tank-hack-darktrace/index.html

81   Mark Jones, "FBI issues dire warning about smart TVs and hackers," komando.com, December 2, 2019, https://www.komando.com/news/hackers-access-smart-tvs/694249/

82   "Global Data Broker Market Size, Share, Opportunities, COVID-19 Impact, And Trends By Data Type…End-User Industry…And Geography - Forecasts From 2021 To 2026," Knowledge Sourcing, June 2021, https://www.knowledge-sourcing.com/report/global-data-broker-market

83   Wolfie Christl, "Corporate Surveillance in Everyday Life," Cracked Labs, June 2017, https://crackedlabs.org/dl/CrackedLabs_Christl_CorporateSurveillance.pdf

84   Megan Molteni, "23andMe's Pharma Deals Have Been the Plan All Along," *Wired*, August 3, 2018, https://www.wired.com/story/23andme-glaxosmithkline-pharma-deal/

85   Christopher Zara, "The Dizzying Number Of CFPB Complaints Against Equifax Since 2012 Should Infuriate You," *Fast Company*, September 18, 2017, https://www.fastcompany.com/40469235/the-dizzying-number-of-cfpb-complaints-against-equifax-since-2012-should-infuriate-you

86   "Understanding Clarity Services by Experian," Lexington Law, April 29, 2021, https://www.lexingtonlaw.com/blog/credit-101/understanding-clarity-services-by-experian.html

87   Selena Larson, "Google will no longer read your emails to tailor ads," CNN Business, June 23, 2017, https://money.cnn.com/2017/06/23/technology/business/google-ad-scanning-email-stop/index.html

88   "Facebook Does Not Use Your Phone's Microphone for Ads or News Feed Stories," Facebook, June 2, 2016, https://about.fb.com/news/h/facebook-does-not-use-your-phones-microphone-for-ads-or-news-feed-stories/

89   "Is your phone listening in? Your stories," BBC News, October 30, 2017, https://www.bbc.com/news/technology-41802282

90   Jefferson Graham, "Is Facebook listening to me? Why those ads appear after you talk about things," *USA Today*, June 27, 2019, https://www.usatoday.com/story/tech/talkingtech/2019/06/27/does-facebook-listen-to-your-conversations/1478468001/

91   Sarah Frier, "Facebook Paid Contractors to Transcribe Users' Audio Chats," Bloomberg, August 13, 2019, https://www.bloomberg.com/news/articles/2019-08-13/facebook-paid-hundreds-of-contractors-to-transcribe-users-audio

92   Sam Nichols, "Your Phone Is Listening and It's Not Paranoia," Vice, June 4, 2018, https://www.vice.com/en/article/wjbzzy/your-phone-is-listening-and-its-not-paranoia

93   Minyvonne Burke, "Amazon's Alexa may have witnessed alleged Florida murder, authorities say," NBC News, November 2, 2019, https://www.nbcnews.com/news/us-news/amazon-s-alexa-may-have-witnessed-alleged-florida-murder-authorities-n1075621

94   "Is YouTube Watching Me? Mozilla Explains: Recommendation Engines," YouTube video, May 11, 2021, https://www.youtube.com/watch?v=pt9YCVX7VOkh

95   Lesley Stahl, "Aleksandr Kogan: The link between Cambridge Analytica and Facebook," *60 Minutes*, April 22, 2018, https://www.cbsnews.com/news/aleksandr-kogan-the-link-between-cambridge-analytica-and-facebook/

96   Sam Meredith, "Facebook-Cambridge Analytica: A timeline of the data hijacking scandal," CNBC, April 10, 2018, https://www.cnbc.com/2018/04/10/facebook-cambridge-analytica-a-timeline-of-the-data-hijacking-scandal.html

97   Lesley Stahl, "Aleksandr Kogan: The link between Cambridge Analytica and Facebook"

98   Ibid.

99   Corinne Reichert, "Clearview AI facial recognition customers reportedly include DOJ, FBI, ICE, Macy's," CNET, March 2, 2020, https://www.cnet.com/tech/services-and-software/clearview-ai-facial-recognition-customers-reportedly-include-ice-justice-department-fbi-macys/

100 Rebecca Heilweil, "From Macy's to Albertsons, facial recognition is already everywhere," Vox, June 19, 2021, https://www.vox.com/2021/7/15/22577876/macys-fight-for-the-future-facial-recognition-artificial-intelligence-stores

101 "Ban Facial Recognition in Stores" petition and data, https://www.banfacialrecognition.com/stores/#sign

102 Ibid.

103 Bennett Cyphers and Gennie Gebhart, "Behind the One-Way Mirror: A Deep Dive Into the Technology of Corporate Surveillance," Electronic Frontier Foundation, December 2019, https://www.eff.org/wp/behind-the-one-way-mirror

104 "How to Remove Yourself from Data Broker Sites," Privacy Bee, September 1, 2020, https://privacybee.com/blog/how-to-remove-yourself-from-data-broker-sites/

105 "Sean Parker—Facebook Exploits Human Vulnerability (We Are Dopamine Addicts)," YouTube video, November 11, 2017, https://www.youtube.com/watch?v=R7jar4KgKxs&t=58s

106 "New Report Finds Teens Feel Addicted to Their Phones, Causing Tension at Home," Common Sense Media, May 3, 2016, https://www.commonsensemedia.org/about-us/news/press-releases/new-report-finds-teens-feel-addicted-to-their-phones-causing-tension-at

107   Andrew Perrin and Sara Atske, "About three-in-ten U.S. adults say they are 'almost constantly' online," Pew Research Center, March 26, 2021, https://www.pewresearch.org/fact-tank/2021/03/26/about-three-in-ten-u-s-adults-say-they-are-almost-constantly-online/

108   Juliana Menasce Horowitz and Nikki Graf, "Most U.S. Teens See Anxiety and Depression as a Major Problem Among Their Peers," Pew Research Center, February 20, 2019, https://www.pewresearch.org/social-trends/2019/02/20/most-u-s-teens-see-anxiety-and-depression-as-a-major-problem-among-their-peers/

109   "Suicide and Self-Harm Injury," National Center for Health Statistics, April 7, 2020, retrieved October 28, 2020, https://www.cdc.gov/nchs/fastats/suicide.htm

110   "Sean Parker—Facebook Exploits Human Vulnerability."

111   Definition of "anxiety," lexico.com, https://www.lexico.com/en/definition/anxiety

112   Sophie Lewis, "Horrified mom discovers suicide instructions in video on YouTube and YouTube Kids," CBS News, February 23, 2019, https://www.cbsnews.com/news/youtube-kids-inappropriate-horrified-mom-discovers-suicide-instructions-in-video-on-youtube-and-youtube-kids/

113   "Shinsei Kamattechan—Ruru's Suicide Show on a Livestream Official Video (Animation)," YouTube video, January 8, 2020, https://youtu.be/hc0ZDaAZQT0

114   Joan E. Solsman, "YouTube recommendations serve up most videos viewers wish they'd never seen, study says," CNET, July 7, 2021, https://www.cnet.com/tech/services-and-software/youtube-recommendations-serve-up-the-most-videos-that-viewers-wish-theyd-never-seen-study-says/

115   MUSTAFA GATOLLARI, "The Roro Chan Challenge Is a Popular New Internet Trend With Severe Consequences," Distractify, July 27, 2020, https://www.distractify.com/p/roro-chan-challenge

116 Jemma Carr, "British schoolboy, 11, is blackmailed into cutting his own wrists by anonymous Instagram user playing sick 'blue whale' suicide 'game,'" *Daily Mail*, July 14, 2020, https://www.dailymail.co.uk/news/article-8521927/British-schoolboy-11-blackmailed-cutting-wrists.html

117 Brooke Auxier, Monica Anderson, Andrew Perrin and Erica Turner, "Parenting Children in the Age of Screens," Pew Research Center, July 28, 2020, https://www.pewresearch.org/internet/2018/05/31/teens-social-media-technology-2018/   and https://www.pewresearch.org/internet/2020/07/28/parenting-children-in-the-age-of-screens/

118 "Responding to Online Threats: minors' Perspectives on Disclosing, Reporting, and Blocking," Thorn.org, 2020, https://www.thorn.org/thorn-research-minors-perspectives-on-disclosing-reporting-and-blocking/

119 Brooke Auxier, Monica Anderson, Andrew Perrin and Erica Turner, "Parenting approaches and concerns related to digital devices," Pew Research Center, July 28, 2020, https://www.pewresearch.org/internet/2020/07/28/parenting-approaches-and-concerns-related-to-digital-devices/

120 Max Fisher and Amanda Taub, "On YouTube's Digital Playground, an Open Gate for Pedophiles," *New York Times*, June 3, 2019, https://www.nytimes.com/2019/06/03/world/americas/youtube-pedophiles.html

121 KG Orphanides, "On YouTube, a network of pedophiles is hiding in plain sight," *Wired UK*, February 20, 2019. https://www.wired.co.uk/article/youtube-pedophile-videos-advertising

122 Max Fisher and Amanda Taub, "On YouTube's Digital Playground, an Open Gate for Pedophiles"

123 "Responding to Online Threats: minors' Perspectives on Disclosing, Reporting, and Blocking"

124 KG Orphanides, "On YouTube, a network of pedophiles is hiding in plain sight."

125 "What Is Addiction?" *Psychology Today*, undated, https://www.psychologytoday.com/us/basics/addiction

126 Caitlin Johnston, "Human traffickers' new tool to lure children: online video games," *Tampa Bay Times*, January 21, 2019, https://www.tampabay.com/news/publicsafety/human-traffickers-new-tool-to-lure-children-online-video-games-20190121/

127 "Responding to Online Threats: minors' Perspectives on Disclosing, Reporting, and Blocking"

128 Definition of "troll," Urban Dictionary, https://www.urbandictionary.com/define.php?term=troll%20definition

129 "American Views 2020: Trust, Media and Democracy," Gallup/Knight Foundation Survey, November 9. 2020, https://knightfoundation.org/wp-content/uploads/2020/08/American-Views-2020-Trust-Media-and-Democracy.pdf

130 Ibid.

131 John D. McKinnon and Danny Dougherty, "Americans Hate Social Media but Can't Give It Up, WSJ/NBC News Poll Finds," *Wall Street Journal*, April 5, 2019, https://www.wsj.com/articles/americans-agree-social-media-is-divisive-but-we-keep-using-it-11554456600

132 Ibid.

133 Ibid.

134 "Americans See Broad Responsibilities for Government; Little Change Since 2019," Pew Research Center, May 17, 2021, https://www.pewresearch.org/politics/2021/05/17/americans-see-broad-responsibilities-for-government-little-change-since-2019/

135 Ibid.

136 Lee Rainie, Scott Keeter and Andrew Perrin, "Trust and Distrust in America," Pew Research Center, July 22, 2019, https://www.pewresearch.org/politics/2019/07/22/trust-and-distrust-in-america/

137 Cary Funk, Alec Tyson, Brian Kennedy, and Courtney Johnson, "Science and Scientists Held in High Esteem Across Global Publics," Pew Research Center, https://www.pewresearch.org/science/2020/09/29/science-and-scientists-held-in-high-esteem-across-global-publics/

138 Ibid.

139 Lee Rainie, Scott Keeter and Andrew Perrin, "Trust and Distrust in America"

140 Ibid.

141 Ibid.

142 Jeff Horwitz and Deepa Seetharaman, "Facebook Executives Shut Down Efforts to Make the Site Less Divisive," *Wall Street Journal*, May 26, 2020, https://www.wsj.com/articles/facebook-knows-it-encourages-division-top-executives-nixed-solutions-11590507499?mod=hp_lead_pos5

143 Ian Sherr and Lin La, "Facebook will ask us to decide what's 'high quality' news," CNET, January 10, 2019, https://www.cnet.com/news/facebook-zuckerberg-news-feed-prioritize-high-quality-and-trustworthy-sources/

144 Jeff Horwitz and Deepa Seetharaman, "Facebook Executives Shut Down Efforts to Make the Site Less Divisive."

145 Ibid.

146 Thomas Brewster, "Sheryl Sandberg Downplayed Facebook's Role In The Capitol Hill Siege—Justice Department Files Tell A Very Different Story," *Forbes*, February 7, 2021, https://www.forbes.com/sites/thomasbrewster/2021/02/07/sheryl-sandberg-downplayed-facebooks-role-in-the-capitol-hill-siege-justice-department-files-tell-a-very-different-story/?sh=2f363fd010b3

147 Ibid.

148 Epstein flight manifests, https://www.documentcloud.org/documents/1507315-epstein-flight-manifests.html

149 "Pizzagate: Gunman fires in restaurant at centre of conspiracy," BBC News, December 5, 2016, https://www.bbc.com/news/world-us-canada-38205885

150 Lois Beckett, "QAnon: a timeline of violence linked to the conspiracy theory," *The Guardian*, October 16, 2020, https://www.theguardian.com/us-news/2020/oct/15/qanon-violence-crimes-timeline

151 Drew Harwell, "QAnon believers seek to adapt their extremist ideology for a new era: 'Things have just started,'" *Washington Post*, January 21, 2021, https://www.washingtonpost.com/technology/2021/01/21/qanon-faithful-biden-trump/

152 Kasey Stricklin, "Why Does Russia Use Disinformation?" Lawfare, March 29, 2020, https://www.lawfareblog.com/why-does-russia-use-disinformation

153 Keir Giles, "Handbook of Russian Information Warfare," NATO Defense College, November 2019, https://weaponizednarrative.asu.edu/system/files/library/docs/fm_9.pdf

154 Miles Parks and Martin Austermuhle, "'None Of This Is True': Protests Become Fertile Ground for Online Disinformation," NPR Illinois, June 1, 2020, https://www.nprillinois.org/politics/2020-06-01/none-of-this-is-true-protests-become-fertile-ground-for-online-disinformation

155 "Exposing Russia's Effort to Sow Discord Online: The Internet Research Agency and Advertisements," US House of Representative Permanent Select Committee on Intelligence, https://intelligence.house.gov/social-media-content/

156 Žilvinas Švedkauskas, Chonlawit Sirikupt, and Michel Salzer, "Russia's disinformation campaigns are targeting African Americans," *Washington Post*, July 24, 2020, https://www.washingtonpost.com/politics/2020/07/24/russias-disinformation-campaigns-are-targeting-african-americans/

157 Salvador Hernandez, "Russian Trolls Spread Baseless Conspiracy Theories Like Pizzagate And QAnon After The Election," BuzzFeed, https://www.buzzfeednews.com/article/salvadorhernandez/russian-trolls-spread-baseless-conspiracy-theories-like

158   "China and Russia spreading anti-US vaccine misinformation, White House says—as it happened," *The Guardian,* July 16, 2021, https://www.theguardian.com/us-news/live/2021/jul/16/us-politics-live-covid-coronavirus-wildfires-biden-latest?-page=with:block-60f184de8f080074230c148c

159   "Exposing Russia's Effort to Sow Discord Online: The Internet Research Agency and Advertisements," US House of Representatives Permanent Select Committee on Intelligence, March 2018, https://intelligence.house.gov/social-media-content/

160   Kathleen McGrory and Neil Bedi, "Targeted. Pasco sheriff created a futuristic program to stop crime before it happens," *Tampa Bay Times*, September 3, 2020, https://projects.tampabay.com/projects/2020/investigations/police-pasco-sheriff-targeted/intelligence-led-policing/

161   Ibid.

162   Randy Rieland, "Artificial Intelligence Is Now Used to Predict Crime. But Is It Biased?" *Smithsonian Magazine*, March 5, 2018, https://www.smithsonianmag.com/innovation/artificial-intelligence-is-now-used-predict-crime-is-it-biased-180968337/

163   Matt Stroud, "Chicago's predictive policing tool just failed a major test," The Verge, August 19, 2016, https://www.theverge.com/2016/8/19/12552384/chicago-heat-list-tool-failed-rand-test

164   Ray Stern, "Was the Backup Driver in an Uber Autonomous Car Crash Wrongfully Charged?" *Phoenix New Times*, July 9, 2021, https://www.phoenixnewtimes.com/news/uber-self-driving-crash-arizona-vasquez-wrongfully-charged-motion-11583771

165   Angie Schmitt and Charles Brown, "Uber Self-Driving Car Death Ruling Sets a Scary Precedent," Next City, September 29, 2020, https://nextcity.org/urbanist-news/entry/uber-self-driving-car-death-ruling-sets-a-scary-precedent

166   Insurance Institute for Highway Safety and the Massachusetts Institute of Technology's AgeLab, "Drivers let their focus slip as they get used to partial automation," November 19, 2020, https://www.iihs.org/news/detail/drivers-let-their-focus-slip-as-they-get-used-to-partial-automation

167   NBCNews, "Tesla Driver Caught On Camera Apparently Asleep At The Wheel," NBC Nightly News, September 9, 2019, https://www.youtube.com/watch?v=NHUZxeSUFUk

168   Matt Egan, "'I begged them for help': Wells Fargo foreclosure nightmare," CNN Business, December 13, 2018, https://edition.cnn.com/2018/12/12/business/wells-fargo-foreclosure-nightmare/index.html

169   Ibid.

170   US District Court for the Northern District of California, Alicia Hernandez v. Wells Fargo Bank, class-action suit. accessed October 3, 2021

171   Penny Crosman, "Weren't algorithms supposed to make digital mortgages colorblind?" *American Banker*, November 26, 2018, https://www.americanbanker.com/news/werent-algorithms-supposed-to-make-digital-mortgages-colorblind

172   Robert Bartlett, et al., "Consumer Lending Discrimination in the FinTech era," research paper, November 2019, https://faculty.haas.berkeley.edu/morse/research/papers/discrim.pdf

173   John Roach. Microsoft AI Blog (January 10, 2018), "Researchers use AI to improve accuracy of gene editing with CRISPR", https://blogs.microsoft.com/ai/crispr-gene-editing/

174   Brian Wang. Next Big Future (June 9, 2015). "Disruptive CRISPR gene therapy is 150 times cheaper than zinc fingers and CRISPR is faster and more precise", https://www.nextbigfuture.com/2015/06/disruptive-crispr-gene-therapy-is-150.html

175   Ibid.

176   Rob Stein. NPR (November 26, 2018), "Chinese Scientist Says He's First To Create Genetically Modified Babies Using CRISPR", https://www.npr.org/sections/health-shots/2018/11/26/670752865/chinese-scientist-says-hes-first-to-genetically-edit-babies

177   Susan Scutti. CNN (June 5, 2019), "CRISPR gene-edited babies may be at increased risk of early death, study finds", https://www.cnn.com/2019/06/03/health/crispr-gene-edit-increased-death-risk-study/index.html

178   Ibid.

179   Rob Stein. NPR (August 18, 2017), "Exclusive: Inside The Lab Where Scientists Are Editing DNA In Human Embryos", https://www.npr.org/sections/health-shots/2017/08/18/543769759/a-first-look-inside-the-lab-where-scientists-are-editing-dna-in-human-embryos

180   Sandy Sufian, Rosemarie Garland-Thomson. Scientific American (February 16, 2021), "The Dark Side of CRISPR", https://www.scientificamerican.com/article/the-dark-side-of-crispr/

181   Ibid.

182   Bret S. Cohen, James Denvil, Filippo A. Raso, and Stevie De-groff, "FTC authority to regulate artificial intelligence," Reuters, July 8, 2021, https://www.reuters.com/legal/legalindustry/ftc-authority-regulate-artificial-intelligence-2021-07-08/

183   Consumer Financial Protection Bureau, "Prepared Remarks of CFPB Director Richard Cordray at the NAACP Annual Convention," July 19, 2016, accessed March 2, 2021

184   Erin Brodwin and Rebecca Robbins, "An Invisible Hand: Patients Aren't Being Told About the AI Systems Advising Their Care," Stat News, July 15, 2020, https://www.statnews.com/2020/07/15/artificial-intelligence-patient-consent-hospitals/

185   Suzy Khimm, "Who gets a ventilator? Hospitals facing coronavirus surge are preparing for life-or-death decisions," NBC News, March 18, 2020, https://www.nbcnews.com/health/health-care/who-gets-ventilator-hospitals-facing-coronavirus-surge-are-preparing-life-n1162721

186   Lisa Rosenbaum, MD, "Facing Covid-19 in Italy—Ethics, Logistics, and Therapeutics on the Epidemic's Front Line," *New England Journal of Medicine*, March 18, 2020, https://www.nejm.org/doi/full/10.1056/NEJMp2005492?query=featured_coronavirus

187   Kei Ouchi, MD, MPH, et al, "Prognosis After Emergency Department Intubation to Inform Shared Decision-Making," *Journal of the American Geriatrics Association*, March 15, 2018)

188 "COVID-19 Pandemic Shifts Innovation Priorities at Health Systems," research report, Center for Connected Medicine, https://connectedmed.com/resources/research-report-covid-19-pandemic-shifts-innovation-priorities-at-health-systems/

189 "Algorithm for COVID-19 triage and referral," World Health Organization, Western Pacific Region, March 22, 2020, https://apps.who.int/iris/bitstream/handle/10665/331915/COVID-19-algorithm-referral-triage-eng.pdf?sequence=1&isAllowed=y

190 Karen Hao, "Doctors are using AI to triage covid-19 patients. The tools may be here to stay," *MIT Technology Review*, April 23, 2020, https://www.technologyreview.com/2020/04/23/1000410/ai-triage-covid-19-patients-health-care/

191 "Study Finds New Commercial AI Devices Often Lack Key Performance Data," American Hospital Association, April 20, 2021, https://www.aha.org/aha-center-health-innovation-market-scan/2021-04-20-study-finds-new-commercial-ai-devices-often